Against the Romance of Community

Against the Romance of Community

Miranda Joseph

University of Minnesota Press

Minneapolis

London

Portions of chapters 1 and 4 appeared in an earlier form as "The Perfect Moment: Gays, Christians, and the National Endowment for the Arts," *Socialist Review* 26, no. 3–4 (1996); reprinted by permission of *Socialist Review.* An earlier version of chapter 2 appeared as "The Performance of Production and Consumption," *Social Text* 54 (Fall 1998); copyright Duke University Press; reprinted by permission of Duke University Press.

"Keeping Things Whole" is from *Selected Poems* by Mark Strand. Copyright 1979, 1980 by Mark Strand. Reprinted by permission of Alfred A. Knopf, a division of Random House, Inc.

Published by the University of Minnesota Press
111 Third Avenue South, Suite 290
Minneapolis, MN 55401-2520
http://www.upress.umn.edu

Library of Congress Cataloging-in-Publication Data

Joseph, Miranda.
    Against the romance of community / Miranda Joseph.
      p.   cm.
    Includes bibliographical references and index.
    ISBN 0-8166-3795-4 (HC : alk. paper) — ISBN 0-8166-3796-2 (PB : alk. paper)
    1. Community. I. Title.
    HM756 .J64 2002
    307—dc21   2002008287

Printed in the United States of America on acid-free paper

The University of Minnesota is an equal-opportunity educator and employer.

12 11 10 09 08 07 06 05 04 03 02   10 9 8 7 6 5 4 3 2 1

Contents

INTRODUCTION

Persistent Critique, Relentless Return

> To give some assistance in wearing away certain self-evidences and
> commonplaces . . . ; to bring it about, together with many others,
> that certain phrases can no longer be spoken so lightly, certain acts
> no longer, or at least no longer so unhesitatingly, performed.
> —Michel Foucault, "Questions of Method"

The self-evidence, the commonplace, that I hope to assist in wearing
away here is community. I hope that this book will give pause, will insert a hesitation into the next sentence you utter that seems inevitably
to require *community*. I hope that hesitation will open a space for creative thinking about the constitution of collective action, where the term
community would operate so effectively to shut down such thought.
Community is almost always invoked as an unequivocal good, an indi-
cator of a high quality of life, a life of human understanding, caring,
selflessness, belonging. One does one's volunteer work in and for "the
community." Communities are frequently said to emerge in times of
crisis or tragedy, when people imagine themselves bound together by a
common grief or joined through some extraordinary effort. Among
leftists and feminists, community has connoted cherished ideals of cooperation, equality, and communion.

Because it carries such positive connotations, community is deployed
by any and everyone pressing any sort of cause. Identity-based social
movements invoke community to mobilize constituents and validate
their cause to a broader public. Both Clintonian communitarianism and

Republican family values rhetoric depend on an image of real Americans living in communities in the "heartland." Even industrial interest groups often call themselves communities to suggest that they and their interests are legitimate sites of empathy and concern.

I am by no means the first to offer a critique of community. As I will outline later in this introduction, many feminist and poststructuralist theorists writing in the 1980s and 1990s described identity political communities as disciplining and exclusionary, while others pointed to the racism, sexism, and violence entailed in explicit or implicit attempts to constitute nations and liberal states as communities. Despite this persistent scholarly critique, a celebratory discourse of community relentlessly returns. My question is, why? Where others have responded to the perceived oppressiveness of community by trying to imagine better forms of community, I undertake to account for the persistence and pervasiveness of community.

Where the earlier analyses of community focused on the internal dynamics of communities, on their efforts to produce unity by universalizing an identity, I attempt to situate communities and the discourse of community in the social processes in which they are constituted and that they help to constitute. In a sense then, I make a classic cultural studies move, shifting from the examination of the text itself to an examination of the production and consumption of the text, which in this case is community. I pursue this account of the production and consumption of community through two related projects. I examine deployments of community, using ethnographic studies and readings of popular, political, and academic texts to explore the relationship of such deployments to capitalism as it expands and evolves. Through these ethnographic and discursive analyses I argue that capitalism and, more generally, modernity depend on and generate the discourse of community to legitimate social hierarchies. But I also undertake to theorize how communities are enacted. While identity is often named as the bond among community members, it is a false name in that communal participants are not identical and many of those to whom an identity is attributed do not participate in communal activities. I argue that communal subjectivity is constituted not by identity but rather through practices of production and consumption.

I propose then that both the rhetorical invocation of community and the social relationships that are discursively articulated as community are imbricated in capitalism. I argue against the idealization of community as a utopian state of human relatedness and, more important, against the idea that communities are organic, natural, spontaneous occurrences. And yet, I do not suggest that invoked communities are false or inauthentic, as if there were some more authentic form of community to be found in some other time or place. Rather, it seems crucial to me to take these invocations and practices of community at their word and to assess the complex complicity with and resistance to capitalism offered by community.

I fully recognize that for most people attachments to particular communities of belonging and activism run deep; they are our sites of hope in a difficult world. It is my own desire for social change that drives my effort to interrupt the reiteration of community. Fetishizing community only makes us blind to the ways we might intervene in the enactment of domination and exploitation. I see the practice of critique, and in particular a critical relationship to community, as an ethical practice of community, as an important mode of participation. I offer then a critique from the inside, not a condemnation from the outside.

Claustrophobia

I will begin this book, as I began my research on the topic of community, with my ethnographic study of San Francisco's gay/lesbian Theatre Rhinoceros. I introduce my book with this ethnographic narrative, which illustrates the exclusionary and disciplining deployment of community, because my participation in identity-political organizations and in activism, as much as the theory I will go on to outline, is the context for my work. I begin with this story in order to make clear, simultaneously, my own investments and frustrations. Like many of the feminist critics of community whose work I was reading as I began this study, I was moved to take up the task of critique precisely because of these investments and frustrations. My experience at Theatre Rhinoceros was symptomatic of the complexities of identity-based activism that those feminists described and responded to; and, in fact, I expect that the story I tell and the analysis I offer in this introduction will be all too familiar to many of my readers. I intend, over the course of the book, to add a new perspective to the critique and not merely reiterate the insights offered by others—and I will draw on this ethnographic study again in chapter 3 in the service of that new perspective. However, my arguments are dependent on those earlier analyses of community, and my first reading of my ethnographic experience—my observation of the oppressive deployment of community—shares a great deal with them.

I fell into this case study somewhat accidentally. For several years before beginning my research, I was an employee of the theater, working intermittently as house manager, box office staff, and telemarketer. I began working there in 1984 when, having just graduated from college, I moved to San Francisco. In the summer of 1990 I began my formal research, which involved attending board and staff meetings as well as performances and interviewing approximately seventy-five people involved in every aspect of the organization, including staff and board members, artists and technicians, audience members, funders, and theater reviewers working at local newspapers. At the inception of my research I ceased being a paid employee, though I continued to help out with various tasks such as a phone-a-thon fundraiser. During my fieldwork, the theater continued to be a central part of my own social world, the site of friendships, sexual relationships, and their aftermath, the site at which I engaged in a large range of acquaintanceships, and gained information about and participated in the arts and politics of the gay community and the city of San Francisco. My position as researcher allowed me to remain silent in moments of conflict and to remain present even when I was uncomfortable with the choices made by the staff and board. However, my notes often reveal my unvoiced feelings, trailing off during heated discussions in which, though silent, I was deeply involved.

Founded in 1977 by two young gay men, Alan Estes and Lanny Baugniet, who began producing plays in gay bars, the theater was originally by and for gay men. In the early eighties, the theater moved into the building in the Mission District in which I found it. This building, in which the theater has two performance spaces as well as its offices, has the atmosphere of an old public school: red brick exterior, beige painted walls, linoleum floors, fluorescent lighting. With a distinguished history as a "labor temple," this building was the home of many nonprofit organizations; among the tenants were a teachers' union, the San Francisco Nuclear Freeze, *Socialist Review, Outlook* magazine, a theater service organization called Theater Bay Area, a gay history archive, and Woman, Inc., a battered women's hotline. In the mid-eighties, women were integrated into the staff and the content of shows as well as into the audience.

By the early 1990s, Rhino was in many ways a typical midsized nonprofit organization, with a staff of five to six, a volunteer board of directors, a loyal following of subscribers, some government and foundation funding, and an annual budget of about $300,000. The theater also employed hourly workers in the box office and house and jobbed in actors and techies for each show, many of whom were regulars.

During the period of my research, the organization understood itself to be in crisis. It was in dire straits financially; relations between board and staff were difficult; the relations between the theater and a number of key artists were troubled; and it was generally understood to be producing poor-quality work. During much of the 1980s, Rhino had been the only venue for gay theater; however, by the early 1990s several other theaters, not explicitly gay identified, were producing gay shows that were better received by both audiences and reviewers. In addition, a for-profit gay cabaret had opened that was presenting well-known touring performance artists to large and enthusiastic audiences, while Rhino persisted in producing its own plays. The neighborhood in which the theater was located, near but not in the gay Castro neighborhood, had absorbed the homeless population produced by Reaganomics and was perceived as a dangerous, drug- and crime-ridden "ghetto."

The theater was started during what was regularly represented to me as the golden age of San Francisco's gay community, before AIDS, before the shooting of Harvey Milk, before the rise of Reagan. That era, I was told again and again by men in their forties, was a period of great optimism and energy. For instance, when, at a board meeting, Edward[1] persisted in saying 1983 and 1984 when he meant 1993 and 1994, others started to kid him about those having been "the good old days . . . when we were making and spending lots of money." When he accurately referred to something in the past as having occurred in 1983, he was asked if he didn't mean 1973: "Those were the *real* good old days." In my interview with him, Lanny Baugniet explained, "When I came to San Francisco in 1970, this was—San Francisco in the seventies . . . it was heaven on earth for gay men. There was never anything, there never again will be anything like that again . . . My life was legitimized by my peers, and I had the opportunity to enjoy everything I ever wanted . . . We refer to it as the Golden Years . . . that's what we call it when we get nostalgic. . . . We thought we could do something, and we did our damnedest, and look what happened. Everyone sold out. The movement died. Nothing

changed." Eric, who was involved in San Francisco gay theater and politics in that era (attending Rhino productions but not himself participating because he found Rhino too conservative), likewise assured me,
in response to my skeptical questions, that it really was an amazing time.
He recalled the pervasive and uplifting optimism about the ability of
that community of gay men to change the world and invent new ways
to live. Many gay organizations, and in fact many gay theater groups,
were started at that time; Rhino was the only theater group from that
era that had survived the intervening hard times, and those hard times,
as much as the preceding paradise, were crucial to the narrative that
constituted the theater's identity with and in the gay community.

Long-time staff members Doug Holsclaw, the assistant artistic director and literary manager, and Adele Prandini, artistic director, had stepped
into staff jobs as the original core group of founders and artists were
dying of AIDS in the eighties. Although neither was present at the founding of the theater, they were, at the time of my research, nearly unique
in having known and worked with the founders (a couple of original
board members also remained) and thus bore the standard of that history
as its guilty/lucky survivors. (Of the original group, only Lanny Baugniet
was still alive when I was doing my research; by his own account he had
been forced out of the theater in the early eighties due to conflict with
his cofounder, Alan Estes, and had never returned, never been welcomed
back.) For them, as for many of the men I spoke with, the communal
narrative was not the story of the glorious beginning but the story of
loss, disappointment, and trauma. Baugniet told me that during his
tenure at the theater there was a regular group of actors who participated in the plays but that "most of them died within a very short period of one another . . . right around the period I left it seemed the whole
company was dying. I'd say there were maybe a dozen people within a
year's time. And our best actors." Adele regularly iterated the numbers
of artists—she sometimes said 30, sometimes 150—lost to AIDS, blam-
ing the current troubles of the theater on the loss of mature talent. Under
Doug and Adele's leadership, the centrality of AIDS to the narrative
constitution of the theater and the gay community was manifested in
the content of Rhino's theatrical productions: they produced at least
one play or musical dealing with AIDS in each subscription season.

"Accident" though it may have been that I found myself already deeply
involved at the theater, much of the basics of an ethnography done be-

fore I officially began, Rhino did turn out to be an incredibly rich site of community discourse. The company understood itself to be by, for, in, and of "the gay community," a metonym for it, a reflection of it, with a responsibility to portray that community to itself and to others (the *mainstream*, in Rhino parlance), but also to help shape, define, and direct that community. Much of this discourse was made conveniently explicit for me at a board/staff retreat, held in 1992, intended to discuss the mission and vision of the organization. This meeting, which included four staff members, twelve board members, and myself, took place in the elegant board room of a real estate company owned by one of the board members. This setting was quite a contrast to that of regular monthly board meetings, which took place around a Formica folding table in a linoleum-floored, fluorescent-lit basement room of the theater building.

Doug launched into the introductory exercise at this retreat with his much touted humor: "I started as a half-time marketing director . . . when I was in my twenties [laughter]. I was doing stand-up at the Valencia Rose when *The AIDS Show* call went out. I had already written this monologue . . . I got sucked in from there [laughter]. I did the monologue in *The AIDS Show*.[2] [Doug went on to codirect the second version of *The AIDS Show* and then joined the staff.] I stayed because you guys produce my work and because of the artistic freedom here. You are not shy of sexual content." Adele's personal history is, similarly, the history of the theater and community. Adele told us that she had come to the theater in 1983. "Chuck [Solomon, part of the core group in the early eighties, now dead] directed my first play at Theatre Rhinoceros. After Alan died, I got involved with *The AIDS Show*, was a playwright-in-residence, and then came on staff as the production manager of the theater. I had always been involved in lesbian work. I had my own company. I moved with the community toward integrated gay and lesbian work. I stayed because I have an 'in' at the theater for producing my own shows. Like Doug, I might not be working if not for Rhino." Adele and Doug gained a great deal of authority by inscribing themselves into the traumatic and oppressed history of the theater and community. It was Doug's habitual role in staff meetings to recall and defend the way things had always been done. And throughout this meeting, both Doug and Adele were able to represent the needs and desires of "the community" in a way that trumped all other suggestions and tended to direct the mission of the theater in very conservative directions.

Interestingly though, they did not in fact have to do very much work to rein in either the vision of gay community operating in the meeting or the mission of the organization in relation to that community. During the initial brainstorming exercise on the mission, led by Liz, a board member, who urged us in vain to "sit some way you don't usually sit, make your brain work in a way it doesn't usually work," the existence of a knowable and known gay/lesbian community was presumed by almost everyone as they suggested that the theater "produce plays, quality plays"; "educate"; "expand"; "develop new talent"; provide "employment opportunities for gay artists and arts professionals"; promote "gay and lesbian visibility within mainstream culture"; be "fun for everyone"; "train artists"; "make an impact—present stuff that is thought-provoking"; "participate in shaping gay identity"; "change with the community"; "document stages of the community"; mark "the importance of sexuality"; provide "sanctuary" and "affirmation"; act as a site of "community ritual" and a site of "community meetings, like around the war and the earthquake"; be an "alternative to family"; "present our dreams and fears in productions"; provide a "sense of acknowledgment, validation—organized acknowledgment"; be financially "sustainable"; offer a "reflection of community," "a social space," "a place to take a date, meet cute girls."

The flow of the brainstorm was disrupted only twice. When Jane, one of the youngest and newest members of the board, offered "unify," Liz broke in to ask her what that meant. Jane did not answer the question herself. Instead, Sue, the board president, jumped in with "brings people together and makes them think." Likewise, when Paula, another new young board member, said, "diversify the community's vision of itself, for itself," she was met by such puzzled looks that she in effect retracted her statement, offering a clarification that was also a dramatic shift in meaning: "diversify ourselves, our personnel, and constituency." Jane and Paula's contributions were disruptive because they both suggested in different ways that "the community" could not be taken for granted. I took them both to be speaking from an experience of conflicts and debates over the very constitution of the community around issues of race, gender, transgender, sexuality (bisexuality, sadomasochism, and so on), and terminology (gay versus queer) that were quite active in San Francisco at that time. In saying "unify," Jane raised the specter of disunity; and, in calling for the theater to diversify its own vision, Paula seemed to be suggesting that the theater's vision of the community might be wrong or inadequate. When Sue interpreted Jane's comment as "bring people together," she bridged a potential breach by reducing the connotation of disunity from conflict or substantive difference to a more acceptable notion of dispersal of people who, once brought together, would in fact evidence unity, identity. When Paula replaced the idea of diversifying our vision with diversifying our personnel, she covered her own potential breach by offering a familiar notion of racial affirmative action or multiculturalism in place of a more disturbing epistemological challenge to the knowability of the community. Their contributions thus stood in stark contrast to the dominant vision of the theater as a ritual or healing space or as mechanism for affirming and documenting the history of a knowable and coherent community, a vision that imagined the theater to be the site at which communal crises and changes were processed and subordinated to an ongoing identity and unity.

The various contributions offered during the brainstorm were summarized as follows: (1) produce quality gay and lesbian plays; (2) maintain a professional work environment; (3) document gay and lesbian life; (4) develop new work by gay and lesbian artists; (5) become a self-sustaining organization. Liz then set off a furor by asking, "Would a funder give money to this?" While most people seemed to think that this would be, as one said, "sturdy," Adele argued that in fact it did not acknowledge "trends in funding." She reported that at her recent meeting with one foundation officer she was told that the foundation's priority was "crossover work, expanding our support base beyond the gay/lesbian community. They want networking, coalition, diversification. This is frightening."

> BARRY: So if we were a gay male theater and a lesbian theater working together then we could get funding for that?

> ADELE: Yes. Our community is extremely diversified. The problem is we don't all have the same definitions of these things.

Adele often spoke in favor of, and worked for, racial inclusiveness, aiming to remedy the fact that the theater staff, board, productions, and audience were not just predominantly white but almost exclusively white, wanting the theater to reflect the diversity of the community.[3] But she interpreted the call for diversification from the "outside" as an attempt by "straight" funders to dilute the focus of the theater. When Sue responded to Adele's comment by saying, "In the plays, sometimes the context is very narrow, insular, there aren't any straight characters," Doug responded by saying, "We can't be duped into courting straight approval. Straight approval corrupts the work. I can just see a playwright adding in the straight brother of the gay character to give the straight audience member something to relate to." And Adele added, "Our mission is for the gay and lesbian community. We exist primarily to communicate within the gay/lesbian community." A brief discussion ensued of whether a gay play had to have a gay author; the answer seemed to be no, that the crucial issue was gay characters.

DOUG: We want to produce plays in which the gay or lesbian content is not incidental. Honesty and truth are important terms here. We don't want a play in which the gay character is just a wacky gay neighbor.

PAULA: As we talk we are limiting ourselves. A play might not have a gay or lesbian character but like *Hidden: A Gender* [Kate Bornstein's play about transsexualism] might still speak to us, address issues relevant to us, like gender.

LIZ: Can we add, "speaks to the human condition and resonates for the gay and lesbian community"?

Various people objected that "resonates" was too broad, that it would, for instance, include a play focused primarily on racism.

DOUG: Anyway, the main character of *Hidden: A Gender* was a lesbian.

ADELE: "Gay/lesbian sensibility." [Adele said this quite sarcastically, quoting a phrase that had been bandied about the theater for years by those who felt that central gay and lesbian characters should not be the only definition of a gay or lesbian play. In the past, the argument for gay sensibility had always lost, thus excluding, interestingly enough, formally experimental works in favor of highly conventional "realistic" renderings of gay life.]

Jane, expressing a discomfort I was also certainly feeling with the way community was being deployed, said, "Let's just say lesbians and gay men rather than lesbian/gay community since given what Adele has been saying, there isn't one community." Following Jane's suggestion that the term *community* be eliminated, Doug resorted to an older and more clinical terminology, saying, "We want to do plays that wouldn't get done elsewhere because of their homosexual content"; and in doing so he reaffirmed the notion that there is an essential and common core to gay

identity rather than opening up the theater to the diversity of gay identities that Jane's comment (which, rather craftily, put her own views in
Adele's mouth) seemed in that context to imply.

This discussion was shortly brought to a rather abrupt halt for a lunch
break, and after lunch the discussion moved on to the planning of up-
coming special events. After the official end of the meeting, as we were
all still gathering our things and saying good-bye, Jane pointed out to
Adele and the financial director, Barbara, that the group had not even
discussed adding bisexuals to the mission. Adele and Barbara responded
almost in unison, "That's right. Let them start their own theater if they
want one."

That is frightening.

No one at this meeting would have explicitly said that they wanted to
exclude gay people of color or gay transgendered people, and in fact bisexuals did participate (were permitted to participate) in the theater as
employees, board members, artists, and audience members. However, as
Jane's last comment seems to notice, the invocation of community served
to articulate what might be called homosexism—that is, the prioritiza-
tion of gayness over other identity features. And this homosexism worked
to limit the theater's orientation to white gays and lesbians of stable
and unified gender identity. As the invocation of a community of women
has often served to produce a white women's movement that could not
adequately address or account for women who were simultaneously or
even primarily faced with oppressions based on race or class or sexuality, the invocation of gay community functioned here to exclude people
of color and transgendered people for whom, though they might in fact
also be gay, sexuality was not an isolated or primary identity. The point
was quite clearly stated by Susan, an African American dancer who had
participated in a Rhino coproduction deliberately arranged to bring
African Americans into the theater, when I interviewed her. Explaining
why she did not feel that she belonged to the gay/lesbian community,
but rather to an African American lesbian community, she said: "Well,
the commonality of being black, understanding the—I hate the word
oppression—the double life we have to lead, the common basis of understanding what's going on. So why I stay with the African Americans
is because I'm more apt to do something with them, if they've got a
fundraiser or something going on. It's not always as easy for people of
color to be out. And also, lots of times when a [white] woman—this is

the first time—they've never had to deal with being told they couldn't do something, or being told that they were like on the wrong end of society. So they're going to jump out there and they're ready to kick butt over it. I deal with thirty-four years of being on the wrong side of this society and what that meant. So being on the wrong side of this society ain't nothing new for me."

As the meeting unfolded and I noted the implicitly exclusionary deployments of community, I wasn't so much alarmed or surprised—I knew these people well—as worried on behalf of the theater, worried that the insistence on community, on gay/lesbian community, was counterproductive in relation to the crises of financial and human resources the theater was experiencing and that this retreat was becoming a missed opportunity. The mission that was reaffirmed there excluded or silenced not only people of color, bisexuals, and transgendered people but also the large numbers of people, myself included, whose sense of identity and community were at that time powerfully mobilized under the name *queer,* whose art and activism were enabled by a term that seemed to embrace flexibility and dynamism of gender and sexuality. And thus at that moment, in that meeting, my own sense was that the theater was excluding to its own detriment a tremendous amount of creative energy as well as particular people in its invocation of an exclusively gay/lesbian community.[4] Despite my worries in the moment, the theater survived the period of crisis in which I observed it, pulling itself out of its financial hole, and it continues now, ten years later, to produce and present theatrical works for and about the gay/lesbian community.

The Critique of Community

> The racist mode of thinking basically produces its own community, the racist community, together with an interpretation of the social world in which this community is situated. . . . Racism and sexism . . . produce *ideals* of humanity, *types of ideal humanity* if you like, which one cannot but call universal.
>
> —Etienne Balibar, "Racism as Universalism"

The conservative, disciplining, and exclusionary effectivity of the invocation of community that so clearly determined the course of events in this Theatre Rhinoceros meeting has been articulated explicitly and repeatedly in much feminist and poststructuralist academic work since the 1980s. Using the term *community* to refer to social practices that presume or attempt to enact and produce identity, unity, communion, and purity, and observing the use of the term *community* in such social practices, critics noted a diverse range of oppressions, including but by no means limited to genocidal violence, that seemed to follow from the idealization and deployment of community. Many scholars and activists observed that communities seem inevitably to be constituted in relation to internal and external enemies and that these defining others are then elided, excluded, or actively repressed. *Community* was in effect articulated as the paradoxical technology for what Balibar calls "racism as universalism," for attempts to universalize one particularity at the expense of others ("Racism as Universalism"). Scholars analyzed and criticized deployments of community-as-unity in diverse political practices: in the identity-political strategies of the left and especially feminist movements that assume communion among those with a shared identity or experience of oppression; in a variety of forms of liberalism, from classical to communitarian to Habermasian, that imagine public spheres as communities or sites of consensus; and in nationalisms, both the nationalisms of white European domination and those nationalisms of anticolonial resistance to such domination, that desire and attempt to articulate nations as organic communities.

The critique of nationalism has a long, complex intellectual history. While, as David Kazanjian points out (personal communication), Marx and Engels vacillated in their readings of national and colonial conflicts in the Hapsburg empire, Poland, India, and Ireland (and later Marxists have debated the question of nationalism), sometimes defending national independence struggles and sometimes defending colonialism, they also subordinated national identities to class identities and thus marked nationalism as historically limited. Where Marx and Engels pointed toward the future limits of nationalism, over the past twenty years many historians of European nation formation and nationalism have marked the limits of its past history. Benedict Anderson (and many others) have located the birth of the nation in the eighteenth and nineteenth centuries and thus marked the narratives of nations as organic communities, forged through some (endlessly reiterated) mythic trauma, as precisely narratives.[5] Meanwhile, Hannah Arendt's *Origins of Totalitarianism* and Theodor Adorno and Max Horkheimer's *Dialectic of Enlightenment* foregrounded the role of nationalist invocations of a *Volk*, of a racially and culturally homogeneous community, in constituting and legitimating the violences of Nazism and totalitarianism more generally. And in fact, for scholars of European nationalism, Nazism would seem to be the paradigmatic case (echoing now in the new nationalisms of Eastern Europe) of universalizing community, of community as a political formation that attempts to eradicate those defined as outside the community.

The two strands of critique—the recognition of the violence of nationalism and the recognition of the historical, modern, specificity of the nation—were brought together in the work of anticolonialist writers such as Franz Fanon, Albert Memmi, and George Padmore. They articulated the pitfalls of anticolonial nationalism, identifying its mimetic relationship to colonialism, its fabricated claims of authenticity, and its simplistic inversion of colonial relations. Postcolonial critics, such as Partha Chatterjee, Ranajit Guha, and other members of the Subaltern Studies collective, have further theorized the role European nationalisms played in imperialist processes as well as the symbiotic relationships that existed between nationalisms of empire and the Third World nationalisms that emerged in anticolonial struggles. Feminist theorists of both Northern and Southern nationalisms have argued that the articulation of national collectivities often depends on the regulation of gender and the control of women, even as women emerge as privileged bearers of "culture" and "community."[6] These arguments suggest that in taking up communitarian nationalist discourse as a discourse of emancipation, of autonomy and authenticity, both Marxist and liberal postcolonial nationalisms have inscribed oppression into their own practices, elaborating and rigidifying hierarchies of ethnicity, caste, class, and gender. In *Nationalist Thought and the Colonial World: A Derivative Discourse,* Chatterjee states, simply: "[Nationalism] has been the cause of the most destructive wars ever seen; it has justified the brutality of Nazism and Fascism; it has become the ideology of racial hatred in the colonies. The evidence was indeed overwhelming that nationalism and liberty could often be quite irreconcilably opposed" (2–3).

Precisely because national formations tend to depend on mythic origin stories, on narratives that aim to restore some imagined historical community as timeless, it is all too easy to imagine that enactments of community are regressive, premodern formations[7] and that Enlightenment, modernization, and liberalism can eradicate the oppressive practices that inhere in the invocation of traditional community. For instance, Chantal Mouffe, in promoting a "return" to a notion of politics in which citizens "recognize themselves as participants in a community," has warned that we must be "careful that we do not go back to a premodern conception of the political" and that we must guard against "nostalgia for the Greek polis and *Gemeinschaft* types of community" (Preface to *Dimensions*, 5). She thus inscribed a progressive narrative in which enlightened pluralist modernity supersedes premodern communities. The danger of such a progressive narrative is that it fails to recognize that, as the trajectory of scholarship from the *Dialectic of Enlightenment* through the historicizations of the nation and nationalisms to postcolonial studies makes clear, the central practices of modernity—Enlightenment rationality, the nation-state, and liberalism in both its political and economic forms—are at best ambivalent about organic community and at worst fundamentally constituted by oppressive communal discourses.

The assessment of liberalism as constituted by and constitutive of community, that is, as universalizing particular norms, rests on a critique of the public/private division on which liberalism depends.[8] In classical liberal theory, the public is a sphere of abstract citizenship in which private interests—communal or individual particularities—are left behind in the construction of a larger political community. Liberalism would thus seem to treat all members of the public equivalently while exhibiting neutrality toward private differences. However, feminist theorists have pointed out that the public sphere is not nearly so abstract or indifferent as its proponents would suggest. Echoing Marx's "On the Jewish Question," they have argued that the liberal public sphere actually presupposes and preserves the hierarchies of the private sphere; but more to the point here, they argue that participation in the public sphere is necessarily guided by norms that are not in fact indifferent or neutral but are rather marked by the particular interests of a dominant group; thus, those who are different from that norm will be disabled in their participation, forced to change, or even fully excluded.[9]

Even, or maybe especially, in its Habermasian reformulation,[10] the public sphere turns out to have the exclusionary and disciplining characteristics of community. In the Habermasian formulation, identity, unity, and consensus are not presupposed but are rather cast as a goal to be achieved through rational discourse protected from the power relations of the market. However, as Nancy Fraser and others have noted, the conditions for such rational discourse turn out to be once again a set of communal norms; thus, the achievement of consensus turns out to be, much like the universalization of an ideal type of humanity, an exclusionary process.[11] While Ranu Samantrai finds that Habermas opens far more space for dissent and in fact has far more desire for dissent than the communitarianism of Charles Taylor, she argues that, nonetheless, "by positing consensus as the desirable goal of communicative action (the universal, rational norms of which also constitute a previous consensus) or as the regulative ideal for political communities, Habermas returns us to the ideal of homogeneity as the model of the successful community" (22).

Such analyses of nationalist and liberal community are important and useful given the dominance and pervasiveness of nationalist and liberal practices around the world; I will offer iterations of such arguments in various places in the book. However, even more crucial to my own work were the self-critiques of identity-political community generated by feminist theorists and activists in the 1980s. Borrowing from anticolonialist analyses of white nationalisms, identity-political movements, like postcolonial nationalisms, have depended on fantasies of community, on stories of traumatic origins and organic unities, presuming always already common essence, experience, oppression, political needs and goals. This presumption of community has seemed to offer extraordinary promise as a ready-made basis for collective action. And in fact, identity-political movements have been able to generate self-worth, purposiveness, and activism in their participants. Identity-political movements have offered an important challenge to the exclusions of liberal practices, winning concrete gains in terms of rights, employment, social and cultural services, and government participation for women, for African Americans, for Chicanos, for gays and lesbians.[12] However, the presumption of community has also been recognized as a liability.

The publication of works such as Cherríe Moraga and Gloria Anzaldúa's *This Bridge Called My Back,* Audre Lorde's collected essays *Sister Outsider,* Anzaldúa's *Borderlands,* and bell hooks's *Ain't I a Woman,* among many many others, raised doubts about singular identity categories as an organizing principle for social change.[13] These works make it very clear that to imagine that women are a community is to elide and repress differences among women, to enact racism and heterosexism within a women's movement that is so marked by a particular (bourgeois) class position that it cannot address the concerns of "other" women. Turning such perspectives toward race-based emancipatory movements, women and queers also asked if Chicano and Black Power movements built on images of masculinity, machismo, and the restoration of "traditional cultures" really included them. At the same time, the very publication of such works made it clear that the deployment of identity, of community-as-identity, as an organizing rubric in fact produced resistance and dissent. To invoke community is immediately to raise questions of belonging and of power.

Unfortunately, where postcolonial theory immediately recognized the implication of postcolonial nationalisms in the oppressive processes of modernity, U.S.-based critics of identity politics have often instead pursued ever more finely grained measures of authentic identity, producing not a critique of community but a proliferation of communities. During my ethnographic research on Theatre Rhinoceros, I had occasion to observe the theater's participation as a representative of the gay community on the San Francisco Cultural Affairs Task Force (SFCATF). The SFCATF was a committee convened by the San Francisco Board of Supervisors to review city arts funding policy in the wake of a very public chastisement for underfunding multicultural, gay/lesbian, and women's arts groups, relative to "the majors" (the symphony, opera, and so on). The composition of this task force was the subject of lengthy political jockeying, with the result that there were more or less formally designated seats for a variety of communities: gays/lesbians, Chicanos, African Americans, Asian Americans, women. Members of an informal group of small and midsized "multicultural" arts organizations—which called itself the Majority Arts Council (MAC), thus asserting that minorities are in the majority—privately expressed concern that the women, people of color, and lesbians and gays on the task force should be "really" from the communities whose positions on the task force they would occupy and not be "white with dark skin." One person offered the hypothetical example that an African American man with the opera should not be counted as the African American representative. And the white heterosexual and lesbian women, Asian American women, and gay men who turned out to be the representatives of most of the major, mainstream arts organizations in the city did not count, to MAC members, as representatives of women, Asian Americans, or gays and lesbians. (Beginning to think toward the question that informs the third chapter of this book, on the relation of nonprofits to capitalism, I wondered how different, how much more authentic, these MAC members, all heads of nonprofit corporations, were from those whom they discounted?)

But the questions of belonging and power that identity-political invocations of community produce are not always framed as questions of purity or authenticity. Many participants in identity-political movements have recognized that rather than simply referring to an existing collectivity, invocations of community attempt to naturalize and mobilize such a collectivity: on both left and right community is deployed to lower consciousness of difference, hierarchy, and oppression within the invoked group. And thus the questions, the resistances, offered in response to incitements to community can be and often are framed as smart questions about tactics and strategy. Sophisticated participants will ask, who wants to know? before labeling themselves, before, for instance, identifying themselves as a "targeted minority" in a given bureaucratic context.[14] The presence of such antifoundationalist, strategic approaches within identity-political movements suggests that such movements cannot simply be dismissed as "essentialist." And in fact, noting that struggles over boundaries, over what one of my interviewees termed "ownership" of the community, may actually be constitutive of identity-political movements, a number of theorists have attempted to redefine community to include all who participate in the constitutive battles whether with acceptance of or resistance to the implied parameters and duties of communal membership.

The feminist and antiracist self-critiques raised serious questions about the goals and strategies of the (multiple, diverse, often apparently contradictory) emancipatory movements in which I participate and in alliance with which I undertake my own work. These self-critiques showed that various emancipatory movements are often (maybe inevitably) implicated in the oppressive practices they seek to resist, not least in the invocation of community. In doing so, they pointed to the extraordinary difficulty of answering the most fundamental questions for any social movement: What does the good society toward which "we" are working look like? And what is the nature of the "we" who undertakes that work? Who is included in the project? How do "we" relate to each other in the work? These are, I would contend, unanswerable questions, or at least there is no answer once and for all. Like the identity-political self-critiques, the arguments I make—for the inevitable implication of community in capital, for the simultaneous support and displacement that community offers to capital, for the complexity and instability of that relation as a dialectic of complicity and resistance—recognize the implication of our communities in the very forces we seek to oppose. With such a recognition comes the realization that there can only be an ongoingly dynamic array of contingent answers to be determined in the course of situated political struggle. I do not then, in introduction or conclusion, propose a singular political program, despite being rather critical of a variety of existing political strategies. This absence may very well be a source of frustration for some of my readers. In a sense it is a source of frustration for me that, faced with the world, after ten years of work, I cannot provide for myself and others "the answer." Nonetheless, when faced with the complexity of social processes as I find them, I have to refuse, can only fail, to satisfy the desire for such a programmatic conclusion. As Eve Sedgwick might say, we cannot know, it is in fact crucial not to know, in advance, where the practice of community might offer effective resistance and where it might be an unredeemable site of cooptation, hegemony, and oppressive reiteration of norms.[15] What we can do though, and must do, is bring our experience to bear; that is, we can try to learn from our mistakes by equipping ourselves with the analytic tools to read the implications of our practices.

Political critiques of community-as-unity were supplemented for me, and for at least some of the theorists I read, by poststructuralist theories that questioned not merely the value but also the very possibility of identity, unity, communion, consensus, purity, and, in sum, community. Foucauldian theories of the subject as an unstable effect of discourse rather than an authentic origin of identity suggested that there was not unity within the individual subject, let alone among members of a community, and put into doubt the authorizing and naturalizing origin stories on which community formation so often depends. Lyotardian and Derridian theories of language and communication as performative action marked by power and by *différance* (that is, by an unpredictable excess) disrupted the imagination of transparent communication on which notions of consensus were built. The deconstructive critique of binary oppositions suggested that the self-other oppositions on which notions of purity depend are in fact constitutive and that therefore the self is never pure but always already incorporates the other. Derrida's critique of presence undermined the fantasies of communion central to many communities. While some scholars have argued that these theoretical tools are only negative, only disabling to progressive movements insofar as they would seem to dissolve the subject, the agent, of political action,[16] others immediately put these tools to use in an effort to reimagine collective action and community.

Alternative Formulations

Recognizing that, as Mouffe has stated, "An organic unity can never be attained, and there is a heavy price to be paid for such an impossible vision" (preface to *Dimensions*, 5), many academic feminists have used poststructuralist theories of subjectivity and communication to call for or propose new notions of communities of difference. Biddy Martin and Chandra Mohanty, for instance, reiterating in some ways the arguments of Bernice Johnson Reagon's "Coalition Politics: Turning the Century" and writing through Minnie Bruce Pratt's "Identity: Skin, Blood, Heart," argued:

> Unity is exposed to be a potentially repressive fiction. It is at the moment
> at which groups and individuals are conceived as agents, as social actors,
> as desiring subjects, that unity in the sense of a coherent group identity,
> commonality and shared experience becomes difficult. . . . Hence the
> need for a new sense of political community which gives up the desire
> for the kind of home where the suppression of positive differences
> underwrites familial identity. ("Feminist Politics," 205–6)

In "A Manifesto for Cyborgs," Donna Haraway described and responded to the experience of difference within academic feminism in terms of antirealist epistemologies and theories of partial and dynamic subjectivity, proposing collective action based on affinity rather than identity, suggesting (in terms reminiscent of Lyotard's) that it makes sense to do our organizing by generating partial and particular—"situated"—narratives, rather than grand universalizing narratives:

> We do not need totality in order to work well. The feminist dream of
> a common language, like all dreams for a perfectly true language, of
> perfectly faithful naming of experience, is a totalizing and imperialist
> one. . . . The play of a text that has no finally privileged reading or salva-
> tion history . . . frees us of the need to root politics in identification,
> vanguard parties, purity, and mothering. (94, 92, 95)

Iris Marion Young described the exclusionary and totalizing tendencies of the ideal of community, using the critique of presence provided by Derrida as a basis for her argument, and sketched a new utopian vision of community based on a model of urban cohabitation (replacing the small township ideal in which the *Volk* vision of community tends to be anchored) (Young, "Ideal of Community").[17] And Judith Butler, having argued that subjectivity is based not only in identification but also in disidentification, proposed that "the map of future community," "hope for the possibility of avowing an expansive set of connections," lies in "tracing the ways in which identification is implicated in what it excludes" ("Phantasmatic Identification and the Assumption of Sex" in *Bodies*, 118, 119).

The most substantial and persistent efforts to articulate a vision of political community based on difference rather than identity, unity, or communion have been undertaken, in rather different ways, by Chela Sandoval and Mouffe. Sandoval seizes on the margins of hegemonic feminism as a "place" in which "new forms of identity, theory, practice, and community became imaginable." These new forms—differential consciousness and social movement—enable linkages between women who are not "the same" as each other, but are also not the same as themselves, whose subjectivities, ideologies, and relations are "mobile," "tactical," and "oppositional"—that is, dialectically constituted in relation to configurations of power—through a process of interpellation (*Methodology*, 69). Mouffe, meanwhile, builds on her earlier work with Ernesto Laclau in *Hegemony and Socialist Strategy*, which offers a poststructuralist rearticulation of Gramsci's theory of hegemony. Gramsci described the political process as a process of hegemony building, of building movements and parties through a combination of persuasion and compromise. Laclau and Mouffe likewise describe the political process as one of hegemony building. But where for Gramsci, in the last instance, the agents of history are expressing their essential class positions and carrying out necessary functions in a teleological course, Laclau and Mouffe argue that the social space is composed of elements without an essence, elements that are subject to articulation into various social/political formations. They argue that the articulatory process is constitutive of social subjects; the constitution of hegemonic formations transforms the subjects of that articulation, rather than merely joining them in a temporary alliance or coalition. But these formations are always vulnerable to rearticulation.

> To construct a "we" it must be distinguished from the "them" and that means establishing a frontier, defining an enemy. Therefore, while politics aims at constructing a political community and creating a unity, a fully inclusive political community and a final unity can never be realized since there will permanently be a "constitutive outside," an exterior to the community that makes its existence possible. Antagonistic forces will never disappear and politics is characterized by conflict and division. Forms of agreement can be reached but they are always partial and provisional since consensus is by necessity based on acts of exclusion. (Mouffe, "Democratic Citizenship," 234–35)

The visions of complex and unstable social fields of multiple and potentially antagonistic articulations that Sandoval and Laclau and Mouffe offer are very powerful and useful, and serve as a basic presupposition in the theory that I offer throughout the book. Less useful to my own work and, I argue, for progressive movements, is the specific strategy of discursive articulation that Laclau and Mouffe offer at the end of the book and that Mouffe has elaborated in her later work. They propose that progressive social movements should proceed by articulating themselves as equivalent subjects of rights within a liberal pluralist political community. It is certainly the case that rights discourse has been useful to a wide variety of social movements, and that such movements often do articulate themselves as equivalent to others who have already gained rights in order to support their own claims. But rights discourse also has important limits. As Butler argues, "If through its own violences, the conceits of liberal humanism have compelled the multiplication of culturally specific identities, then it is all the more important not to repeat that violence with a significant difference" (*Bodies*, 119). And the logic of equivalence, of analogy, by which such an articulation proceeds is in itself quite problematic insofar as it does necessarily reaffirm that very proliferation of discrete positive identities.[18] Given the instability and complexity of the social field that they describe, it does not make sense to foreclose the range of useful articulatory strategies ahead of time by declaring that one such strategy is *the* right one for progressive movements.

It is, however, crucial for those of us who are concerned to generate social change to actively articulate active collectivities. The various efforts to rearticulate community I have described here are valuable (if limited in ways that I will discuss below) precisely because, in recognizing the discursivity of community, they acknowledge the work that is necessary to produce collective action for emancipatory social change and undertake to think through how to do that work in a way that is in itself humane. By contrast, two important contemporary theorists of community, Jean-Luc Nancy and Giorgio Agamben, propose that the solution to the violently universalizing tendencies of community is to abandon such work.

In *The Inoperative Community,* Nancy argues that we should imagine community as unworked and unworking: "Finitude, or the infinite lack of infinite identity... is what makes community. That is, community is formed by the retreat or by the subtraction of something: this something, which would be the fulfilled infinite identity of community, is what I call its 'work'" (xxxix). For Nancy, the violence of community is generated precisely through the efforts made to produce community and make community productive: "In the work, the properly 'common' character of community disappears, giving way to a unicity and a substantiality... It yields its being-together to a being *of* togetherness... (Nothing indicates more clearly what the logic of this being of togetherness can imply than the role of *Gemeinschaft,* of community, in Nazi ideology)" (xxxix). Thus far, his analysis accords well with the poststructuralist assessments of the impossibility of community as unity, presence, communion, and the dangers of attempting to fulfill such an impossible fantasy. However, unlike the other theorists I have reviewed here, he does not propose that we undertake finite, situated, or processual efforts to articulate political projects. Rather, having made this analysis, he proposes that we must give up all political projects. He argues, "All our political programs imply this work: either as the product of the working community, or else the community itself as a work" (xxxix). He offers, in place of political projects, a vision of community as the condition of being in social relations simply because we are always already in such relations, always already socially constructed: "It is the work that the community does *not* do and that it *is* not that forms community" (xxxix).

In *The Coming Community,* Giorgio Agamben quite similarly suggests that in order to displace the discriminations that constitute community we should approach the experience of community with an attitude he calls "whateverness." For Agamben, "whatever" is not "indifference" but rather "being *such as it is*. . . . In this conception such-and-such being is reclaimed from its having this or that property, which identifies it as belonging to this or that set, to this or that class (the reds, the French, the Muslims)—and it is reclaimed . . . for belonging itself" (1–2). His project is, like Nancy's, to refuse universalizing ambitions, common properties, and identities in favor of what both refer to as *exposure:* "If humans could, that is, not be-thus in this or that particular biography, but be only *the* thus, their singular exteriority and their face, then they would for the first time enter into a community without presuppositions and without subjects, into a communication without the incommunicable" (Agamben, 65). While Agamben claims that "[whatever being] is neither apathy nor promiscuity nor resignation" (10), in working to evoke "the impotent omnivalence of whatever being" (10), he excludes the possibility of articulating even contingent subjects and political goals. He celebrates the Tiananmen protests for "the relative absence of determinate contents in their demands (democracy and freedom are notions too generic and broadly defined to constitute the real object of a conflict . . .)" (85).

While I generally disagree with those who argue that poststructuralist theory promotes political passivity or paralyzing relativism, Nancy and Agamben would certainly seem to offer grist for that complaint since in fact they do quite explicitly promote passivity. But, more important to me, they seem to miss the whole reason that community is interesting at all, which is to say the fact that community generates not an attitude of "whatever" but rather the strongest of passions. And those passions cannot be erased with a theoretical magic wand. Community is one of the most motivating discourses and practices circulating in contemporary society. While attempts to imagine alternative forms of collectivity can be valuable as acts of discursive articulation—and the feminist theorizations of community of/as difference have been to a limited degree effective in shifting the practices of feminists—Nancy and Agamben's theories share with the feminist rearticulations of community reviewed here the important flaw of failing to appreciate the extraordinary power and persistence of a dominant discourse of community.

Collectivities often persist in their projects despite the catachrestical and disputed nature of the identity terms under which they are mobilized; despite the ontological impossibility of identity, people do work together. Further, while a few of us on the left have shifted, somewhat, our strategies for collective action, the not-surprising truth is that the critique of community offered by feminist poststructuralists has made not a dent in the pervasive and celebratory deployment of community in popular culture and even on what used to be the left.[19] In attempting to recuperate by giving new meaning to *community,* both of these approaches fail to address one of the most important implications of the critical literature on community I have reviewed here. What the critiques of community imply, and what some state explicitly, is that fundamental practices of modernity—liberalism, the nation-state, identity political emancipatory movements, and, I argue, most important, capitalism—depend on and generate community.

Before any progressive or resistant reimagination of community will be efficacious, we need to account for the relentless return of the dominant discourse and practice of community. What is the motor driving this discourse ever onward, despite our best efforts to shift it? What makes all these smart theorists want to salvage a term and practice they themselves recognize has been a crucial tool in the very violences they wish to stop? It is these questions that my project attempts to answer. My analysis of how community is produced and consumed, rather than what community ought to be, should make it possible to build movements based on the connections we do have, rather than yearning for lost or impossible utopias. Based on my reading of community as articulated through capitalism, I propose that progressive movements would be well served by articulating themselves through a critique of capitalism.

Community and the Performativity of Capitalism

Insofar as they characterize community as traditional, conservative, regressive, irrational, or oppressive, the assessments of community I have described (and in which I participate) are themselves imbricated in a progressive narrative of Enlightenment that defines itself through the othering of community, even as it generates Romantic nostalgia for that lost past other. Like the celebration of community, this "othering" of community seems to run across the political spectrum. In popular discourse, community appears as a negative where some community seems to offer resistance to assimilation, modernization, or capital penetration. But if community is the defining other of modernity, progress, and capitalism, then it is always already inside modernity. I can begin to account for its relentless return in the relentless elaboration of capitalism and the liberal nation-state formations that characterize modernity.

Where the earlier analyses of community focused on the tendency of community to universalize particularities, I argue that the work of community is to generate and legitimate necessary particularities and social hierarchies (of gender, race, nation, sexuality) implicitly required, but disavowed, by capitalism, a discourse of abstraction and equivalence. In shifting from the familiar analytic dyad, particularity/universality, to a less familiar hermeneutic pairing, particularity/abstraction, I mean to shift focus from the question of sameness and difference to the question of social processes. Where particularity/universality poses the question of (static or essential) identity, particularity/abstraction poses questions of equivalence, translatability, communication, and circulation, questions of social relations and social activities as mobilized for particular political and economic purposes.

I propose (most directly in chapter 1) that community—the Romanticized "other" of modernity—supplements capital, that community is deployed to shore it up and facilitate the flow of capital. But I also argue, in chapter 2, on the performativity of capitalism, that capital supplements community. I propose that social formations, including community, are constituted through the performativity of production, that capitalism is the very medium in which community is enacted. These are related but distinct arguments. The first describes the constitutive significance of community for capitalism, the dependence of capitalism on community. And it seeks in effect to answer the question of why community persists.

The second argument, for the performativity of production, describes the significance of capitalism for community; in describing the multivalent social relations enacted through our participation in production and consumption, it attempts to recognize the extraordinary power of capitalism in shaping our social relations. (This second chapter also retreads in rather different theoretical language the argument of the first chapter: it expands the purview of production to include activities that go on outside the factory, outside of commodity production, arguing for the productivity of performance—that is to say, arguing that our cultural, our communal practices are generative for capitalism and not only or even primarily outside or against capital.) The second chapter addresses then the question of how community is constituted.

The distinction between the two arguments is crucial in that I do not mean to offer a structural-functionalist analysis. I do not argue that the communal formations enacted through capitalist processes exist only in service to capitalism; rather, the supplementarity of community with capital suggests that community both supports and displaces capitalism. I bring the two arguments together in chapter 3, where, through an ethnographic as well as theoretical exploration of the constitution of community at the site of the nonprofit organization, I am able to track most closely the displacements, the ways that communal subjects constituted for capitalism also fail to be only subjects of capitalism.

However, I do mean to suggest that community is complicit with capitalism and also that communities are, through capitalism, complicit with each other. This theoretical strategy—that is to say, my implication of community in capital—enables an understanding of the relationship between sites of value that otherwise seem to be discontinuous: gay consumers in the United States and Mexican maquiladora workers; Christian right "family values" and Asian "crony" capitalism. While for some my move to mark community as "complicit" may seem a loss of an imagined space of authenticity and opposition, I find this complicity a relief, opening up space to imagine collectivities unimaginable from within the repressive space of community. In marking the complicity of heterogeneous social practices, identities, and communities with capitalism, I hope to make it possible to imagine alliances across those differences.

I make these arguments through an interweaving of discourse analysis with theoretical exposition. I develop my claim for the supplementarity of community with capital through readings of Marx's theory of value, of the relation between value, the abstract equivalence of commodities with each other, and use value, the concrete material bearer of value. Likewise, I articulate production as performative, and thus able to generate polyvalent individual and communal subjectivities, through readings of several of Marx's key arguments, beginning with his fundamental claim in *The German Ideology* that social relations are implied in material relations of production and ending with his discussions of the production of conscious classes in *The Manifesto of the Communist Party* and *The Eighteenth Brumaire*. Both within the first two chapters and in chapters 3, 4, and 5, I elaborate these theorizations through analyses of a wide range of materials: debates in the popular media and in the U.S. Congress over arts and education; popular and academic narratives of economic transformation ("globalization"); and most important, my own ethnographic studies of the gay/lesbian nonprofit Theatre Rhinoceros and of the controversy over the National Endowment for the Arts (NEA).

The case studies featured in chapters 3, 4, and 5 explore the supplementarity of community with capital and the performativity of production in diverse sites and across different scales. Chapter 3 treats these issues at the scale of a single organization, Theatre Rhinoceros, exploring the ways that participation in nonprofit and nongovernmental organizations (NGOs) constitutes individual subjects. Chapter 4 shifts to the scale of the nation, examining the renegotiation of the relation between nation and state in the context of the economic transformations of the 1980s and 1990s. Chapter 5 takes on the narratives of that economic transformation directly, examining discourses of globalization. While these chapters would seem to move progressively from smaller to larger scales, in some sense they also move from larger to smaller scales. My analysis of the constitution of communal subjectivity at the site of the individual nonprofit organization in chapter 3 is situated in an analysis of the deployment of NGOs in international economic development practices, and my discussion of globalization in chapter 5 focuses on the role of gender, sexuality, and kinship formations.

In attending to the discursive deployments of community throughout the chapters, I explore the narrative mechanisms by which community is naturalized or "culturalized" and thus enabled to legitimate the hierarchies of capitalism. In chapter 1, I begin a discussion of the temporal legitimations of community as an ideal social formation predating the fall into "society," a temporal story that renders community as autonomous from capital, the site of values rather than value, and as a complement (rather than supplement) to capitalism. In chapter 2, I describe the fetishization of community through the elision of the labor involved in producing community. Chapter 3 takes on the currently popular discourse of civil society (defined as the realm of voluntary associations), arguing that rather than being the expression of already formed subjects, nonprofits and NGOs are in fact sites at which subjects are formed as subjects of capital, even as the existence of nonprofits indicates a crucial

subjectivity gap in capitalism, an absence of subjects constituted as capitalist subjects. It argues that while participation in nonprofits is articulated as gift-exchange, such exchange is not external to for-profit economic exchange but rather is a supplement to such economic exchange.

Chapter 4, in examining the constitution of gay and Christian communities through their participation in the NEA controversy, deconstructs
the binary opposition between gays and Christians that has marked the
political efforts of both groups. I argue that gay and Christian communities are more similar than they might at first appear insofar as they
both enact themselves as niched producers and consumers and are thus
similarly symptomatic of post-Fordist capitalism. At the same time, I
contest the conflation of the two as simply discountable extremes in relation to which some political middle ground seems the only reasonable
choice. Rather, I point out the ways that each carried part of the discursive burden of an unresolved crisis over the shifting relation between
nation and state, between the nation conceived as a particular community, and the state, ambivalently operating as an apparatus for constituting national subjects and as an abstract administrator of rights.

Chapter 5 reads the discourse of globalization as structured by analogics, that is, as a narrative that articulates the inclusion of diverse
particularities into capital through an apparently open-ended logic of
equivalence. It argues that analogy presupposes the autonomy of each
incorporated community, thus erasing the prior history and current
dynamics by which the community is constituted. And it explores the
ways that such analogics work in concert with binary oppositions to
produce and legitimate the hierarchical arrangement of the incorporated communities. It thus argues that the narrative of a historical break
between Fordist capitalism based on the binary logics constituting nations and post-Fordist capitalism articulated through analogics—a narrative that can be found in both cultural studies and popular discourses
of globalization—is problematic insofar as it offers a temporal supplement to the spatial hierarchies of globalized capital (international divisions of wealth and labor).

The ethnographic material figures differently in different chapters.
In the NEA chapter (chapter 4), I read small quotations from interviews
much as I read direct mail advertisements or other artifacts of the controversy, that is, as symptomatic of the discourses through which the relationships between the actors in the controversy were articulated. In

chapter 3, I deploy longer selections from my Theatre Rhinoceros materials (transcripts of meetings and interviews). In that chapter my own turn toward particularity, my recourse to ethnographic detail, is meant to perform the relation of particularity to abstraction as well as to demonstrate the work of particularity in capitalism that I describe in chapter 1. The concrete particularity of the ethnographic materials supplements my theoretical argument, giving it substance and mobility, even while marking its insufficiencies and discontinuities, displacing the theory by being alternately excessive and too particular, the only case to which the theory applies. Viewed through the lens of my theoretical apparatus, this particular case appears equivalent with, exchangeable for, others, supporting my abstractions, allowing them to circulate. At the same time, the ethnographic material, in its particularity, presents certain kinds of resistances and contradictions to the totalizing tendencies of my theoretical argument, presenting it with challenges to be overcome, opening it up to the openness of performative production.

CHAPTER ONE

The Supplementarity of Community with Capital; or, A Critique of the Romantic Discourse of Community

Deployments of community, both verbal invocations and practices, are conditioned by a larger discourse of community, a pervasive way of thinking and doing community that would seem to answer all the important questions before they have even been asked, that sets the terms in which we might ask questions, and that shapes what we can see and do and even who we are. What I call the discourse of community positions community as the defining other of modernity, of capitalism. This discourse includes a Romantic narrative of community as prior in time to "society," locating community in a long-lost past for which we yearn nostalgically from our current fallen state of alienation, bureaucratization, rationality. It distinguishes community from society spatially, as local, involving face-to-face relations, where capital is global and faceless; community is all about boundaries between us and them, boundaries that are naturalized through reference to place or race or culture or identity, while capital would seem to denature, crossing all borders and making everything, everyone, equivalent. Further, this discourse contrasts community to modern capitalist society structurally: the foundation of community is supposed to be values, while capitalist society is based only on value (economic value). Community is posited as particular where capitalism is abstract. Posited as its other, its opposite, community is often presented as a complement to capitalism, balancing and humanizing it, even, in fact, enabling it.

Community and capital, posed as complementary binary opposites; an invitation to deconstruction, an invitation I cannot refuse. The community/capital binary implies both that the domain of community is autonomous from capitalist society and that particular communities are discrete and autonomous from each other. In this chapter I will begin an exploration, which I will pursue throughout the book, of the discursive techniques by which the opposition and autonomy of community and capital are constructed. I argue that in being articulated as discontinuous from each other and "society," communities are actually linked to capitalism and through capitalism to each other. I propose that, precisely through being cast as its opposite, community functions in complicity with "society," enabling capitalism and the liberal state.

I describe the relation between community and capital as supplementary. Derrida defines supplementarity this way: "The supplement adds itself, it is a surplus, a plenitude enriching another plentitude.... But the supplement ... adds only to replace. It intervenes or insinuates itself *in-the-place-of*; if it fills, it is as if one fills a void.... its place is assigned in the structure by the mark of an emptiness" (*Of Grammatology,* 145). A supplementary reading notes the void, the absent center, of any structure, suggesting that a given structure cannot be by itself coherent, autonomous, self-sustaining, or what Gayatri Spivak calls "continuous." The structure constitutively depends on something outside itself, a surplus that completes it, providing the coherence, the continuity, the stability that it cannot provide for itself, although it is already complete. But at the same time, this supplement to the structure supplants that structure; insofar as the structure depends on this constitutive supplement, the supplement becomes the primary structure itself; its own logic becomes, or at least may become, dominant or destabilizing, a blockage to the continuity, a sign of crisis or incompleteness.

A supplementary reading of community and capital reverses the order of continuities and discontinuities. While community and capital are each posited as internally coherent (continuous) structures, autonomous (discontinuous) from each other—and communities are likewise taken to be discrete and whole vis-à-vis other communities—in a supplementary reading, community and capital are both internally incoherent and externally connected. Community and capital appear to be mutually dependent structures and, likewise, communities are revealed to be dependent on each other. But at the same time, a supplementary reading sustains the discontinuities between community and capital, noting the ways that they exceed and displace each other in a dynamic process, rather than merely complementing each other to form a complete and stable system.

I propose that Marx's theory of value describes the supplementary relation of community with capital quite precisely in its articulation of the relation between use value and value, between, that is, particularity and abstraction. However, making Marx's theory useful as a description of the relation between community and capital requires disentangling his structural account from his historical account, which in orthodox Marxist and Frankfurt School appropriations does tend to support the notion that capital has superseded community. And, as it turns out, the construction of the community/capital binary—a structural relation— is often (not only in Marx and Marxisms) supported, supplemented even, by problematic temporal and spatial accounts, which are themselves often deployed as supplements of each other.

In this chapter I explore the temporal problem.[1] I examine the narratives that claim that capitalism, modernity, society have replaced or destroyed community. I discuss the ways such temporal narratives are used to constitute a relation between community and capital as a structural relation operating in the present. I then begin to offer an alternative account of the relation between community and capital through a reading of Marx's theory of value, and in that section also examine the ways that Marxist historical accounts have supplemented the theory of value to produce "one-dimensional" visions of society. In the third section of the chapter, I examine recent political debates over pluralism, multiculturalism, and diversity, examining the changing ways that the discourse of community is deployed in those debates as an intervention into the changing social relations of capitalism in crisis and expansion.

The Romantic Discourse of Community

Much twentieth-century scholarship on the place of community in American society invokes Tocqueville's *Democracy in America* as the quintessential statement on the topic.[2] Tocqueville describes the United States (as he observed it in the 1830s) as built on the base of the "township system": the "township was the nucleus round which the local interests, passions, rights and duties collected and clung. It gave scope to the activity of a real political life, thoroughly democratic and republican. . . . In the New England town . . . the affairs of the community were discussed, as at Athens, in the marketplace by the general assembly of the citizens" (vol. 1, 42). While such passages are often deployed by contemporary advocates of localism,[3] such uses of Tocqueville miss what I would argue is his more important analytic argument. He posits the township as ideal not to argue that face-to-face relations are in themselves some sort of magic bullet but rather because, as townships functioned politically in the historical moment in which he observed them, they are the context within which two potentially problematic aspects of American political culture, equality and democracy, work together productively.[4]

Tocqueville argues that equality leads people to see inside themselves the only relevant authority and to act only on behalf of themselves and their immediate circle. While on the positive side such individualism promotes tremendous energetic entrepreneurial activity, Tocqueville suggests that it may lead on one hand to political and social anomie and on the other to too much conformity, since people lacking a real external authority turn instead to social convention for many of their personal beliefs. Democracy, he argues, acts as an antidote. Rather than positing democratic process as the realm of the abstract liberal subject who has left his private interests at home, he articulates it as the realm in which individual interests are elaborated. Opportunities to participate in local government and freedom of political association encourage and enable people to organize, to engage in collective action to further their interests (see especially vol. 2, second book). "As soon as several of the inhabitants of the United States have taken up an opinion or a feeling which they wish to promote in the world, they look for mutual assistance, and as soon as they have found each other out, they combine" (vol. 2, 117).[5] Tocqueville's "communities" then are resolutely modern sites in which equality and democracy together produce a highly active citizenry. He emphasizes the modernity of these social formations by contrasting them with the traditional authoritarian structures of Europe, where "political existence . . . commenced in the superior ranks of society" (vol. 1, 42) and trickled down, resulting in a notable lack of "local public spirit" (vol. 1, 69).

Tocqueville's position would seem to bear some resemblance to that of Raymond Williams as articulated in Williams's discussion of the impact of enclosure laws on community formation in the late eighteenth and early nineteenth centuries in England. Against the idealization of preenclosure communities that he reads in the literature of the period, Williams argues that while such villages may have provided certain opportunities for independence for laborers, nonetheless, "the inequalities of condition which the village contains and supports are profound, and nobody, by any exercise of sentiment, can convert it into a 'rural democracy' or, absurdly, a commune. The social structure that will be completed after enclosure is already basically outlined" (*Country and City*, 102). But even more importantly, and in concert with Tocqueville, he argues against the notion, likewise apparent in the literature of the period, that the possibility of community was destroyed by enclosure. "Another thing we can learn is that community must not always be seen in retrospect.... In many villages, community only became a reality when economic and political rights were fought for and partially gained, in the recognition of unions, in the extension of the franchise, and in the possibility of entry into new representative and democratic institutions. In many thousands of cases, there is more community in the modern village, as a result of this process of new legal and democratic rights, than at any point in the recorded or imagined past" (104).

But Tocqueville and Williams are lonely voices against the dominant view that political and economic modernity has destroyed or replaced community. When Tocqueville is cited, as he is relentlessly in the extensive mid- to late twentieth-century genre of crossover academic/popular assessments of American society, he is invoked for the sake of a contrast between a problematic "modern" present and a "premodern" past that is generally articulated as a Golden Age of community. Texts such as Reisman's *The Lonely Crowd*, Sennett's *The Fall of Public Man*, Lasch's *Culture of Narcissism*, Bell's *The Cultural Contradictions of Capitalism*, Bellah and others' *Habits of the Heart*, Etzioni's *The Spirit of Community*, Putnam's "Bowling Alone," and Dionne's edited collection *Community Works* all insist that a once-vibrant communality is absent from or in crisis in contemporary society.[6] Tocqueville is credited with pointing out the dangers of modernity that these texts argue have now overtaken us (see, for instance, Sennett, *Fall*, 30–31, or Bell, *Cultural Contradictions*, 100), and he is primarily deployed to invoke a lost era in which face-to-face local and familial relations infused with "biblical and republican traditions" (Bellah et al., *Habits*, 37) counterbalanced such dangers: "In Tocqueville's still-agrarian America, as indeed throughout the nineteenth century, the basic unit of association, and the practical foundation of both individual dignity and participation, was the local community.... American citizenship was anchored in the ethos and institutions of the face-

to-face community of the town" (Bellah, *Habits,* 38–39). While many of
these texts explicitly disavow nostalgia—Reisman's 1969 preface for instance says that while "most readers seem to have regarded [the changes
we described] as changes for the worse . . . we viewed both the American
past and present with irony and ambivalence" (xiii)[7]—most do in fact
portray an idealized past against the present and seek to "build—and re-
build—community" along the lines of models drawn from an imagined
past (Dionne, "Introduction," 3).

That particular genre of texts is of course hardly unique in opposing
an idealized community of the past to a problematic contemporary society. Williams, in describing the literary history of the idealization of
country life (the site of community) traces the recurrence of such retrospective and nostalgic narratives back to Hesiod (though he does suggest
that it takes on a particular intensity as a response to the social transformations of emergent capitalism).[8] And the temporal sequencing of community and society is the authoritative sociological narrative. Thomas
Bender traces the development of this narrative from Maine to Tonnies's
theory of the transformation from *Gemeinschaft* to *Gesellschaft* to
Durkheim's opposition of mechanical and organic solidarity to Redfield's
distinction between folk and urban cultures to Parson's elaboration of
the opposition in terms of four dichotomies: affectivity vs. neutrality,
particularism vs. universalism, ascription vs. achievement, and diffuseness
vs. specificity (*Community and Social Change,* 16–24).[9] Weber's narrative
of rationalization and Habermas's story of a "lifeworld" increasingly
encroached on by "system" *(Theory of Communicative Action)* are also
versions of the community/society opposition posed as a temporal sequence in which society replaces community. One might plausibly argue
that the oppositional sequencing of community and society is constitutive of the field of sociology. But as Williams points out, the retrospective idealization of community against modernity is articulated differently and for different purposes in different historical moments; thus,
the point is to understand how it is being deployed at a particular historical conjuncture.

What the Romantic discourse of the second half of the twentieth century in the United States shares with the pastoral tradition that Williams
describes as characteristic of the eighteenth and early nineteenth centuries
in England is that idealizations of community operate as conservative
critiques of changes in the given social hierarchy.[10] While one might

read Tocqueville as emphasizing the importance of democratic processes, of real opportunities for people to pursue their interests by participating in collective action and decision making, those texts tend to pick up on the other side of Tocqueville's argument, that is, on the dangers of equality in its simultaneous encouragement of solipsism and conformism. They decry the "evils of untrammelled individualism" (Lasch, *Culture and Narcissism*, 37) and yearn for moral codes and families; they seek to replace self-interest with self-reliance, to pair "rights" with "responsibilities" (Etzioni, *Spirit of Community*, 4) and "commitment" to "community" (Bellah et al., *Habits*, 197). Their arguments slip very fast to the right, to implicit and even explicit affirmations of social hierarchies of gender, race, and class. This slippage occurs both within and across texts. While Etzioni specifically claims that community need not be authoritarian, since in a community people voluntarily obey internalized moral codes, he also calls for an end to the extension of civil rights; Bellah eschews a return to "intolerable discrimination and oppression," but his ideal community is an all white middle-class town (*Habits*, 144). Donald Wildmon of the American Family Association (a conservative Christian media-watch organization) quotes Bellah, thus producing and revealing a slippage from Bellah's civic republicanism to fundamentalist Christianity, from commitment to community to submission to god. According to Wildmon, Bellah, "at a recent national church meeting, painted a scary picture of individualism (humanism) gone rampant. Robert Bellah said he found the typical attitude was: 'You're responsible for yourself and no one else.' Such a freedom, he stated, finds that 'marriage, friends, job, community, church are all dispensable'" (*Home Invaders*, 26–27). Wildmon's parenthetical interpretation of individualism as humanism performs the rightward slide: the problem with humanism for Wildmon (and conservative Christians more generally) is that it expresses a belief in the authority of humans rather than god. Meanwhile, Alan Ehrenhalt, in an essay in Dionne's collection, argues, simply, that authority is constitutive of community:

> We don't want the 1950s back. What we want is to edit them. We want to keep the safe streets, the friendly grocers, and the milk and cookies, while blotting out the political bosses, the tyrannical headmasters, the inflexible rules, and the lectures on 100 percent Americanism and the sinfulness of dissent. But there is no easy way to have an orderly world without somebody making the rules by which order is preserved. Every

dream we have about recreating civil society in the absence of authority will turn out to be a pipe dream in the end. . . . To worship choice and community together is to misunderstand what community is all about. ("Where Have All the Followers Gone?" 96–97)

What differentiates the late-twentieth-century deployment of community from that of the early nineteenth century is its relation to capitalism. The early-nineteenth-century articulation is not merely reactionary, not merely a yearning for older social formations in which all people knew their proper place, but is specifically anticapitalist, rejecting the commodification of culture and human relationship (Sayre and Lowy, "Figures"). By contrast, the twentieth-century U.S. discourse does not mobilize its concern for community against capitalism. Some of these texts, especially those midcentury texts written in the context of Fordist mass production and consumption, such as Reisman's *The Lonely Crowd* or Lasch's *Culture of Narcissism,* might be read as a critique of monopoly capitalism. And some of their authors do claim to be anticapitalist: in *The Cultural Contradictions of Capitalism,* Bell claims that his concern is with the breakdown of cohering moral values, traditions, and/or asceticism that might temper capitalism and their replacement by modernism and postmodernism, cultural movements that he claims are promoted by and useful to capitalism because they celebrate change and hedonism. However, for the most part, these analyses focus more on the bureaucratic nature of the large corporation than on capitalism per se, and they are more often turned against the welfare state than against capitalism. Bellah says, "The bureaucratic organization of the business corporation has been the dominant force in this century" (*Habits,* 45), and Lasch argues, "Modern bureaucracy has undermined earlier traditions of local action, the revival and extension of which holds out the only hope that a decent society will emerge from the wreckage of capitalism" (*Culture of Narcissism,* 20), bemoaning the replacement of the family by various social service and psychological industries and the replacement of "traditions of self-help" with "dependence on the state, the corporation and other bureaucracies" (37). They are concerned that bureaucracy produces what Reisman calls "outer directedness" or as Lasch says, "a society that demands submission to the rules of social intercourse but refuses to ground those rules in a code of moral conduct" (41). In fact, entrepreneurial capitalism—"the activist individual entrepreneur" (Bellah, *Habits,* 45)—is often celebrated. Wildmon says,

"Capitalism, nurtured by Christian ethics, is the finest system ever devised by mankind . . . 'The free enterprise system is set up to reward your energy'" (*Home Invaders,* 40–41). And capitalist consumption is cast as the site of democratic action: Wildmon urges boycotts as an exercise of the "rule of democratic capitalism," which provides that "the consumer can spend his money where he desires" (49). The nostalgic discourse of community would ultimately seem to propose that capitalism be precisely nurtured—"tempered" in the sense of strengthened—not challenged or constrained, by community.

Joined as they are in these texts, the critique of bureaucracy and the critique of individualism perform a radical transformation of Tocqueville's notion of balance and complementarity between individualism and community. The critiques of bureaucratic conformism promote differentiation, while the critiques of individualism promote subordination to existing social norms and structures. Taken together, differentiation and subordination would seem to yield hierarchy. Whereas Tocqueville describes the ways that the integrating tendencies of democracy complement the isolating tendencies of equality, in these texts it becomes a question of complementing the freedom and equivalence generated by capitalism with social hierarchy. However, I will argue, capitalism does not simply entail freedom and equivalence. In fact, it is precisely in generating and legitimating social hierarchy that "community" supplements (enables, fills a void in) capitalism. But far from articulating community as a supplement, this Romantic discourse of community-less modernity renders community and capitalism quite independent of each other.

To imagine that a long-lost communality might return to nurture contemporary capitalism requires detaching community from the social, economic, political, and historical conditions that enabled the particular forms of sociality that would seem to be so appealing. And, in fact, the Romantic discourse of community does this precisely by placing community in an idealized past, disconnected from the present as if by epochal break. In representing a temporal discontinuity between community and modern society, it elides the material processes that have transformed social relations (material processes that, like Williams, I would and will propose have generated new communities). As Thomas Bender says of the sociological tradition he outlines, one might say of this popular discourse: "Its sense of the past is made up of ideal types linked only by logical necessity. This logic conveniently supplies a history without obliging the theorist to analyze structural change as a tempo-rally and culturally situated process" (*Community and Social Change*, 16). Rather than ascribing community participation to the historical and hard-won emergence of a particular form of democracy, as Tocqueville does, these twentieth-century texts ascribe such public spirit to "virtues and values generated neither by the state nor by the market" (Dionne [paraphrasing Wolfe], "Introduction," 5), to a more or less explicitly Christian morality posited as timeless. Community ceases to be a set of social relations and becomes "a particular and private sensibility, the individual moral action" (Williams, *Country and City*, 180). Where for Tocqueville and Williams community connotes collective action—a group joined in common cause, fighting for economic gain or against some form of economic or political oppression—in much of this liter-ature community is rendered quite passive, static, conservative: commu-nity describes that network of people who inevitably know your name and your business because you interact with them every day, rather than those you have sought out as allies (Dionne, "Introduction," 10); com-munity is founded in values held and inherited, "passed along to chil-dren" (4), rather than purposes or goals to be achieved. Having elided the material basis for and the historical process of social transformation, "community" floats free of its location in the idealized past and appears to be independent of but potentially complementary (and for that mat-ter complimentary) to capitalism in the present.[11]

Oddly enough, once community has been articulated as "values" that are autonomous in relation to material (that is, economic and political) conditions, it suddenly appears that "rumors of the death of older forms of community had been greatly exaggerated" (Dionne, "Introduction," 4; see also Wolfe, "Is Civil Society Obsolete," 20). It seems that we can turn to community itself to solve problems—poverty, crime, drug use, single-parent families—that are taken to be both evidence and cause of the crisis of community: "family breakdown, neighborhood violence, and a weakening of traditional local institutions and constraints" (Dionne, "In-troduction,"4). Rather than intervene in political or economic processes, since in this view such processes have little bearing on "community," the contributors to Dionne's collection turn to a combination of moral ex-hortation and nonprofit organizations, most especially churches, to solve social problems (see, for instance, the contributions by DiIulio, Rivers, and Himmelfarb).[12] This, of course, as Dionne points out and celebrates, is the perspective that brought us the Moynihan Report and the "culture of poverty"; the Personal Responsibility Act of 1996, which ended welfare as we knew it (and which is defended by Senators Rick Santorum and Dan Coats in an article in Dionne's collection); and the many other efforts to devolve social welfare of various kinds onto individuals and nongovernmental organizations. Arguments such as these, which presuppose the independence of community from capital, suggest that capitalism should not be held accountable for poverty or social dislocation. And in fact such arguments elide the role of capitalism; for instance, the discussions by Dionne and Coats and Santorum ("Civil Society") of the dismantling of welfare in the United States give no hint that this dismantling is a structural adjustment policy of precisely the type that the International Monetary Fund imposes on developing countries to make them safe for globalizing capital (by further impoverishing the already poor).

The screw turns a bit further, though not without splitting the board. In his widely acclaimed but also widely disclaimed essay "Bowling Alone," published in 1995 in the *Journal of Democracy*, and even more explicitly in his earlier piece, "The Prosperous Community" in *The American Prospect* (1993), Robert Putnam argues that community is not merely a good unto itself, a realm for the good life that is independent of and to some extent protected from or a protection against the state and the market (as Barber, for instance, claims). Rather, he says that "Americans' sense of their own communityness" (Hauser, *Opening*, 11) is "social capital," a stock of "trust, norms and networks" (Putnam, "Prosperous Community," 35) to be invested, both politically and economically.

Much of Putnam's argument is par for the course of this literature. Whereas I (and Foley and Edwards) read Tocqueville as claiming that a civically engaged community is an outcome of democracy, Putnam argues conversely that "when Tocqueville visited the United States in the 1830s, it was the American's propensity for civic association that most impressed him as the key to their unprecedented ability to make democracy work" ("Bowling Alone," 65). Typically, he thus renders Americans' tendency to associate as a "cultural" characteristic, a value, independent of its political and economic conditions, arguing that the source of a healthy associational life is primarily to be found in traditions of association ("Prosperous Community," 37). He explicitly says that "investments in physical capital, financial capital, human capital and social capital are complementary" ("Prosperous Community," 40). That is, despite the fact that he recognizes that "dramatic technological, social and economic progress" as well as "massive waves of immigration" (Hauser, *Opening*, 11) has disrupted existing communal formations, he sees no role for political or economic change in generating community.

Defining "communityness" or social capital as "trust, norms and networks," he, again typically, presents a highly conservative view of community, where "trust" of one's government and fellow man is a good regardless of the trustworthiness of the government or fellow men and in which economic cooperation is a good regardless of the conditions of subordination or exploitation the cooperation might entail. Putnam argues, of course, that our collective stocks of social capital have been depleted, claiming to document a falloff in participation in parent-teacher associations, bowling leagues, and unions ("Bowling Alone").[13] Putnam's claim of a decline in social capital formation depends on excluding or discounting political organizations and national organizations, organizations driven by inequities of power or wealth and aimed at contesting the dominant "community," as well as family, school, and workplace, as sites of community formation (see Foley and Edwards, "Escape," 554–5, and Newton, "Social Capital"). Instead, the voluntary associations that generate "social capital" (the ones that count, that we should count and, more importantly, fund) are primarily local face-to-face organizations aimed at mutual benefit or recreation (thus bowling) and that, as he repeats again and again, reinforce norms, networks, and trust.[14] He is not interested in promoting dissent or conflict. And, in fact, as Foley and Edwards point out, social harmony would seem to be the goal of Putnam's vision of community. The social value of local community formation, for Putnam, is not in the challenges that such communities might offer to dominant regimes but rather in that they are sites of incorporation into hegemonic regimes.

But Putnam goes further, and this is the crucial point: he argues that the health of democratic states and economic prosperity both depend on social capital, saying, "The social capital embodied in norms and networks of civic engagement seems to be a precondition for economic development, as well as for effective government" ("Prosperous Community," 37). In arguing that economic progress (he means but doesn't say capitalist economic progress) and "democracy" depend on community (or rather on the hegemony-producing functions of community), he points to the supplementary, and not merely complementary, role that community plays in relation to capitalism, and thus begins to make my argument for me, although he does so as a fan of capitalism, where I will do so as a critic.

The Supplementary Relation of Community with Capital

Marx's theory of value, elaborated in the opening pages of *Capital*, volume 1, and in the *Grundrisse*, can be read, and I read it, as articulating the ongoing structural supplement that community offers to the abstract determination, circulation, and realization of capital. In other words, Marx articulates the necessary role that historically particular and differentiated social formations play as the bearers of capital, as the medium within which capital circulates, without which it cannot circulate.

In the first chapters of *Capital*, Marx describes the commodity as simultaneously a use value and a value; the commodity thus joins two different orders of value. Value, the "exchange relation of commodities, is characterized precisely by their abstraction from use value" (vol. 1 [Fowkes], 127). As values, he says, commodities "do not contain one atom of use value" (128). Value is what remains when use value, the particularity and concreteness of the commodity, is "subtracted," that is, when particularities become irrelevant in a given moment of exchange. Marx suggests that use values are merely "material bearers" of exchange value (126): "As old Barbon says, 'one sort of wares are as good as another, if their value be equal'"(127). Marx would seem here to be dismissing use value as irrelevant to capital accumulation. However, in the *Grundrisse* ("The Chapter on Money") as well as in volume 2 of *Capital*, the role of use values as material bearers of exchange value resurfaces as a relevant function. Rather than focusing as he does in the first volume of *Capital* on the process of production alone, in these texts he has the whole circuit of capital in mind; he is looking not only at production but at the distribution and consumption of the commodities produced. And for capital to travel through this circuit, values must be embodied in use values.

In "Scattered Speculations on the Theory of Value," Spivak notes that the common reading of the "labor theory of value" describes the determination of capital as a chain of increasing abstraction, grounded positively in labor: labor is represented by value, which is in turn represented by money, which then appears transformed as capital. However,

Spivak argues that this chain is discontinuous, open at each moment of representation or transformation. It is open at the origin in the sense that value is not only determined positively by labor, but negatively, differentially, as an abstraction from use value.[15] Likewise, for money to represent value, it has to be separated from its own being as a commodity. However, if money is not simply to be hoarded, this separation, the abstractness of money, must be negated as it is exchanged for commodities. And finally, the transformation of money into capital depends not only on prior accumulations of (abstract) capital but on what Marx calls original or primitive accumulation, the separation of labor from the means of production through domination, and, further, on the super-adequation of labor, its ability to produce surplus value, that is, its use value (Spivak, "Scattered Speculations," 158–62). So, while the determination of capital would seem to be a continuous and therefore independent chain of representation and transformation, in fact, at each stage, the movement toward abstraction—that is, the predication of capital itself—depends on the intervention of other orders of value or on an investment in particular use values.

The indeterminateness of capital, its openness to determination by use value, is an opening to "community," to determination by social relations and "values" in exchange, production, and consumption. Marx says, "Nothing can be a value [that is, exchangeable] without being an object of utility" (vol. 1, 131). But utility is socially and historically determined: "Every useful thing is a whole composed of many properties; it can therefore be useful in many ways. The discovery of these ways and hence the manifold uses of things is the work of history" (125). Likewise, the production process itself is dependent on historically particular social relations. Production, as Marx says, is "conditional on reproduction processes outside the reproduction process of the individual capital" (vol. 2, 154), that is, the producer must be able to obtain the necessary materials (raw and otherwise) for his production process. While Marx is here referring to the dependence of one capitalist on other capitalist producers, the dependence of capital on other orders of value is also made obvious, especially, since, for Marx, the important commodity is labor power. For production to be possible, a process of social distribution must assign some but not all, at birth, to wage labor and distribute the members of society among the different kinds of production (*Grundrisse*, 96). And, as "the object is not an object in general but a specific object which must be consumed in specific manner" (*Grundrisse*, 92), consumption as well can only occur within a particular social formation, in which particular desires for particular commodities, produced by particular acts of labor, are operative.

This reading of the theory of value suggests that the particularities of historically and socially determined use values, which include particular social relations and "values," supplement the discontinuous circuit of abstract value, enabling its circulation. In this structural account, "community" is quite crucial to capitalism. Where Romantic anticapitalism, as Moishe Postone argues, selects for attack only the abstract side of capital (value) and does not comprehend the whole dialectic of abstraction (value) and particularity (concrete use-value) through which capital operates, this analysis of the role of use value in capital circulation indicates that particular communal formations must also be subject to critique. Postone suggests that the Romantic misapprehension is encouraged by capital itself, that commodity fetishism presents, materializes, value and use-value, abstraction and concreteness, as a naturalized antinomy of money and commodities.

> Forms of anticapitalist thought that remain bound within the immediacy of this antinomy tend to perceive capitalism, and that which is specific to that social formation, only in terms of the manifestations of the abstract dimension of the antinomy; so for instance, money [or bureaucracy] is considered "the root of all evil." The existent concrete dimension is then positively opposed to it as the "natural" or ontologically human, which presumably stands outside the specificity of capitalist society. Thus, as with Proudhon, for example, concrete labor [or family or local community] is understood as the noncapitalist moment opposed to the abstraction of money. That concrete labor itself incorporates and is materially formed by capitalist social relations is not understood. ("Anti-Semitism and National Socialism," 309)

As Postone goes on to argue, in his account of fascist antisemitism, this allows industrial production or, I would argue, individual and family-based entrepreneurship to be celebrated (as it is in the texts discussed in the previous section) as rooted in "Community *(Gemeinschaft)*, *Volk*, Race," while finance capital and the bureaucracy of the multinational corporation appear rootless (310). While Marx's structural account of the value/use value relation makes it impossible to posit sites of value such as "community," "culture," "family," or "values" as offering a pure or resistant alternative to capitalism, this account does make it possible (as I hope to demonstrate throughout the book) to trace the complicity of race, ethnicity, gender, nation, and sexuality with capital.

However, Marx's structural account does not stand alone. It is supplemented by a historical argument that might seem to undo the complex view of the relation between community and capital that his structural account of value provides. As Negri points out, Marx's account of circulation in the *Grundrisse* is literally interrupted by a historical digression that would seem to suggest that capitalism destroys community, or at least destroys the particularity and differentiation of social identities and communities. Without any sign of the nostalgia that is characteristic of the Romantic discourse of community, Marx describes a course of diachronic development from precapitalist communities based in natural bonds of flesh and blood, language, division of labor, and personal dependence to capitalism, which severs those bonds and replaces them with universal, impersonal, individual but alienated—"objectively dependent"—bonds. Interdependence and communality are alienated to a realm of abstract liberal citizenship and fetishized in the market as a relation between things. Marx argues that, through the extension of the division of labor across the globe and thus the interdependence of all upon all, capitalism puts the individual into universal rather than particular relations, such that when the alienation of capitalism is transcended, these individuals will be able to experience fully that universal relatedness and thus reach their full individual potential. Marx's story is an optimistic one: precapitalist communal bonds are characterized as constraining and oppressive, so their replacement by the universal if alienated bonds of capital is an improvement to be improved on further by the unalienated, "subjective" universal bonds of communism. In this story, the relations of personal dependence, of explicit political and social domination, are transcended in capitalism. He claims that in order for labor to be sold as a commodity, people must be abstracted from their relations of dependence and operate as independent individuals, able to sell their labor freely. While he reads this freedom as, at one level, a hoax, since it is really about freedom from the means of production and thus entails the dependence of wage labor on capital, he nonetheless seems to buy the idea that there is some real emancipatory process under way.

This notion—that capitalism frees individuals from particular relations of domination—depends not only on the equivalence and abstraction of exchange value and thus its exchangers, but also on a very specific imagination of capitalism, of its technologies and strategies, one in which the particularities of labor are imagined as homogenous and equivalent. The strategies of capital that Marx describes in *Capital,* volume 1, are fundamentally based in economies of scale: like Adam Smith, in describing capitalism as characterized by the massing of labor in factories in which each laborer is assigned to one small piece of the production process that he does repetitively and efficiently, Marx seems to anticipate what in the twentieth century was called the Taylorization of production. In such a production system, the tasks of production become deskilled and one worker becomes equal to any other; anyone can do any job. The abstract equivalence of labor power as a commodity, as an exchange value in the market, is imagined as penetrating the realm of production; abstraction becomes particularity within capital, its particular nature; the particular social formation capitalism produces is one in which individuals are equivalent.

Until quite recently, this narrative appeared to be simply the truth of capitalism.[16] However, a new account of capitalism has surfaced in the past twenty years or so. An array of narratives describing a shift from Taylorized industrial mass production to "post-Fordism" and "flexible specialization" suggest that capitalism no longer produces conformity but rather addresses us in our cultural particularity. I will analyze the implications of this narrative of transformation in chapter 5; I note the existence of this new narrative here in order to suggest that Marxist accounts that render capitalism's tendency to produce increasingly an identity of particularity with abstraction as its only, central, and pervasive implication for social formation are in fact overgeneralizing from one historical period and, even with regard to that period, miss the full complexity of capitalism's technologies of hegemonization and oppression. If we view contemporary narratives of "flexible specialization," which emphasize the significance of particular communities for capital (and Putnam's work is a good example here), as precisely narratives, stories that capital tells about itself, then we must also recognize mass production as a narrative, a story that capitalism told about itself, a story worthy of examination and critique.[17] The failure to offer such a critique allowed

Adorno and Horkheimer, in *The Dialectic of Enlightenment*, to produce an account of history and structure that is as totalizing and one-dimensional as the capitalism they describe.

In *The Jargon of Authenticity*, Adorno poses critical rationality against Romantic nostalgia, which he characterizes as a form of escapism from the political battles of the present: "The jargon [of authenticity] must defend, so as not to be lost, transitory social forms which are incompatible with the contemporary state of the forces of production. If it wanted to mount the barricades itself, then it would have to engage itself . . . for that rationality which the exchange society both promises and denies, and through which that society could be transcended" (47). This critique of Romanticism would seem to suggest that even as capitalism destroys social formations, it generates new formations—rational exchange society—that might pose a challenge to capitalism itself; in other words, Adorno seems to describe history as a dynamic process, driven forward by the contradictions of the present. However, in *Dialectic of Enlightenment*, he and Horkheimer describe, in effect, the end of history, in which all such dialectical processes are brought to a halt by the enforced identity of the particular with the universal. Characterizing their contemporary culture, they argue, "The actual working conditions in society compel conformism" (37). Generalizing from the tendency of industrial/monopoly capitalism to massification and homogenization, they argue that "in the enlightened world . . . the individual is reduced to the nodal point of the conventional responses and modes of operation expected of him" (28). And even where there would appear to be nonconformism, it is merely an appearance: "Pseudo individuality is rife: from the standardized jazz improvisation to the exceptional film star whose hair curls over her eye to demonstrate her originality. What is individual is no more than the generality's power to stamp the accidental detail so firmly that it is accepted as such" (154).

As the Romantic claim for the autonomy of and complementarity between community and capital in the present is supplemented by the Romantic temporal opposition of community and modernity, Adorno and Horkheimer likewise supplement their account of the identity of the particular with the universal in the present with an account of history that describes all moments of history, from Greek prehistory as described by Homer to their own moment, as instances of the same dialectic in which Enlightenment turns into its uncritical other. While they say in the introduction that "the issue is not that of culture as a value, which is what critics of civilization have in mind ... The task to be accomplished is not the conservation of the past, but the redemption of the hopes of the past" (xv), they produce in this text an account of history that undermines any such hopes. They argue for the identity of all "the turning points of Western civilization, from the transition to Olympian religion up to the Renaissance, Reformation, and bourgeois atheism, whenever new nations and classes more firmly repressed myth, the fear of uncomprehended, threatening nature ... was reduced to animistic superstition, and the subjugation of nature was made the absolute purpose of life" (31–32). This synchronic account of history supplements the dialectical movement that would seem to be the universal characteristic of the history of enlightenment, rendering, in the place of historical transformation, an inevitable return to the "jurisdiction of myth" (32). In thus shoring up their account of totalization in their present of fascistic capitalism with an account of history that makes all particular moments simply exemplars of a universal process, they exclude from the present the possibility of transformational contradiction. While their account of the dialectic of Enlightenment recognizes the constitutive and ultimately displacing role of Enlightenment's "other"— irrational nature, myth—in proclaiming the final displacement of Enlightenment by myth, they actually exclude the supplementary particularity that might displace or disrupt, as well as constitute, the generality. Despite their critique of Romanticism, Adorno and Horkheimer leave us with nothing but nostalgia for a time when the penetration of capital was less complete.

In arguing for the absolute continuity of particulars (particular communities, identities, individuals) with capitalist rationality, Horkheimer and Adorno's argument lends support to my critique of the discourse of autonomous community and "values." But what their account, and mine to this point, does not account for is the fact that, as Stuart Hall has written, "capitalism only advances, as it were, on contradictory terrain. It is the contradictions which it has to overcome that produce its own forms of expansion" ("The Local and the Global," 29).

I have described the role played by use value, and community, in facilitating the flow of capital and have thus suggested that community is complicit with capital. But Marx's discussion of the relation between value and use value emphasizes not only or even primarily their complicity; rather, he generally describes them as contradictory or antagonistic: "The simple form of value of the commodity is the simple form of the appearance of the opposition between use value and value which is contained within the commodity" (*Capital*, vol. 1, 153). In the simple equation of two commodities (x coats $= y$ linen), each commodity can only be either in the role of the relative form or the equivalent but not both. The relative form would seem to express only value, while the equivalent form appears to express only use value. But in the process of exchange, a given commodity must metamorphose from its appearance as value into use value and vice versa. A thing that is not useful to its owner is sold to someone for whom it does have a use value: "The commodity itself is here subject to contradictory determinations. At the starting point it is a non-use-value to its owner; at the end it is a use value" (207). The realization of capital depends on the resolution of these opposed determinations through successful exchange. Should the joining/metamorphosis of value and use value fail, capital accumulation will fail. For instance, if useless goods are brought to market, they will not be purchased; conversely, if useful goods are not brought to market, they do not participate in the social exchange process, and they will fail to have value. Marx describes these potential failures at length in *Capital*, volume 2, where he discusses the time and space obstacles in the circuits of capital (to the circulation of capital).

The fact that value is an abstraction, that it is what is left when the particularities of a commodity are subtracted, makes it appear to be mobile and dynamic, able to change its form and location at the will of the capitalist. But, as I have argued, value can do nothing without embodiment. And this embodiment that enables its movement also weighs it down and obstructs its movement through time and space. In *The Urban Experience*, David Harvey's discussion of overaccumulation, where overaccumulation takes the form of a built environment that is no longer the most efficient environment for capitalism, implies a contradiction between value and use value: buildings and transportation infrastructures that were designed to facilitate the flow of value become encumbrances to that flow and have to be destroyed to free the capital and make room for new embodiments, new infrastructures. The contradiction of particularity and abstraction operates not only at the level of the individual commodity but also in more complex forms such as money and capital. The development of technologies for overcoming the obstructions presented by the necessary embodiment of capital is a history that hardly needs repeating here. Possibly the most interesting development for my purposes is the mobility of labor, which indicates that the contradiction between abstraction and particularity must be solved for social formations as well as for the built environment.[18] The solution to such contradictions is, pace Adorno, not solved once and for all through the enforced conformity of the particular with the universal, but is rather a constant struggle, engaged discursively through ongoing rearticulations of the discourse of community.

"Particular Voices": Pluralism, Multiculturalism and Diversity

Keeping Things Whole

In a field
I am the absence
of the field.
This is
always the case.
Wherever I am
I am what is missing.

When I walk
I part the air
and always
the air moves in
to fill the spaces
where my body's been.

We all have reasons
for moving.
I move
to keep things whole.[19]

A reading of the debates over pluralism, multiculturalism, and diversity reveals the work assigned to community within modernity. While I will argue that the deployment of community works in the service of maintaining or elaborating domination and exploitation, in recent years political conservatives have expressed a concern that too much communality, named multiculturalism or tribalism, would seem to threaten those processes. In the 1990s, as in the first decades of the twentieth

century, the threat was perceived to come from immigrants and by analogy a variety of other identity-based groups.[20] In the early part of the
twentieth century, cultural pluralism, as Carrie Tirado Bramen argues,
was first disseminated in popular national discourse through a profu-
sion of metaphors of melting pots, mixing bowls, orchestras, and sani-
tation as a way "to absorb the cosmopolitan differences produced by an
emergent global economy"; cultural pluralism was deployed to help the
existing society to "digest" massive immigrations to the metropolises of
the United States (Bramen, personal communication; see also *Finding
"An Innocent Way Out"*). Bramen draws on Harvey's work[21] to argue
that cultural pluralism functions, through a rhetoric of community, to
"mediate" the increasing class polarization coincident with immigration. Cultural pluralism is a discourse of assimilation, articulating a
process whereby "community" members become individual American
citizens.[22] As such, it is a Fordist strategy for regulating and generating
the mass culture of mass consumption and production on which that
form of capitalism depends. And it has been elaborated (not without
opposition) in the policies and practices of the national state itself,
most explicitly with regard to social welfare, cultural, and educational
programs. But assimilation not only produces sameness; it also depends
on difference, positing both a prior "other" communal affiliation and an
ongoing balance of local, familial, or ethnic community in the lives of
the assimilated individuals.

Like pluralism, the corporate embrace of multiculturalism and diversity
is a strategy for the production of subjects for capitalism. (Multiculturalism was, I think, a transitional term between pluralism and diversity
used primarily by nonprofits, especially arts and educational institutions,
that has since been eclipsed by the language of diversity, generated principally by for-profit corporations.)[23] Corporations have taken up a discourse of diversity as a strategy for extending and intensifying the articulation of social elements within capitalist practices; diversity discourse
deploys existing differences and elaborates new ones as occasions for
the voluntary and enthusiastic participation of subjects as niched or individuated producers and consumers. In a speech to the national convention of the LEAGUE (Lesbian, Bisexual, Gay, and Transgendered
United Employees at AT&T), the gay employees association of AT&T,[24]
AT&T's senior vice president for human resources, Hal Burlingame, said,
"I've been working to understand your issues and concerns. Kathleen

Dermody [a LEAGUE officer] helped me understand the journey she's been on in her personal and professional life. Margaret Burd [another LEAGUE officer] has courageously shared her concerns as some attack your orientation.... These learnings have been very helpful to me. They've raised my sensitivity level ... It's been an enriching experience" (4). But, he explained,

> For me, it always comes back to one main point: the business imperative of valuing and managing diversity.... Diversity fuels creativity... Diversity fuels business growth opportunities ... Our diversity strategy is not aimed at transforming our larger society in our own image ... AT&T has not—and should not—be left, right or centrist.... By valuing diversity we can experience greater marketplace success, make better decisions, and win and keep the best people. (1–2, 5)

Diversity, like pluralism, is—explicitly—a strategy for the expansion of capital. However, diversity discourse locates the production of the communal formation necessary to that expansion directly in the marketplace, rather than running it through the nation-state, and posits various particular identity communities, rather than national community, as the goal of the process. Like pluralism, diversity performs a kind of assimilation—an assimilation to corporate culture, to production and consumption—that is simultaneously the articulation of sameness and difference.

The debates in the early 1990s over government policy on arts funding and education are oddly positioned between these two moments and strategies. Arthur M. Schlesinger Jr., in his 1991 book *The Disuniting of America* (considered by the *New York Times* the reasonable center of the debates over multiculturalism in education [Kermode, "Whose History Is Bunk?" 3, 33]), explicitly tries to hold the pluralist line against multiculturalism, which, in his characterization, consists of Afrocentric curricula and bilingual education. Community occurs in three places in his argument: original ethnic community membership is positioned as a step along the path toward a goal of American national community, and then reappears as an explanation of one's place within that American community. He complains that "instead of a transformative nation [a nation able to transform "individuals of all nations into a new race"], with an identity all its own ... a nation composed of individuals making their own free choices, America increasingly sees itself composed of groups more or less indelible in their ethnic character" (Schlesinger,

Disuniting, 2).[25] "'Multiculturalism' arises as a reaction against Anglo- or Eurocentrism; but at what point does it pass over into an ethnocentrism of its own? . . . When does obsession with differences begin to threaten the idea of an overarching American nation? . . . Will the center hold?" (40). The center, he acknowledges, is white Anglo-Saxon Protestant. Ethnic community is the raw material, the necessary base on which American individuality is built: "Ethnic enclaves served as staging areas for regrouping and basic training before entry was made into the larger and riskier American life" (8) but must be left in the past. He cites Tocqueville in arguing that participation in civil society is what will generate national community; ethnic or racial communal membership is positioned here in relation to participation in the American community as an excess, which, like the potential excess of individualism described by Tocqueville, results in social anomie. Participation in the nation—the process of becoming abstract individuals who make their own free choices—paradoxically does not mean simply abandoning one's community of origin but, as his insistence on education in English about Western Civilization suggests, it means trading one set of communal particularities and constraints for another. To the extent that Schlesinger recognizes Americans' ethnic inheritances in the present in his pluralist historical scholarship, they do not function as celebratory narratives sustaining ethnic or racial pride; instead, these ethnic histories become explanatory stories for the unequal location of individuals in the hierarchy of American society: Jews and Asians are successful; African Americans are not.

All of this would seem to be the classic formulation of cultural pluralism, and yet there is something else going on in Schlesinger's book. I became aware of *The Disuniting of America* because my mother, an attorney at a large New York law firm, passed along to me the copy she had received as a gift from Federal Express. The edition she received, published by Whittle Books, has advertisements for Federal Express interspersed between and within the chapters. Each ad is two full pages, one page a photo of a Fed Ex employee, the other a short sentence in quotation marks, attributed to the employee, who is identified by job title and location. The ads emphasize the worldwide reach and diversity of Fed Ex. The first is a photo of a white male pilot, of Indianapolis, in the cargo area of his plane; the second a black man of Toronto, Canada, displaying a handheld package-tracking device; the third shows a white male courier of Sydney, Australia, in shorts standing next to a kangaroo on some rocks, saying "Born to carry." An African American female customer service agent, of Sacramento, is posed amid clocks showing times in Munich, Dubai, and Memphis, among other locations. An Asian male courier, of Tokyo, is bowing in front of a Japanese-style wooden gate; his quote is printed in Japanese and translated in small print as: "When it comes to the international shipping business, we know our way around like the natives. Because we are the natives." The final photo shows a large number of Fed Ex employees posed in rows as for a class photo in front of an airplane, accompanied by the quote: "We didn't just start an air express service. We started a revolution." These ads jerry-rig Schlesinger's pluralist argument to a corporate diversity strategy with no attempt made to work out the important differences between them. The book simply enacts the displacement of the nation-state by the market as the container for and manager of difference. But in doing so it reveals the dynamism of the social formations generated by capitalism—in this case a shift in the role of the nation-state—and of the efforts to control such dynamic social formations through novel yet familiar invocations of community.

Congressional debate over the National Endowment for the Arts (NEA) likewise reveals both the persistence and the diversity of the iterations and effects of the discourse of community. Like Schlesinger's arguments against multicultural education, the Congressional debate over arts funding began from the premise of an imagined "Nation"—imagined to have a unique and coherent cultural life, value system, history, and place in an international community of nations. And as in Schlesinger's text, in this debate as well, that coherence was cast as "at risk." Both those in favor of unrestricted NEA funding and those seeking to either cut that funding or restrict the content of funded art claimed to be trying to promote the interests of that national community. They elaborated different though complementary strategies: the conservatives were explicitly exclusionary, while the liberals suggested inclusionary pluralist policies; the conservatives thus marked the external boundaries, the liberals the internal structure of that national community. Both of these approaches produced contradictory outcomes in relation to the nation. Conservatives enabled a dismantling of the apparati of the state that help to produce the nation as a community by cutting the budget of the NEA, and thus, despite their highly nationalist rhetoric, helped to relocate the power to constitute social formations from the state to the market. Meanwhile, the pluralism of the liberals, despite their nationalist rhetoric, promoted the elaboration of the nonnational niched communities embraced by post-Fordist capital.

Those members of Congress critical of the NEA funding practices claimed a commonality among Americans based on adherence to what Representative Baker called "basic tenets of the American value system" (*Cong. Rec.* 10 May 1989 H 1797). During one debate Representative Rohrabacher proposed legislation to establish what he called "commonsense standards," suggesting that there is a common national sense, while Representative Roth seemed to know that "the American people have really been outraged . . ." and Representative Pashayan that "this Nation's citizens are scandalized . . . this nation's religious and moral values are subject to . . . ridicule" (*Cong. Rec.* 11 October 1990 HR 4825). They imagined the nation as a Tocquevillean township of face-to-face interaction. Representative Rohrabacher spoke of and for "those people working out in the hinterland" (*Cong. Rec.* 1 February 1990 H 194). Senator Gorton made Congress itself a metonym for that community, asking, "Where is the consensus for 'Piss Christ'? Is there anyone in this body who will stand to declare that Americans should subsidize religious bigotry?" (*Cong. Rec.* 31 May 1989 S 5806). Likewise, Representative Pashayan declared: "I dare say that the Congressional Arts Caucus would not even think of displaying the works under question here upon the walls of the tunnel leading from the Cannon Building to the Capitol. The members would be scandalized and deservedly so" (*Cong. Rec.* 11 October 1990 H 9407). And Senator Helms, most pointedly, began each speech against the NEA with the statement, "I do not know [Andre Serrano, Annie Sprinkle] and I hope I never meet him [or her]" (*Cong. Rec.* 18 May 1989 S 5596 and others).

In casting the nation as a community, they define its boundaries. But the articulation of external boundaries is only half the job that community does in relation to the modern state. As I began to point out in my discussion of Schlesinger, the other half is to articulate the social structure within that state. Liberal discourse explicitly preserves a space for religious and cultural difference by distinguishing private from public. However, particularities of race, religion, and culture are not just a private residue. Those making pluralist arguments in favor of an unrestricted NEA made use of this public/private distinction in the form of a defense of free speech (that is, a realm of privacy) to smuggle hierarchical difference into the core of the supposedly horizontal national space.

Like the conservatives, liberals such as Senator Pell also spoke of "our national cultural community" (*Cong. Rec.* 26 July 1989 S 8814), but cast the communality as a goal to be achieved and maintained, and suggested that arts were the means for accomplishing that goal. Representative Towns contended, for instance, that "artists... shore up the national spirit and move the country towards prosperity.... Art allows us to... understand the life and experiences of others" (*Cong. Rec.* 19 June 1990 H 3804). Those in the inner city might produce a more harsh vision than "we" would, but it is good for us to reach beyond ourselves and empathize with that experience. Representative Downey said, "Artists tell us the truth about ourselves... making America more creative, more beautiful and more sensitive..." (*Cong. Rec.* 11 October 1990 HR 4825).

The argument for the social bonding function of art was common in the "arts community," not only in Congress. Its call to humanistic empathy is certainly a fine sentiment. But in this congressional context its meaning was somewhat less noble. "We" authentic Americans, who need to understand "others," still inevitably live in "communities," such, as "Wynne, Horseshoe Bend, Earle Morrilton, and Brinkley," small towns in northeast Arkansas cited by Representative Alexander as benefiting from NEA funding (*Cong. Rec.* 11 October 1990 H 9428). And as "we" townspeople are metonymically represented by "we" congresspeople, a slippage is produced between Joe sixpack and upper-class culture consumers, for whom the experiences of oppression and otherness expressed in the controversial works of art are apparently, according to these congressmen, objects of voyeuristic pleasure and enrichment. The stance of respectful cultural relativism with regard to the experiences of racism, sexism, homophobia, and AIDS, an appreciation of the public expressions of private differences, leaves those material inequalities in place, positioning the artist/speaker as an "other" within the nation.

Senator Moynihan made the connection between NEA funding and the assimilation narrative explicit in his argument against restricting the NEA: "Are we so little mindful of the diversity of our Nation and the centrality of censorship in the experience of not just a few but I would almost say every religious and ethnic inheritance in this land?" (*Cong. Rec.* 26 July 1989 S 8815). Like Schlesinger, he seems to reduce difference to an origin, as in Representative Williams's declaration: "We place a great value on the variety of our origins..." (*Cong. Rec.* 11 October 1990). Moynihan equates the now fearsome groups—sexual and racial minorities whose art was most at issue in the NEA controversy—with the groups that are now relatively nonthreatening to the status quo, that is, white ethnic groups[26]; gays become yet another ethnic group.[27] Through this equation, Moynihan implies to his colleagues that government funding, the lack of censorship, will induce those funded to make that same equation, to read themselves into the narrative of assimilation, and I think he is not entirely wrong. Moynihan holds out assimilation as a beneficial carrot to potentially disruptive social agents, and many of us run after it, with complex consequences.

The fact that, in the pluralist assimilation narratives constructed by Schlesinger, Moynihan, and Williams, community is posited as the origin of the journey toward individualism is crucial here. In order to be recognized as a potential recipient of (subject to) the goodies that come from a pluralist state one must first constitute oneself as a legitimate community. But in so doing, one inscribes oneself into the machinery that turns the raw material of community into subjects of the nation-state and capital. That machinery is the bureaucratic and capitalist apparatus that community must inhabit in the United States; to participate in a community in the United States is to participate in a group with certain standardized features, such as businesses (bars, bookstores, restaurants and foodshops, small-scale manufacturing) and often more importantly, civil voluntary organizations (churches, schools, arts organizations, lobbying groups, employees associations) that are frequently organized as governmentally regulated and state-sanctioned not-for-profit corporations. If the group does not operate in this way, then it is a "gang" or an "underground network"; it is not given the status of a "community." The practical as well as rhetorical deployment of community makes one group equivalent to another and produces equivalent subjects, even when there are drastic power differences between them (white ethnic groups versus African Americans) and discrepant logics organizing the various collectivities (gays and lesbians versus Christians).[28]

In *The Urban Experience,* Harvey argues that new "traditions of community" based on cultural and lifestyle distinctions, neighborhoods, or ethnicities have been invented, or quite literally built (as in "suburban communities") to counter the antagonisms of class and to consume the overproduction induced by the cycles of capitalism (87).[29] But community is not only invoked as Harvey describes to organize populations (and their consumption patterns) in physical space and to focus their attention on local boosterism rather than class conflict. The results of community participation are interestingly ambivalent. Subjects are produced whose reasonable behavior, such as voluntary cooperation in interest group organizations, marks them as individual citizens and members of the American community. On the other hand, the elaboration of the community group as a distinct, different, particular community makes it available for insertion into a particular slot in the hierarchy of capitalist exploitation. In combination with the discourses of equality and rights that articulate capitalism and democracy, such formations may be or become sites of resistance to the flows of capital. The various, importantly diverse, and yet relentless, deployments of community that I have sketched here point to the constant discursive and practical effort required to articulate social formations that supplement, by supporting rather than supplanting, capitalism.

CHAPTER TWO

The Performance of Production and Consumption

Production and Performativity

This chapter offers what might be called a general theory of social formations, though it is specifically concerned to articulate the formation of those groupings called *communities* and even more specifically those contemporary identity-based communities that social theory refers to as "new social movements." The theory I offer brings the insights of poststructuralism with regard to the performativity, constructedness, and discursivity of identity together with a modified but nonetheless substantially Marxist view that social organization is implicit in the organization of production. The argument moves in two directions, showing the performativity of production and the productivity of performance. On the one hand, I expand the definition of production to include a range of activities not normally considered production; on the other hand, I am concerned with the central role of capitalist production and of products that flow through the marketplace in producing identity and community. For most of the chapter, I proceed through readings of Marx's central arguments. At the conclusion, I shift focus from Marx's texts to a set of texts that argue an opposing view, that try to distinguish performativity from production. These antiproductivist theories see production as only reproductive, not dialectical or dynamic, and locate freedom and liberation (from production) in an exterior space, a representational excess frequently named *performance*. Through an analysis of these texts, I suggest that rather than attempting to escape production, emancipatory projects need to undertake a critical engagement with capitalist production.

As I did in chapter 1, I address here the relationship between the economic and the cultural. In expanding the definition of production, I displace the oppositions between the economic and the social, production and signification, exploitation and domination, in order to emphasize that the relation between these processes is one of complicity rather than analogy. In a sense then, this aspect of my argument elaborates, in rather different language, the argument of chapter 1 for the supplementarity of community with capital. But in naming social/cultural activity *production* and in attending to the broad social effectivity of capitalist production more narrowly construed, I mean to emphasize the tremendous power of capitalism as the site at which identity and community are enacted and generated.

While Marx's texts can be used—I will use them—to stave off both economic and linguistic determinism, poststructuralism and Marxism have frequently arrayed themselves against each other to the detriment of each. As many theorists have pointed out, orthodox Marxist social analysis has been plagued by a tendency toward economic reductivism, determinism, and one-dimensionality[1]; in eschewing the play of signification, such a Marxism is simply unable to address the complexity of contemporary social formations. In its appreciation of signification, poststructuralism is very good at accounting for the complexity of cultural processes but tends not to give production its due as arguably the most powerful generator of signification and thus social organization. As Mary Louise Pratt has said, anybody can make a meaning, but not anybody can give that meaning efficacy in the world (personal communication). By articulating a performative theory of social relations with an analysis of the specific practices of production and consumption, expanding the notion of exploitation as I expand the notion of production, I gain the ability to analyze such systems of power difference while maintaining a vision of social and cultural complexity.

Gayatri Spivak argues (with, not against, Marx) that use value (especially the use value of labor) cannot be used to ground or close off a chain of signification, much the way Judith Butler argues (against Lacan) that materiality in general (and the penis and the phallus in particular) cannot be the guarantor or stabilizer of the signifying chain that seems to follow from it, but rather that materiality can only seem to be that guarantor by being posited as such within discourse, which puts discourse before and not only after materiality (Spivak, "Scattered Speculations," 158–59; Butler, "The Lesbian Phallus," *Bodies*). The point of both of these difficult deconstructive arguments is to show that the posited origins of meaning are in fact socially constructed and historically determined and that in their particular forms they tend to support particular arrangements of power. Spivak's project, in showing the social (discursive) determination of use value, is not to empty it of its materiality or to make use values appear expendable, as if people don't need to subsist. Rather, the point of her argument is to create a version of Marxian analysis that ties the "political economy of the sign" (the realm of domination), which seems to have so captured the minds of First World academics, to a more traditional Marxian analysis that can see the exploitation occurring in the international division of labor. Like Spivak, I want to read the discursive aspects of commodity production not in order to leave the realm of needs, inequality, exploitation, and oppression but rather to offer an adequate account of the social relations produced therein. I want to show the ways that domination is enacted through the technology of exploitation. And, displacing the domination/exploitation binary, I want to show that the production of monetary surplus values depends on social production, broadly construed.

I posit Marx as a social constructionist, as offering a theory of the way people make themselves and their relations with each other. In order to enable Marx's theories to account for "new social movements" or "communities" and not only for a binary class division, I recoup the notion, present in Marx's early texts, of labor as all human doing and not just contributions to the gross national product. I include as acts of making, as production, activities that go on outside the factory, the production of all sorts of things beyond traditional material objects, and even beyond the commodity, which has become, in any case, less and less material. I use feminist arguments—for the productive value of reproduction, specifically, and for the recognition of values other than monetary exchange as the measure of productivity, more generally—as a basis for including supposedly unproductive acts such as nonprocreative sex, especially but not only the anonymous public sex that was so central in producing the urban gay male community in the 1970s and early 1980s. Likewise, I include in production the voluntary as well as paid participation in nonprofit corporations that absorbs the bulk of political and cultural activism in the United States. Having recognized the diversity of production, I recognize the diversity of subjects produced therein: I emphasize that production produces not only workers but Americans, loyal and proud General Motors employees, women, and gays and lesbians. In my reading, Marx's dialectical theory is a theory of a necessarily nontotalized society in which multiple articulations of the society contradict each other and yield new arrangements. The new in this story comes not from some external nonrationalized realm of emergent truth and freedom but from the constraints of the present. Reading Marx in this way allows me to construct production as performative, in the sense elaborated by Butler.

Butler argues that gender and bodily sex itself are performative constructions; in so doing she offers a notion of performativity that can usefully be applied to identities other than sex and gender and in relation to social formations other than identity.[2] She invokes the speech act definition of "a performative [as] that discursive practice that enacts or produces that which it names" (*Bodies*, 13); the performative act does not enact preexisting meanings but rather constitutes meanings through action ("Performative Acts," 521). But she also employs the dramatic connotations of performance as "a stylized repetition of acts" witnessed and believed by an audience ("Performative Acts," 519–20), a "reiterative and citational practice" (*Bodies*, 2), reiterative of social norms and discourses rather than a dramatic text. Unlike speech act theory, which, as Butler and Mary Louise Pratt ("Ideology") have both argued, tends to assume the existence of a "choosing and constituting subject," Butler uses the theatrical, witnessed aspect of performativity to shift focus and see "the social agent as an object rather than the subject of constitutive acts" ("Performative Acts," 519).[3] In this she echoes Hannah Arendt's notion that while one may be the hero of one's life story—that story being the product of one's acts and speech—one is nonetheless not the author. The story, the identity of the actor, can only be constructed by others (*Human Condition*, esp. 159–64) or by oneself, retrospectively.

In *Bodies That Matter*, Butler regularly defines performativity by emphasizing that it is "production,"[4] and not "consumerism," by which she means to point out that it is the retroactively constituting enactment of discursive constraints and not the free act of a fully constituted subject

(2).[5] By using the term *consumerism,* she invokes the liberal, individual, willing, choosing subject: "The account of agency conditioned by those very regimes of discourse/power cannot be conflated with voluntarism or individualism, much less with consumerism" (15). Performativity is not exemplified in the whimsical wearing of one drag, one set of clothes, one day and another drag the next, but rather in the punitively circumscribed enactment of gender roles (x). Kath Weston argues that understanding gender as a performance, as drag, focuses too much on the display of consumer goods such as clothing and not enough on gendered roles in relation to production, employment opportunities, or their absence ("Do Clothes Make the Woman?"). Weston is quite right to point us to the significance of production, and I would argue that, in Butler's account, restricted and differentiated participation in production would be accounted for as one of the central performances that is productive of gendered subjects. At the same time, it will be important to recognize *consumption,* not merely as *consumerism,* but rather as a site of performative production, that is, as a highly constrained site of collective as well as individual subject constitution.

In Butler's analysis, it is in the productive reenactment of norms that the possibility or even the necessity of the production of innovation occurs—a potentially, though not by any means necessarily, subversive change. Butler locates (oppositional) "agency as a reiterative or rearticulatory practice, immanent to power, and not a relation of external opposition to power." "The subject who would resist such [regulatory, constraining] norms is itself enabled, if not produced, by such norms" (Butler, *Bodies,* 15). Rather than thinking of production as a mechanical or rule-bound system of reproduction of sameness, what Butler calls *norms* might usefully be understood in Pierre Bourdieu's terms as "habitus, the durably installed generative principle of regulated improvisations," which are subject to an "art of performance" in order to be successfully reproduced (*Outline,* 78, 20). The habitus may tend to reproduce itself, to produce "practices which tend to reproduce the regularities immanent in the objective conditions of the production of the [habitus]" itself, but there is plenty of room here for things to go other ways as well (78). The multidimensionality of the habitus, or the multiple articulations determining any given situation, creates contexts in which conflict, innovation, and change are frequently features of the production of social relations.

In taking up Marx's analysis of production, in expanding production to apply to a wide range of practices, and in interpreting production as a performative practice, I hope, with Butler, to emphasize the opportunities for liberatory social change made available within production even while offering a critique of the constraints—often oppressive innovations rather than preservations—imposed by the mode of production.

The Relationship between Production and Social Relations: Discourse, Materiality, and Practice

In *The German Ideology,* Marx argues that subjecthood and social relations are implicit in the production of the means of subsistence and in the new needs that each new product brings into existence, which in turn generate new production.[6] Marx states that individual subjects are the simultaneous product of the production of objects:

> Production must not be considered simply as being the reproduction of the physical existence of the individuals. Rather it is a definite form . . . of expressing their life. As individuals express their life so they are. (150)

And not only is the individual's identity expressed and thus formed in production but the collectivity, social relations, are also determined through the mode of production. "There exists a materialistic connection of men with one another which is determined by their needs and their mode of production" (157). Divisions of labor are immediately social divisions as well as technical divisions, which differentiate the interests of individuals from one another and create "cleavage between the particular and the common interest" (160).

Marx's argument against the primacy of consciousness in producing society is not now cogently an argument about the immateriality of consciousness but rather an argument against claims for its independence or a priori status vis-à-vis the social. Marx does not wield materiality against the claims of social construction but rather in his arguments for it; for Marx, materiality equates with human practice, and thus materiality is inseparable from discourse:

> From the start the 'spirit' is afflicted with the curse of being 'burdened' with matter, which here makes its appearance in the form of agitated layers of air, sounds, in short, of language . . . language is practical consciousness, that exists also for other men, and for that reason alone it really exists for me personally as well . . . Consciousness is, therefore, from the very beginning a social product. (158)

He insists on placing materiality in the determining role and makes consciousness its byproduct specifically to tie consciousness to society, to the actions and practices that people engage in and not to make a moral point about the importance of material survival over and above the life of the mind, nor a logical point reaffirming the mind/body split. By emphasizing the production of new needs Marx makes it clear that he is not talking about some sort of biologistically necessary material subsistence production but rather the production of whatever has come to seem necessary in a given society. Later, in discussing the commodity, I will show that Marx argues that materiality is always already discursive. In the passage quoted here, Marx argues that discourse is always already material.

As Raymond Williams argues, quoting this same passage, Marx does not relegate language use, and signification more broadly, to a secondary reflective realm of ideology or superstructure but rather sees signification as "practical, constitutive activity" (*Marxism and Literature*, 29). In fact, Williams points out, Marx distinguishes his form of materialism from other inadequate materialisms (such as Feuerbach's) precisely on the ground that they do disconnect signification—consciousness as an activity—from "reality" and thus posit the ideal, rather than the material, as the active realm.[7] For Marx, consciousness, culture, religion, language, and politics are all social (and thus material) products, products of people making their world together through their actions and interactions.

The implicitness of subjectivity, social relations, and consciousness in production might seem to suggest an essentialist notion of identity and collectivity, in other words, that identity and collectivity have one necessary determination; but that is true only if the objects being produced have a stable essence, can be reduced to some singular identity or effectivity in relation to which only one subjectivity redounds to the producer. While it is possible, even typical, to read Marx in this manner— the teleological narrative in which the theory is embedded certainly suggests that Marx read himself in that way[8]—that reading is reductive and specifically flattens out the dialectical analysis of social processes Marx offers. Marx's theory of the simultaneity of the production of objects and subjects (or of the multivalence of every productive act) can more interestingly be taken as a phenomenological theory; as for Butler, for Marx, you are what you do (and how you are done). In this view, it is the potentially diverse performativity of productive activity and of products that matters.

The Multivalence of the Commodity

The capitalist form of the subject/object dialectic is commodity production and is described by Marx's theory of value. According to the theory of value, not only is production multivalent in that it produces both objects and subjects, but under capitalism it is multivalent in the sense that it produces use value, value, and a potentially infinite array of exchange values. Marx's opening move in *Capital* is to analyze this multivalence.

As I pointed out in chapter 1, Marx argues that the commodity must have a social use value, that is, it must be recognizably useful in a given society (since to be a commodity it must be exchangeable, if not actually exchanged); the use value of a commodity, the commodity in its particular, concrete, apparently material (but nonetheless socially constructed, historically developed) aspect, is thus one crucial site at which domination enters the process of capital accumulation, at which exploitation depends on social production.

But more important to Marx in many ways than use value is what he names simply *value*. This value is determined not through the social process of inscribing the object as useful in its particulars, but through the social process of production itself; this value is an account of, an expression or "form of appearance" of, the labor that went into making the commodity.[9] While Marx emphasizes that value represents only the (abstract socially necessary) quantity of labor, because that quantity is dependent on the level to which productive forces have been developed in a given society (that is, on how the thing was made), value also, in a sense, expresses the quality of labor involved. (It is, then, not only possible to show that use value is dependent on value but, conversely, that value folds back into material specificity as well.) The development of productive forces is based not only on some naturally increasing human ability but on the historically contingent need to control labor and labor's resistance.[10] Marx saw the production process itself as recast through the reinterpretation of it as a battle between classes, as opposed to, for instance, a competition among workers. So while abstract value is determined by concrete productive forces, those productive forces are again not some essential origin of meaning but rather a product of social practices and struggles.

Exchange value (as opposed to value, which is abstract labor in its abstract state) is the form of appearance of value in the particular language, the particular coin, of a particular society or at least of a specific transaction; an exchange value is so many dollars or yen or coats. It is therefore precisely a discursive articulation, a culturally and historically specific manifestation of value.

In examining all aspects of the commodity, Marx makes it clear that what is being produced are meanings, that is, social values, things that perform in the context of social practices, for example, a consumption or an exchange. But how many practices or potential meanings did Marx take into consideration? While use value is potentially a wide-open category, Marx shows relatively little interest in its potential diversity; he is primarily interested in the use to which labor power in particular is put, how its use value produces surplus values. Marx's discussion of surplus value—especially when that value appears in the form of profit or money and is used for private consumption rather than as capital— points to an array of social meanings and values distinct from a narrowly defined economic sphere but not independent or autonomous of it. In the *1844 Manuscripts*, for instance, Marx describes the ability of monetary wealth to act as the equivalent of beauty, intelligence, physical capability, talent, morality, and so on.

Marx, however, doesn't theorize these other values adequately; as many feminists have pointed out, by focusing, especially in *Capital*, on the use value of labor power and on exchange value, Marx limits his analysis to a very narrowly drawn economic realm. He does this for a particular reason: to provide a basis for the revelation of exploitation through wage labor, which he sees as the primary form of oppression under capitalism. Exploitation depends on the interplay of use value and exchange value. (The use value of one day's labor minus the exchange value of one day's labor equals a quantity of surplus value.) But as has become widely apparent, exploitation has not displaced other forms of oppression; capitalism has in fact incorporated all sorts of other social hierarchies into its operations.

In order to account for the diversity of oppressions inhabiting capitalism, it is necessary to look beyond direct commodity production and beyond a dualistic analysis of value. In undertaking this task, I will build on feminists' analyses of the productive labor that goes on outside the factory and monetary market contexts. And I will also deploy the insights of theorists of "consumer" society who have analyzed the many other kinds of value besides use and exchange that travel with the commodity in its production, distribution, and consumption circuit; these theorists also recognize labor outside the factory that is done in great part by women though in fact it must be done by everyone—the labor of consumption.

Feminists such as Christine Delphy and Marilyn Waring have observed that neither Marxist nor neoclassical economics manages to value (as products of socially necessary labor) or account for (in national economic statistics) large categories of goods and services that are central to the lives of people and, for that matter, to the functioning of capitalism: these categories include human reproduction, housework, subsistence farming, the environment, and volunteer work (generally for nonprofit organizations). They note that not only are these goods and services not recognized as values, but the producers, frequently women, are not recognized as valuable either. Government policies do not respond to the needs of these producers, who live in subordinate positions within families whose monetary market participants are its ranking members and public face.[11]

The point of these feminist arguments is to suggest that gender oppression has a determining role in relation to the economy. Delphy, for instance, describes women in French peasant households who produce goods that cannot be distinguished from commodities (they may be brought to market or used at home) and who produce these goods not for a wage but in a sense for free, or for subsistence only. Delphy claims these women can be considered slave labor, while husbands or fathers are petty bourgeoisie, trading goods in the marketplace. The distinctions here do not depend on the nature of the product/production but primarily on gender.

Rather than mark determination in one direction or another, I am interested in noticing that gendering occurs through productive practices, through the performance—the enactment, witnessed and inscribed monetarily or not—of production, understood to include these nonmonetarized activities. What is important in this analysis is the fact that the goods and services and the producers of those goods and services share an evaluation that articulates neither use in any narrow sense, nor labor time, nor exchange value, but rather discourses of gender, of public and private, of the monetary and nonmonetary. The marking of gender depends on one's role in relation to production and even specifically to capitalism. Social divisions and gendered individual and collective subjectivities do not have some independent preexisting life but are fully immanent in (produced by and productive of) this productive activity.

Feminist arguments that nonmarket activities, especially reproduction, are production open the possibility (with which these feminists were not particularly concerned) for a huge range of private, social activities to be considered production. If child socialization or heterosexual sexual activity (inscribed as monetarily valuable productive practices only in the demimondes of paid childcare and prostitution) can be recognized by these feminist arguments as valuable labor, then gay sex is also certainly analyzable as a valuable, productive act: productive of relationships, identities, communities, and social spaces. Even that most devalued sexual practice, anonymous public gay male sexual activity, has at certain points in gay history operated as a technology producing an imaginary expanse of identification, not unlike the newspaper in Benedict Anderson's *Imagined Communities.* This sexual activity has defined and claimed a variety of public places (certain streets, blocks, and parks as well as bars and bathhouses) as gay communal space.

Such social production feeds almost immediately back into production in the narrower sense of monetary surplus value production. Donna Haraway has said that "the body is an accumulation strategy" (Haraway and Harvey, 510), a point that Harvey has elaborated in his recent work, exploring the construction of the body as variable capital through the sites of production, exchange, and consumption (Harvey, "The Body"). However, the strategic production of specific but diverse bodies as capital requires the complicity of discourses not normally named *production.* As Janet Jakobsen puts it, with reference to Weber's *The Protestant Ethic and the Spirit of Capitalism,* the realm of values (that is, religion, culture, and domination in the form of "family values") enters—at the site of the body—the supposedly value-free realm of value, the economic (Jakobsen, "Embodying," 7–8). I would simply add here that not only are individual bodies an accumulation strategy and thus the site of this values-laden production process, but social bodies, social formations, families, and communities are also accumulation strategies.

But one needn't look outside commodity production for the production of values other than use and exchange and thus of subjects other than wage-laborer and capitalist. The importance of social production for economic production is evident in the elaborate efforts made by capitalists to influence identity and community structures. While some feminists argue that Marxism has failed to give adequate attention to something going on simultaneously with, but external to, direct commodity production (that is, reproduction), theorists of consumer culture make a more historical argument, suggesting that capitalism itself has changed, that the nature of the products being produced has changed, and that what is significant about the products has changed.

Jean Baudrillard and others have described a shift to a stage of capitalism in which profit depends not on the production process, or the exploitation of labor, but rather on the control of consumer desire through advertising, through control of "the code," the entire symbolic order (Baudrillard, *Mirror*, x). Fredric Jameson argues that the production of culture "has become integrated into commodity production generally" because it has such a significant role to play in the production of innovative commodities, so that "cultural production [has become] an arena of fierce social conflict" and there is a "new role for aesthetic definitions and interventions" (quoted in Harvey, *Condition of Postmodernity*, 63). But as I see it, the issue here is not so much the commodification of discourse, of media, art, and information, but the discursivity of the commodity.

Pierre Bourdieu has described not use or exchange value in the Marxian sense, but status or what he calls the "distinction" value of the commodity, arguing that commodities are consumed and traded with the goal of accumulating "cultural capital." Baudrillard notes that the status- or identity-conferring quality of the commodity is not manufactured in the factory but rather in the consumption process. Thus, it is control over consumptive rather than productive labor (through advertising or, less overtly, through cultural products like television programs rather than through time clocks and shop floor managers) that is important to the production of surplus value. The labor of the consumer contributes the greater share of surplus value, an unlimited share since it is based on signification and not on human labor capacity within the twenty-four-hour day.

The status-, identity-, and community-conferring aspects of a commodity might be seen as part of its use value, or alternately as part of its
exchange value, in the sense that the commodity is traded in a marketplace of status, identity, or community (a market that is not merely
metaphorically related to the commodity market but is crucially enabling to it). To view it in either of these ways raises questions about the
distinction between use value and exchange value. Exchange looks like
just another possible use for a commodity or all uses look like exchanges
in the sense that a commodity (an expression of value) is being invested
(exchanged) to produce a given result, which will then be turned around
and invested again to turn another profit of some sort. The problem
with this conflation of use and exchange value is that, while it conforms
to Marx's definition of exchange value as a socially determined value
abstracted from the particulars of the object, it doesn't conform to his
definition of exchange value as an abstraction of labor, unless labor is
redefined to include sign production. This redefinition of labor puts
the appropriating consumer on a theoretical par with the factory worker,
the so-called producer. Marx recognized this consumptive labor in the
Grundrisse:

> The product only obtains its "last finish" in consumption. A railway on
> which no trains run, hence which is not used up, not consumed, is a
> railway only [potentially], and not in reality. . . . Consumption produces
> production . . . because a product becomes a real product only by being
> consumed. . . . the product, unlike a mere natural object, proves itself to
> be, *becomes,* a product only through consumption . . . only as object for
> the active subject. (91)

Marx, however, also recognized that the identity of production and consumption that one could arrive at theoretically was merely theoretical
identity, based on seeing a society as a singular subject. Once seen as the
activity of many individuals, production and consumption are clearly
separated by distribution: "The producer's relation to the product, once
the latter is finished, is an external one, and its return to the subject depends on his relation to other individuals" (94). So while the expansion
of production to include consumption is crucial, it is also important to
note that production is a differentiated process.

Consumptive labor is productive, but it is organized very differently
from productive labor: it is not organized, procured, or exploited as wage
labor. In expanding production to include women's work, private activ-

ity, and signification or performance, the definition of the technology of oppression that Marx called *exploitation* also must be expanded.

First of all, exploitation must be distinguished from appropriation, a term that has been used to accuse dominant groups of taking and profiting from cultural forms that belong to some subordinate group. As Amy Robinson argues, the logic of appropriation invokes and relies on a discourse of private property, which is precisely the discourse that functions to separate subordinate groups from social goods ("Forms of Appearance of Value"). According to Marx, exploitation is not appropriation; it is not the taking of property that properly belongs to someone else. One should be able to enjoy seeing someone else make good use of the product of one's labor, and in Marx's view, one would if one did not see that someone as Other, if one recognized one's communal relation to that Other. The wage labor system is technically fair: the full exchange value of the labor is paid to the laborer. As Marx argues in "The Critique of the Gotha Program," its exploitativeness would not be cured by increasing the portion of goods distributed to the direct producer; the direct producer would still be exploited because he would still not control the means of production. He would still be controlled by, opposed to, the capitalist Other; he would still be in competition with other workers and would still be subject to a division of labor that divided his particular interest from the general interest. The key to exploitation, then, is that it is a practice participated in by both the dominant and subordinate parties for the apparently voluntary and fair transfer of power to the dominant party.

How does this work when applied to consumption? Consumptive labor is procured and exploited through active subjection in the expression of needs, desires, self, identity, and community; as producers seem to freely sell their labor, consumers freely choose and purchase their commodities. With regard to production, Marx says: "The owner of money must meet in the market with the free labourer, free in the double sense, that as a free man he can dispose of his labour-power as his own commodity, and that on the other hand he has no other commodity for sale, is short of everything necessary for the realisation of his labour-power" (*Capital*, vol. 1 [Tucker], 338). In consumption, exploitation occurs insofar as by freely choosing, the consumer who is free of, short of, the means to meet her needs without choosing a commodity contributes to the accumulation of capital—and thus to the power of the owners of the means of production—and enacts the cultural and social formations in which her choices are embedded but which she does not control. The consumer's free choice is constrained and productive of further constraints.[12] Status, for example, as Bourdieu recognizes, is not only a consequence of specific economic factors, factors that limit or enable a variety of social performances such as the purchase of status-conferring commodities, but is a moment in a trajectory. Status itself opens or shuts off economic opportunity, jobs, education, and social access (Bourdieu, *Distinction, x*).

As conditions of productive labor are the site of struggle between worker and capitalist, so the conditions and implications of consumptive labor have been the site of struggle. A body of work in the field of cultural studies has attended to the deployment of mass products in particular or innovative ways in the elaboration of the subcultural community identity.[13] But the redeployment of such communal images by the corporate producers of the commodities has also been notable.

> The ephemerality of such images can then be interpreted in part as
> a struggle on the part of oppressed groups of whatever sort to establish
> their own identity (in terms of street culture, musical styles, fads and
> fashions made up for themselves) and the rush to convert those
> innovations to commercial advantage. (Harvey, *Condition of
> Postmodernity*, 289)

The problem with the Gap-ification[14] of gay culture, or with the incorporation of hip-hop into sneaker ads, is not that someone has stolen a cultural form that properly belongs to one group but that corporate deployment of the given form or style makes it at least in part alien to and against those who generated it. Queer Nation, for instance, felt that it had to "out" the Gap for its use of gay celebrities and styles. As Lauren Berlant and Elizabeth Freeman explain,

> The New York Gap series changes the final P in the logo of stylish ads
> featuring gay, bisexual and suspiciously polymorphous celebrities to
> a Y.... The reconstructed billboards ... address the company's policy of
> using gay style to sell clothes without acknowledging debts to gay street
> style. ("Queer Nationality," 168)

In speaking of "debts," Berlant and Freeman suggest that Queer Nation is objecting to appropriation, as if gays had property in the styles they developed by consuming mass culture products such as blue jeans and white T-shirts. But if the question of exploitation is more a question of control than one of acknowledgment or debt, then one must ask what social relations are advanced when gays and lesbians purchase their jeans, white T-shirts, and leather jackets in the first place. And in analyzing the reappropriation of the style by Gap, the crucial issue is whether gay people are empowered, their articulation of society promoted along with the particular clothing items, or whether the existence of gays and lesbians is erased or closeted. Finally, in assessing the intervention by Queer Nation, it is important to note that, while hijacking the corporate means of production of the discursive value of commodities can be a powerful intervention, participation in discursive production can also be "conciliatory, [in the] mode of, for instance, [Marshall] Kirk and [Hunter] Madsen's plan to market 'positive' (read 'tolerable') gay images to straight culture" (163). In either case, the very differentiations that communities may seek to enact with their consumptive production may not be external to or oppositional to capitalist production but may very well be the elaboration of its own necessarily increasingly dense articulations of difference, of niches, and of communities of consumers and producers.

Capitalism Produces Multidimensional Social Relations

Out of the multivalence of the commodity Marx draws a dynamic and multidimensional social space. He describes a historical evolution of social relations toward individuation and universalization, a dialectical relation between simultaneous and contradictory articulations of social relations, and a discursive process through which social movements, a class conscious of itself, may be constituted.

The Evolving Relation of Capitalism to Community

Marx describes (repeatedly in various texts) a historical process of the progressive reformation of society under capitalism, which breaks down existing communities and communal forms, freeing (and obliging) individuals to sell their labor and to be refunctioned as necessary for the capitalist development of productive forces. He notes that

> big industry ... destroy[ed] the former natural exclusiveness of separate nations ... and resolved all natural relations into money relations. In the place of naturally grown towns it created the modern, large industrial cities which have sprung up overnight. (*German Ideology*, 185)

Ultimately, this turns out to be a good thing: the conditions have been created so that under communism individuals are free to act according to their desires in relation to a "universal," "world-historical" human association, unimpeded by locality or relations of hierarchy, dependence, or dominance.

> Only then will the separate individuals be liberated from the various national and local barriers, be brought into practical connection with the material and intellectual production of the whole world and be put in a position to acquire the capacity to enjoy this all-sided production of the whole earth (the creation of man). (163–64)

Unlike many late-twentieth-century leftists, Marx is not nostalgic for older communal forms; describing the extraordinarily destructive effects of the introduction of industrial technology and capitalist logic by the British in India, he writes,

> We must not forget that these idyllic village communities . . . restrained the human mind within the smallest possible compass, making it the unresisting tool of superstition, enslaving it beneath traditional rules, depriving it of all grandeur and historical energies. . . . These little communities were contaminated by distinctions of caste and by slavery, that they subjugated man to external circumstances instead of elevating man to be the sovereign of circumstances. ("On Imperialism in India," 658)

Likewise, after discussing the fact that the English Parliament had finally decided to regulate the economic exploitation of children by their parents and thus destroy the traditional rights of parents over their children, Marx argues:

> However terrible and disgusting the dissolution, under the capitalist system, of the old family ties might appear, nevertheless, modern industry, by assigning as it does an important part in the process of production, outside the domestic sphere, to women, to young persons, to children of both sexes, creates a new economic foundation for a higher form of the family and of relations between the sexes. (*Capital*, vol. 1 [Tucker], 415)

As I argued in chapter 1, this narrative of the transformation of social relations toward individualization and universalization has a very problematic status in Marx's theory when it functions to supplement a structural account that focuses exclusively on the production of equivalence and exchange value and seems to suggest that all qualitative difference, of commodities, subjects, and social formations, is erased or becomes irrelevant under capitalism. I recount the story here to make precisely the opposite point—to show that the evolution of the modes of production produce evolutions in social formation. The evolution Marx describes does not simply destroy communities; as his description of the re-formation of the family suggests, it also generates new social formations. The positive opportunities provided by the disintegrative effects of the development of capitalism have been noted by feminist and gay historians. These historians have shown that industrialization did not simply bring homogeneous workers together in factories but freed young women from parental authority, bringing them together in cities and factories, where they created not just labor movements but also feminist movements, and likewise allowed gay people to congregate in urban centers outside the reach of the patriarchal and communal situations from which they had come. This research does not suggest that capitalism, in dissolving communities, left people "alienated" but rather that it enabled them to create communities on new (and, in their accounts, more voluntary) grounds.[15] However, these new communities also serve an evolving capitalism in particular ways.

Marx's story of the evolution of capitalism has been updated by historians and theorists who have described the emergence of the corporation, of Fordism, and now post-Fordism. These narratives can, like Marx's narrative, be deployed in quite problematic ways; as I will describe in chapter 5, the claims for epochal shifts in the structure of production, much like Marx's claim for the destruction of community by capital, can be used to suggest an opposition between community and capital, or at least the autonomy of community from capital. However, as Marx's description of the evolution of social formations can be used to show the complicity of community with capital, of culture with economy, likewise I will here use the descriptions of the twentieth-century transformations of capitalism to emphasize the ways that capitalism generates social formations and is inhabited by such formations.

Alan Trachtenberg points out that the dissolution of local and idiosyncratic communities and the development of industrial factory production coincided with the process of corporation building, as the necessary financial and organizational structure for the rationalization and massification of production. The development of a corporate capitalism based in mass production and consumption has been narrated as culminating in Fordism,[16] which involved not only the rationalization of

production through the Taylorization of work processes and the introduction of assembly lines, but also of consumption (the family wage
and the eight-hour day were meant to encourage workers to consume
the products they made). Gramsci describes Fordism as involving as
well the rationalization of the psychophysical, moral, and sexual lives of
workers. Gramsci's description of the resistance to "Americanism" posed
by economic "parasites" in Italy—historical remnants of feudal classes—
suggests that the rationalization of Fordism requires the destruction
of prior social formations. However, the social formation generated
through Fordism was not simply antagonistic to communal differentiation (Gramsci, *Prison Notebooks*, 279–318).

While, according to Trachtenberg, the massing of capital and of labor
tended, as Marx predicted, to articulate a relatively obvious and simple
division between workers and capitalists (*Incorporation of America*, 70–
100), this simplicity was complicated by the emergence of a vast class of
managers and professionals necessary to make these corporations run.
And, as Harvey points out, Fordism created a class of relatively privileged
white male (if often immigrant) workers and underclasses of African
Americans, Asians, and women (*Postmodernity*, 138). Further, as Piore
and Sabel note, particular industries and industrial labor unions were
often strongly articulated by particularities of ethnicity, family, and
gender. Corporations, then, have from their birth been sites of complex
subject construction, a complexity that cuts against any simple binary
oppositions and certainly against the notion that capitalism simply destroys differentiated social formations. But the evolution of capitalism
does not stop with Fordism, and in fact, what is most interesting about
contemporary innovations in corporate capitalist practices is that they
make corporate subject construction explicit and obvious.

Harvey dates from approximately 1973 the breakup of "Fordist-
Keynesian" "configurations of political-economic power" and a shift to
"new systems of production and marketing, characterized by more flexible labour processes and markets . . . geographical mobility and rapid
shifts in consumption practices" (*Postmodernity*, 124). He argues that,
starting in the 1970s,

> technological change, automation, the search for new product lines and
> market niches, geographical dispersal to zones of easier labor control,
> mergers and steps to accelerate the turnover time of their capital surged
> to the fore of corporate strategies for survival. (145)

According to Harvey, the merging of massive multinational corporations has come to depend on diverse communally structured production and consumption. The proliferation of corporate strategies to promote rather than suppress diversity, ranging from affirmative action to
diverse representation on television, operates to stabilize, not disrupt,
the system.[17]

Niche marketing and the shift from durable goods to services and
media have been the popularly recognized aspects of flexible accumulation. So there has been, for instance, a proliferation of long-distance
telephone services that operate under the sign of some particular community, in some cases claiming to contribute some part of their income
to organizations promoting the interests of that community. I am aware,
for instance, of services claiming identification with progressive causes
in general, women, Latinos, gays/lesbians, and Christian conservatives.
Over the past few years, the American Family Association has sent out
several direct mailings promoting the "Lifeline" long-distance service.
One such mailing read in part,

> Dear Friend,
>   It is not my intent to make you feel guilty, but I thought you would
> want to know: If you are a customer of AT&T, MCI or Sprint, you are
> helping promote the immoral, anti-family causes that the American
> Family Association has been fighting for seventeen years. . . .
>   The good news is that there is a way to fight back—and help AFA at
> the same time . . . Lifeline is deeply committed to helping Christian
> ministries like AFA.

Meanwhile, in 1994, AT&T did in fact target-market gays and lesbians
with a direct mail campaign (Figure 1). The packet they sent out included
a lavender and rainbow-colored brochure (colors widely used to sig-
nify gay culture and "gay pride") featuring pictures of gay couples, and
gay people with, or talking on the phone to, their parents. These images
were accompanied by the slogans "Let Your True Voice Be Heard" and
"It's Time for a Change." This packet also included a fact sheet on the
history of AT&T's gay employees association. What is being sold is not
so much phone service as participation in a given community.

Post-Fordist flexible accumulation involves shifts in the articulation
of production as well as consumption. One of the principle trends of
corporate capitalist activity has been the relocation of hard-core industrial production away from more "developed" regions and into formerly

less industrialized areas where labor is cheaper and regulations are fewer (Harvey, *Postmodernity,* 147). This trend creates a new relationship between labor and capital in the developed areas such as the United States. Workers are articulated as being in competition with workers elsewhere in the world, both those employed by the same company and by other companies. The corporation can claim that the other companies will use their cheaper foreign labor to put this company out of business, which will be bad for these workers too. (And in fact such competition has even been fomented between workers in different regions of the United States.)[18] Corporations use this situation to elicit a cooperative approach to collective bargaining (that is, to gain concessions), to encourage a sense of investment on the part of the workers in the profitability of the company, which the company backs up with more or less token profit sharing and management sharing. This process tends to articulate both nationalist discourses and discourses that ask workers to identify with the corporation itself as a family or community.[19]

Interestingly, these efforts to articulate worker and company interests as coincident come precisely at the moment in which worker loyalty is profoundly threatened by the increasingly evident lack of loyalty on the part of the corporation toward its employees. Not only are corporations willing to move plants overseas; they are busy downsizing and outsourcing, replacing full-time, benefited workers with part-time, temporary labor. Jobs that once seemed to carry lifetime tenure are now vulnerable to the latest economic news. Michael Moore's documentary film *Roger and Me* bemoans precisely this loss of a sense of company loyalty, as well as the loss of actual jobs, among General Motors (GM) workers in Flint, Michigan, who were subject to a seemingly endless series of plant closures in the 1980s. In its own public relations efforts, a series of full-page ads in the *New York Times* (probably not the paper most frequently read by GM workers), GM displaces responsibility for loyalty onto the worker. Workers are articulated as participants rather than merely wage laborers in that corporation; and as participants, they are shown identifying with the corporation (Figures 2 to 4). This vision of a unified corporation, within which workers have a home, runs counter to the actual effects of outsourcing, which distances workers from the large corporation and situates them in local/communal employment.

Large corporations acting as market coordinators encourage culturally distinct small and diverse groups to coalesce and incorporate. Outsourc-

Figure 1. "Let Your True Voice Be Heard." AT&T advertising brochure.

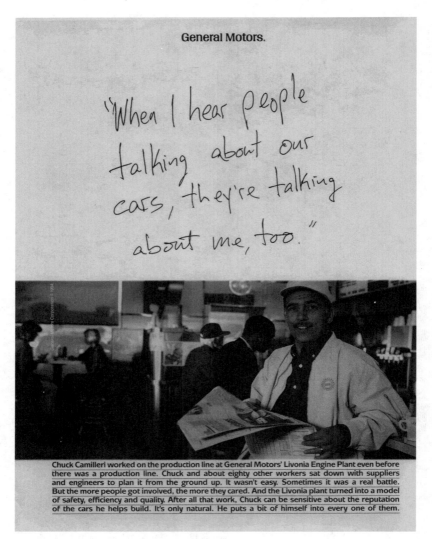

General Motors.

"When I hear people talking about our cars, they're talking about me, too."

Chuck Camilleri worked on the production line at General Motors' Livonia Engine Plant even before there was a production line. Chuck and about eighty other workers sat down with suppliers and engineers to plan it from the ground up. It wasn't easy. Sometimes it was a real battle. But the more people got involved, the more they cared. And the Livonia plant turned into a model of safety, efficiency and quality. After all that work, Chuck can be sensitive about the reputation of the cars he helps build. It's only natural. He puts a bit of himself into every one of them.

Figure 2. "When I hear people . . ." From the General Motors "Handwriting" newspaper and magazine advertisements.

ing and subcontracting to small businesses means that production can be organized in diverse ways, "permitting older systems of domestic, artisanal, familial (patriarchal), and paternalistic ('god-father,' 'gov'nor,' or even mafia-like) labour systems to revive and flourish" (Harvey, *Postmodernity*, 152). The shift away from mass production opens the way not only for older kinship structures to reinhabit production but also

General Motors.

"I sell these cars, so it's right that I have a say in how they're built."

Lisa Schomp, a third generation Oldsmobile dealer in Denver, spends a lot of time fielding questions from her customers. But these days, Lisa gets almost as many questions from the people at General Motors. They want to know: "What do people love about our cars? What are their gripes?" And they're not just asking for her advice. They're acting on it. Which makes sense. Because General Motors is out to build the cars and trucks customers really want. And who knows more about GM customers than the dealers, like Lisa, who make their living listening to them?

Figure 3. "I sell these cars . . ." From the General Motors "Handwriting" newspaper and magazine advertisements.

for newer social groupings to inhabit the corporation, to manifest themselves as a corporation. The diversity of groups useful as niche market consumers can turn around and understand themselves, assert themselves, as producers. Various communities—gay, racial, ethnic/immigrant, religious, and so on—make perfectly good corporate-productive rubrics; and so Korean markets, lesbian auto repair shops, Indian gas

General Motors.

"If the people who make the car don't fit together, the car won't either."

Welcome to the Excel training course. Before it's over, Saturn's Dennis Bowman will take these General Motors employees on a real adventure. They'll scale walls. Walk across high wires. Plunge backwards into the waiting arms of their coworkers. And take away some valuable lessons about trust, cooperation and seeing things from the other person's point of view. Developed by Saturn, Excel is now used throughout General Motors. It's turning out graduates who know the power of teamwork. Who go a little further to build quality automobiles. And who believe that the right way to treat a customer is the way you'd want to be treated yourself.

Figure 4. "If the people who make the car don't fit..." From the General Motors "Handwriting" newspaper and magazine advertisements.

stations, "minority-owned" (African American) engineering and construction firms, and Asian American sweatshops are examples of production and distribution sites that facilitate the flow of capital by organizing themselves on the basis of, and thus producing, the community with which the business is identified. They become the site and structure through which the community enacts its very existence.

Kath Weston and Lisa Rofel's study of labor conflict in a lesbian workplace argues that the communal structure was ultimately displaced by a labor-capital split, but what, for me, is most telling about their narrative is that the communal formation itself, as well as the labor-capital split, was articulated by capitalist discourses. The business was established precisely in order for its owners to escape the fate of wage labor; entrepreneurship seemed to offer independence, an opportunity to create a business that would have the characteristics of private space, in which lesbians could be out of the closet and treat each other according to a "politics of trust," inscribed as feminine. When the owners violated the trust and treated employees as subordinates, the employees, maintaining the discourse of the private, invoking trust and friendship among themselves as a technique of solidarity, gradually began to deploy another discourse on which capitalism depends, that is the discourse of the contract and "rights." "Because the politics of trust masked power inequalities . . . it had encouraged workers to consider all points negotiable and to believe they could ask for whatever seemed 'fair' and 'reasonable' according to their own needs" ("Sexuality, Class, and Conflict," 215). As I will explore in the next section, it seems clear here that neither the particular community formation, nor the employees' resistance to exploitation, were mobilized from outside the capitalist mode of production. Instead, in fact, they were the products of it.

The Dialectical Dynamics of Social Formations

In Marx's narrative, the new social formations being generated, even as the disintegrative process of individuation occurs, are on the one hand the relations of production (that is, the relations within the factory among workers and between workers and owners) and on the other hand the relations of the marketplace and the bourgeois "liberal" state. What are the relations between these simultaneous but divergent new social formations?

Marx argues that under capitalism, the realms of production (construed as manufacturing) and exchange (the marketplace) appear to be independent of each other.

> Accompanied by Mr. Moneybags and by the possessor of labour-power, we therefore take leave for a time of this noisy sphere, where everything takes place on the surface and in view of all men, and follow them both into the hidden abode of production. . . . This sphere that we are deserting, within whose boundaries the sale and purchase of labour-power

goes on, is in fact a very Eden of the innate rights of man. There alone rule Freedom, Equality, Property and Bentham.

On leaving this sphere of simple circulation or of exchange of commodities . . . we think we can perceive a change in the physiognomy of our dramatis personae. He, who before was the money owner, now strides in front as capitalist; the possessor of labour-power follows as his labourer. The one with an air of importance, smirking, intent on business; the other, timid and holding back, like one who is bringing his own hide to market and has nothing to expect but—a hiding. (*Capital*, vol. 1 [Tucker], 343)

In drawing production narrowly and representing these two realms as independent, Marx is here—dripping with irony—showing us capitalism as it sees itself. Within capitalism, the inequities of production appear to be limited to the factory and appear not to determine (or be determined by) social relations, which appear to be free. It is precisely the implication of the realm of exchange in production that Marx needs to argue for in *Capital*. To say this another way, Marx is here making an argument much like the one I wish to make for the complicity of production in a broad sense (the whole social organization of production, exchange, and consumption) with production in a narrow sense (manufacturing in this quote, the production of monetary surplus value in my argument).

Marx characterizes the ideological process that makes the marketplace and the state appear independent of production as fetishism. Fetishism is a two-step process: first the subject objectifies itself in some way, through some product; then this product is alienated, that is, it appears to have, in fact does have, an independent life and acts as a power over the producer. The commodity is a fetish in that the value of the commodity in exchange (that is, its relations with other things) seems to inhere in it and seems not to be a product of the producer. This results from the fact that the commodity's value is social; it is only as a product of the whole society's productive abilities and relations that the particular commodity gets its value; its value is not due to the actions of the individual producer alone. But the producer thinks he is producing the product by himself and isn't aware of his relations with others in the society (or at least that is how Marx's story goes).[20] "A definite social relation between men . . . assumes, in their eyes, the fantastic form of a relation between things" (*Capital*, vol. 1 [Tucker], 321).

I would suggest that many social formations might be analyzed on the model of fetishism: communities created through production (through labor or participation) appear to be independent, organic entities over and against the subjects who produced them. This is true for identity-based groups in two ways. First of all, the participation and activism of group members is erased in the appearance of the group, the community, as an organic and eternal effect of identity. Second, because of their supposedly organic nature, ethnic-, national- or identity-based communal formations are frequently articulated as providing an alternative to the alienated realm of production; in other words, they are understood as independent of the larger social relations of production within which they are situated. As Marx says, civil society (his term for the realm of production when contrasted with the state rather than with the market) seems by contrast with the fetishized communality of the state to be a realm of "atomistic, antagonistic individuals" ("On the Jewish Question," 51), when in fact civil society is where people enact their mutual dependence and have their real relations. Likewise, I would suggest that while civil society appears to be a realm of organic and independent communities, it is in fact where these communities are constituted through their interdependent productive practices.

Marx's analysis of fetishism might make it seem that the market (or state) is merely the ideological projection of the production process, in which the equality and interdependence of producers that ought to exist and be explicitly acknowledged have become the equivalence and interchangeability of things (or citizens). But as he analyzes the interdependence of these two realms it becomes clear that the relation between these two spheres is not a relation of unidirectional determination in which the reality of production determines the ideological marketplace. They coproduce and support each other: the marketplace is the realm of individualism and apparent free choice through which individuals freely enter into exploitative (productive) relations. Surplus value cannot be generated without the interplay of the two processes.

In addition, production and exchange yield two very different and equally consequential visions of the world. While the production realm yields an articulation of class subordination, the marketplace and the state provide any situation with alternative potential articulations: the discourses of rights and of nation are salient examples. The realm of production and the marketplace exceed each other; civil society and the state exceed each other and come to be antagonistic, dialectical, dynamic forces. It may be that only in combination with rights discourse can class subordination be articulated as class conflict. And the inequality of the production process makes the enactment of equality in exchange impossible; people's ability to participate in the market can become extremely limited, thus creating a segment of the population that does not buy the discourse of equality. Both views of social relations are equally real, and although they are both necessary for the realization of capital they are not structurally stable or coherent. They are in a relation of antagonism as well as coproduction, in which, as two very different articulations of society, they generate social change.

The Discursive Production of an Oppositional Movement

Marx elaborates a third theory of social relations (counting the evolutionary and dialectical as the first two) in describing the development of the revolutionary proletariat. This class is produced through a process of (practical) consciousness raising based on participation, first in production and then in resistance.

> The co-operation of the wage labourers is entirely brought about by the capital that employs them. Their union into one single productive body and the establishment of a connexion between their individual functions, are matters foreign and external to them, are not their own act, but the act of capital that brings and keeps them together. (*Capital,* vol. 1 [Tucker], 395)

The transformation of this collectivity from working for capital to working for itself, ultimately in the production of goods but immediately as a revolutionary force, is a lengthy process:

> [As] the various interests and conditions of life within the ranks of the proletariat are more equalised ... the collisions between individual workman and individual bourgeois take more and more the character of collisions between two classes. There upon workers begin to form combinations (Trade Unions) against the bourgeois; they club together in order to keep up the rate of wages; they found permanent association in order to make provision beforehand for these occasional revolts. ... The real fruit of these battles lies, not in the immediate result, but in the ever expanding union of the workers. This union is helped by the improved means of communication that are created by modern industry and that place the workers of different localities in contact with one another.
> The bourgeoisie find itself involved in constant battle. ... In all these

battles [the bourgeoisie] sees itself compelled to appeal to the proletariat . . . and thus to drag it into the polifical arena. The bourgeoisie
itself, therefore, supplies the proletariat with its own elements of political and general education. (*Manifesto of the Communist Party*, 480–81)

The story told here can be read in a couple of different ways. It can be
and has been read as a story of essentialism and determinism—of real
material conditions (as some real essence or truth) producing a necessary result. Or it can be seen as describing and rhetorically promoting a
process of consciousness raising, in which people both within and without the given class must witness, narrate, or practically inscribe, not
necessarily verbally, the conditions and collectivity of the class in order
for the class to form as a self-conscious actor. Marx's description of the
evolution of the revolutionary class from geographically local rebellion
to a worldwide revolution, through means of communication, supplemented by "experience" of collectively taken actions and "political and
general education," suggests that at each crucial turn it is the discursive/
practical inscription of experience through/in the appropriation (learning, education, enactment) of existing forms and methods of collective
action (i.e., political parties) that allows the movement to grow.

The textual locus for the argument I am making about the discursive
formation of classes in Marx is usually the *Eighteenth Brumaire,* and
especially its discussion of the lumpenproletariat. Marx sees the proletariat forming through "rubbing together in the factory," which is why
he does not see a revolutionary role for the lumpenproletariat, a diverse
and dispersed mass (not quite a class and not producers). The lumpenproletariat have not been brought together into a productive collectivity, which they can then reappropriate or renarrate for new ends; they
lack the prior connection within the realm of production that would
support an economic determinist theory of their functioning as a coherent class. As Peter Stallybrass explains, "The lumpen seems to figure
less a class in any sense that one usually understands than a group that
is amenable to political articulation" ("Marx and Heterogeneity," 88).
The lumpenproletariat is constituted as a class by and for Bonaparte's performance of political hegemony. Marx's presentation of "Bonapartism . . .
opens up the domain of politics and the state as something other than a
reflection" (91). It is not clear that Marx was ready to recognize the full
import of the discursive, participatory, performative process of class
formation that he describes. Its full import is that capitalist societies

are not split along one single axis but rather generate collectivities that align or agonize on many incohèrent, unassimilable fronts. While Marx's theory offers a glimpse of the multidimensional dynamics of social formation, by (most frequently) limiting his view to the factory and the process of monetary exchange, Marx deemphasizes other important sites of production, exploitation, and class formation.

Because of these limitations in Marx's texts (limitations that were elaborated and reified in later orthodox Marxisms) many theorists have rejected his analysis altogether, finding a source of subjectivity and social relations outside of production. While I argue that production, especially when taken to include activities outside the factory, such as consumption or reproduction, can be analyzed as generating a great diversity of social relations, others have chosen instead to reject productivism as a mode of analysis and look elsewhere. Laclau and Mouffe and Samuel Bowles and Herbert Gintis, for instance, see the discourse of rights rather than the discourse of class as the more potent force for social change, as able to both generate and coordinate, into a unified counter-hegemonic formation, various "new social movements." My own argument is that this is not so much of a break with Marx as Laclau and Mouffe would suggest and that the discourse of rights appears within a productivist analysis. However, accounting for rights discourse is not enough. It is the particular diversity of collectivities and conflicts that really needs to be accounted for. I want now to turn to theories that account for heterogenity by locating it outside of production, by opposing production and performance, production and liberation.

A Queer Interlude—Performativity: Productive or Antiproductive?

There is a line of argument running from the Frankfurt School to some recent queer theory that attempts to account for the diversity of social movements, the diversity of axes of antagonism, by positing an exterior to production; these critiques posit production as creating a "one-dimensional," rationalized, homogenized, and hegemonized society, and they look for expressions of heterogeneous—connoting "free"—human intelligence, spirit, imagination, and sexuality to break through the discipline of production. "The 'heterogeneous' includes everything 'resulting from unproductive expenditure,' everything that 'homogeneous' society defines as 'waste' or that it is 'powerless to assimilate'"

(Stallybrass, "Marx and Heterogeneity," 81, quoting Bataille). In this view, the unproductive, equated with the heterogeneous, is celebrated as having a liberatory potential. The association of homogeny with hegemony is a false one, as the explicit promotion of diversity in contemporary capitalism demonstrates, but it is pervasive in this line of theorizing. The current version of this critique can be found in scattered assertions of the "heteronormativity" of production (meaning not that it is based on or produces heterogeneous norms, but just the opposite, that it is based on and reproduces the hegemonic homogenizing norm of heterosexuality), and in celebrations of heterogeneity, homosexuality, and theatricality as subversive of dominant discourses.

In "Unthinking Sex," Andrew Parker weaves together the various threads of contemporary arguments that characterize unproductivism, performance, and homosexuality as heterogeneous and thus liberatory practices. His weaving technique is that of suggestive slippages, of metonymic associations: he states that Marx's notion of productivity is modeled on procreation[21] and that, citing the Marx-Engels correspondence, Marx sees homosex as anal ("lumpy"), wasteful, and thus unproductive (34–35); Parker argues that Marx sees homosex as a mere recirculation (rather than production) of goods, adding no value (25), such as goes on amid the lumpenproletariat, the scum, the heterogeneous, metonymically associated mass. Parker further associates this lumpensexuality with theatricality, with the parody of production[22]: he claims that, in the *Eighteenth Brumaire,* Marx criticizes the French political scene as a "farce" because politics seems to have lost its realist representational relationship to class divisions, that is, to production.[23] While Parker is correct in pointing out that Marx does link performance and unproductiveness, echoing Adam Smith's claim that theatrical performance, like all service work, is unproductive in the technical sense that "it perishes in the very instant of its production," it is clear that such vanishing products are precisely what contemporary capitalism thrives on (Smith, *Wealth of Nations,* quoted in Parker, 25). And Stallybrass's reading of the *Eighteenth Brumaire* suggests that Marx did recognize the productivity of Louis Bonaparte's farcical performance ("Marx and Heterogeneity," 87).

Parker claims that he is doing something different, in generating this chain of verbal associations that ultimately connects homosexuality (very narrowly evoked as male-male anal penetration and a queeny theatricality) with unproductiveness, from prior Marxist (Frankfurt School) dealings with sex, which see natural sexuality as repressed under capitalism (that is, a regime of productivism). But Parker's rhetoric, which condemns Marx for his (indisputable) homophobia and his (highly disputable) antitheatricalism, enacts a very similar move; it seems also to condemn production and productivism. It's just that it is Marx's productivism rather than capitalist production that is doing the repressing of subversive sexuality.

Associations between unconventional sexuality and heterogeneous, free, subversive, unrationalized unproductivity are well established in the earlier Frankfurt School theory to which Parker refers. In *The Dialectic of Enlightenment,* Theodor Adorno and Max Horkheimer reject the notion that sexual perversion in itself is liberatory. While stating that "in so far as the flagrant violation of the taboo, which was once allied to the bourgeois revolution, has not adjusted proficiently to the new reality, it lives on with sublime love as faith in that now proximate utopia which makes sexual pleasure free for all" (109), they argue that the separation of physical sexuality from love that Sade's characters articulate epitomizes rationalization in its most perverse form, where organization for the sake of organization has overshadowed any substantive content (88).

> By praising genital and perverted sex to the disadvantage of unnatural, immaterial, and illusory sexuality, the libertine throws himself in with that normality that belittles and diminishes not only the utopian exuberance of love but its physical pleasure, not only the happiness of the seventh heaven but that of the immediate reality. The rake without illusions (whom Juliette stands for) transforms himself with the assistance of sex educators, psychoanalysts, and hormone physiologists into the open and practical man who extends his attitude to sport and hygiene to his sexual life. (109)

For Adorno and Horkeimer, the irrational sexuality that would stand as utopian, as a refusal of the capitalist logics of equivalence and productivity, is the joining of lust and love in a passion for a specific individual that overrides concerns for self-preservation (109). Such combinations of lust and love would seem to represent the positive side of the dialectic of Enlightenment in that they represent a relationship between nature and Enlightenment prior to the Enlightenment's absolute domination of nature, or rather, its absolute subordination to its drive to master nature.

By contrast, in *Eros and Civilization,* Herbert Marcuse does celebrate sexual perversion in itself as a form of resistance. Marcuse argues that "the performance principle" is "the prevailing historical form of the reality principle"(32); "the reality principle," as defined by Freud, is the conformation of man's drive for pleasure to the social and natural realities in which he finds himself. As Marcuse explains it, *performance* has none of the liberatory connotations that it takes on in contemporary queer theory; rather, performances are portrayed as entirely constrained by their audiences.

> We designate it as the performance principle in order to emphasize that under its rule society is stratified according to the competitive economic performances of its members.... Men do not live their own lives but perform pre-established functions... Libido is diverted for socially useful performances.... His erotic performance is brought into line with his societal performance.... The perversions thus express rebellion against the institutions which guarantee this order. (40–42, 45)

What Adorno and Horkheimer and Marcuse share in their analyses of sexuality is a celebration of heterogeneity. Love for a "specific individual" and "the perversions" are utopian impulses in that they refuse sameness of sexuality as a capitalist performance. Understanding capitalism one-sidedly, that is, simply as a regime of homogenization, heterogeneous sexuality would necessarily seem to stand outside it. However, because of the intensive reach of the regime of production into every nook and cranny of subjectivity, that "outside" is very difficult to find. In making recourse to individual love (as well as to relatively private artistic expressions such as lyric poetry or to the obscurantism of the avant-garde [and his own prose]), Adorno suggests, in fact, that resistance must not be found; the condition for freedom would seem to be privacy from the audience that would turn one's actions into a performance.

In *The Mirror of Production,* Baudrillard, like Parker, develops the critique of the totalizing and repressive nature of production in the direction of Marx, arguing that like the political economists, Marx celebrates production and thus does not expose the way in which man is alienated by being identified with his labor power (and not just by the sale of that labor power) (31). It is not the organization of production (which he very narrowly imagines as wage labor) but the system of meaning that values only production that is oppressive in Baudrillard's analysis. According to Baudrillard, freedom is to be found not, as Marx would suggest, through production (that is, through binary class conflict), but through subversion of the code by diverse oppressed groups: ethnic minorities, women, youth, sexual perverts. Revolution must involve heterogeneous expression, wasteful gift exchange (pure expenditure rather than accumulation, final consumption rather than productive consumption), and nonprocreative sex. What Baudrillard misses here of course is the very usefulness of final consumption and of gift exchange to capitalism: final consumption is useful in clearing space for new production, that is, for managing overaccumulation; and gift exchange, as I will argue in the next chapter, forges the social bonds that enable the flow of capital.

For Baudrillard the exteriority from which this heterogeneous expression can occur is a product of the system itself:

> Subversion is born there, an *elsewhere*. . . . Segregated, discriminated against, satellitized—[youth, blacks, women] are gradually relegated to a position of non-marked terms by the structuration of the system as a code. (131–35)

And yet Baudrillard does ascribe a peculiar freedom to this forced exteriorization; the "unmarked" are able to rebel against the code rather than demanding equality within the terms of the code, so these groups would seem to have some source of subjecthood other than their exclusionary construction by the code. My question is what that source might be.

The link between performance and unproductiveness found in contemporary queer theory such as that of Parker and Peggy Phelan, whose work I will address shortly, is made by constructing two analogies: first between representation and production, and second between political and symbolic representation. As Spivak points out, the structure of analogy is problematic here, producing a conflation of the two terms that elides their complicity. Cultural representation, she says, has the structure of subject predication, while political representation relies on "rhetoric-as-persuasion." It is the work of critique to see when these two things work together, when hegemonizing political representation "behaves like" subject predication. In eliding this complicity, Spivak argues, the analogy obscures discontinuities within the subject and defers that subject to a space of silent unrepresentability ("Subaltern," 275–77). Representation is then understood as a (re)productive technology operating within the symbolic. The relationship, the complicity, between representation (the political economy of the sign) and production (the division of labor) is here, likewise, elided. The falsity, the insufficiency, oppressiveness, and homogenizing character of any realist (political or cultural) representation of a social group is emphasized, based on (post)structuralist arguments against the referentiality of the signifier (this is to go no further than Baudrillard), and theatricality is promoted as a nonrealist and thus a less hegemonized, repressive, possessable, co-optable form of signification. A Brechtian sort of performance is singled out for praise here: a performance that announces its own constructedness and thus disrupts the realist truth claims of productive/representational hegemony. Parker and Stallybrass focus on Marx's discussions of farce and parody; Phelan talks about performance that includes "the marked reproduction of the real production" (that is, representations of things used to make the artwork are included in the work itself) (*Unmarked*, 8).

These theorists disagree about what antirealist theatricality makes possible. Parker seems to suggest that it is the free play of signification. Stallybrass is interested in giving the political relative freedom from economic determination, making available diverse forms and sites for social protest and political activity. Phelan and Baudrillard, however, suggest that theatricality frees political subjects from representation altogether and thus offers access to the (supposedly) inaccessible (Lacanian) Real. Brecht did not see his work as antirealist but rather antinaturalist—in disrupting the illusion of reality it revealed the real reality—and Phelan likewise believes in the possibility of a performance that really exposes the Real.

In *Unmarked*, Phelan celebrates the political potential of the invisible, which she claims is relatively free, as against the co-opted, predetermined, preassimilated visibility that identity-based political movements make the mistake of endlessly striving for. Her argument makes Baudrillard's Lacanian formulation explicit (135–36).[24] In her terms, "the code" is "the Symbolic," and that which is unmarked, or unsymbolized, exists as the unappropriated Real, "full being itself... forever impossible to realize within the frame of the symbolic" (3).

Phelan's argument depends on splitting the world into two levels. But unlike Marx's levels, the marketplace and production, which are dialectically agonistic articulations, equally real and equally constructed, Phelan's levels are ranked, with false and oppressive representation standing against the good but unrepresentable reality. The Real that is being (mis)represented, both excessively and inadequately, is a truth, an origin, a guarantor of some sort. For her and for Baudrillard this Real is the source of unrationalized subjecthood. It is the locus of liberatory exteriority.[25]

Phelan sets up a dichotomy that is very similar to that proffered by the Frankfurt School theorists: on the one hand a totalizing homogenizing production system and on the other the liberatory un(re)productive, named here "performance."[26]

> Performance, insofar as it can be defined as representation without reproduction, can be seen as a model for another representational economy, one in which the reproduction of the other as the Same is not assured. (3)
>
> Performance clogs the smooth machinery of reproductive representation necessary to the circulation of capital. . . . Live performance . . . disappears into memory, into the realm of invisibility and the unconscious where it eludes regulation and control. (148)

The notion that performance is unproductive because it is live, because it is produced and consumed in the same moment, because it is not a material commodity (even while, as the Real, it is in the structural position of pure materiality, unmediated by discourse) is, as I think I've made clear by now, simply wrong: performance is just as well able to bear value (use, exchange, surplus, status) and to produce subjects and social formations as any material commodity, arguably better able: "The commodification of images of the most ephemeral sort would seem to be a godsend from the standpoint of capital accumulation" (Harvey, *Postmodernity,* 288).

In order to claim that performance resists exchange value, or equivalence, and thereby approaches the unrepresentable Real itself, Phelan discounts the work of the audience; their productive consumption of the work, their act of witness, is for her the mere memory of something presented by someone else. She cannot recognize the audience's consumption as production, for then it would not offer the escape from regulation and control that she seeks.[27] In losing the audience, though, she loses the theatrical aspect of the artwork's performativity (both its reiterative and witnessed, and therefore social, aspects) and is left with the speech act connotations (that it enacts that which it names).[28] As Mary Louise Pratt points out, by focusing on "excessively private" dyadic

examples of communication, speech act theory loses the ability to recognize that "people always speak from and in a socially constituted position . . . in which the subject and context mutually determine each
other ongoingly" ("Ideology and Speech Act Theory," 63). Performance,
for Phelan, appears to be the act of a fully constituted subject, a subject
thus unavailable for articulation with a liberatory collectivity and unable
itself to articulate resistance. Against Adorno, Phelan, and Baudrillard, I
would suggest that resistance is enabled by (inevitable) participation in
the system rather than in escape from it.

Conclusion

The reading of Marx I have offered works against the view that production would produce a totalized society and against the view that representation or production would ever be reproduction of the same. But I
am also very doubtful of the existence of some sort of heterogeneous
exteriority to production from which subversion might come. Butler,
using Laclau's formulation of social dynamics as antagonistic articulations, argues that what appears to be exterior, to be "the Real," what can
bring one particular social formation into crisis, is actually just another
discursive schema (*Bodies*, 194). As Parker correctly points out, it is

> impossible to repeat after Foucault . . . [a story of] how a natural or
> potentially liberatory sexuality has been set upon, repressed, commodi-
> fied or otherwise constrained by the institutions of capitalism: as if
> sexuality were not always already institutional, existing only in his-
> torically sedimented forms and discourses. ("Unthinking Sex," 21)[29]

Likewise, Stallybrass, citing Georges Bataille to describe a Marxian view,
argues that "'social heterogeneity does not exist in a formless and dis-
oriented state,' but is itself structured through its relation to the dominant homogeneous forces" ("Marx and Heterogeneity," 81).

What Laclau and Butler's arguments, circumscribing subversion within
signification and social relations (making it a product of sociality),
mean to me is that critique needs to continue to focus on production.
But what all the theorists I have reviewed here have made clear is that a
critique of production needs to look at sign production as well as material production, at the performativity of production, at the circulation
of social formations as well as goods. From the Frankfurt School through
Baudrillard to Phelan, concern shifts from production as a rationalizing

system to the Lacanian Symbolic and its reproductive capacity as the system by which subjects are operationalized. In place of this shift, my own argument intends to put production and signification into a necessary relation with each other and not posit the political economy of the sign as superseding political economy. Attending to the productivity of performance, Baudrillard and the Frankfurt School theorists argue that sign production primarily functions in the service of capitalism (they just also think it can have an independent existence) and that capitalism mobilizes, enforces, and materializes discursively articulated social divisions. Attending to the performativity of production, a Butlerian reading of Marx makes it possible to recognize the opportunities as well as the constraints available within production.

CHAPTER THREE

Not for Profit? Voluntary Associations and the Willing Subject

A specter is haunting Europe—the specter of communism.
—Karl Marx and Frederick Engels, *Manifesto of the Communist Party*

The problem of our age is the proper administration of wealth, that the ties of brotherhood may still bind together the rich and poor in harmonious relationship. . . . The Socialist or Anarchist who seeks to overturn present conditions is to be regarded as attacking the foundation upon which civilization itself rests, for civilization took its start from the day when the capable, industrious workman said to his incompetent and lazy fellow, "If thou dost not sow, thou shalt not reap," and thus ended primitive Communism. . . . In bestowing charity, the main consideration should be to help those who will help themselves; to provide part of the means . . . but rarely or never to do all.
—Andrew Carnegie, "The Gospel of Wealth"

It is necessary to speak *of the* ghost, indeed *to the* ghost and *with* it, from the moment that no ethics, no politics, whether revolutionary or not, seems possible and thinkable and *just* that does not recognize in its principle the respect for those others who are no longer or for those others who are not yet *there*.

And this being-with specters would also be . . . a *politics* of memory, of inheritance, and of generations.
—Jacques Derrida, *Specters of Marx*

A reckoning with nonprofit organizations is inevitable in this project on the relationship of community with capitalism. Nonprofits would appear to have a very important relation to community. In 2000 the Web site of the Independent Sector—"A national leadership forum working to encourage giving, volunteering, not-for-profit initiative and citizen action"—claimed that "It is difficult to imagine a community without a community Food Bank, a Mothers Against Drunk Driving chapter, a community museum, or a Friends of the Zoo." At least in the United States, when the imaginary of community is invoked, nonprofits are a central feature and, conversely, nonprofits are imagined to be expressions of community. In my research process, wherever I looked for community, what I found were nonprofits. Nonprofits often stand in for community metonymically. One gives to one's community or to "the community" by contributing labor or money to a nonprofit; nonprofits are asked to represent communities politically, to speak for the communities for which they are metonyms. Written into the Romantic narrative, nonprofits are imagined to be the formal sites for communal behavior, for caring and giving, supposed once upon a time to have taken place informally among neighbors (Wuthnow, "Rediscovering Community"). At the same time, nonprofits are defined through their relation to capital. Nonprofits are supposed to be *not* for profit—the capital they accumulate cannot be distributed as profit—but they are also not non-capitalist and especially not anticapitalist. Nonprofits are often posited as the institutional form in which community complements capital. "Markets have a harsh side and a sharp edge to them; consequently nonprofit associations are held up as a softer and more compassionate alternative" (Powell and Clemens, *Private Action*, xiii). Largely run on women's voluntary and low-waged labor and providing services once thought to be women's work (religion, education, social welfare), nonprofits might be seen as a site of reproduction that supports for-profit production in much the way women's domestic labor has done.[1] I will argue that nonprofits play a crucial role in the supplementarity of community with capital.

The significance of formally incorporated nonprofit organizations to "community" on the one hand and to capitalism on the other emerged for me during a research trip to Tupelo, Mississippi, the hometown of the American Family Association (AFA); the organization, run by Donald Wildmon and his brother Allen, is largely responsible for instigating the controversy over the National Endowment for the Arts (the topic of the following chapter). In a brief phone conversation with Allen Wildmon, I asked whether his work was intended to be community building. His response was to say that he would not work for an organization that was not building community and that in fact he was so insulted by my question that he did not want to continue talking. Had I known more about Tupelo, I might have known to expect such a response. I spent most of my time in Tupelo at the offices of the local newspaper, the *Northeast Mississippi Daily Journal,* which had rich files on the AFA. My primary informant, Ann, a reporter at the paper, told me that "community is everything here." She explained that what "community" meant in Tupelo, as exemplified by the statements of the politicians in the mayoral race she was covering, was economic development. Tupelo's "progressiveness"—its relative economic well-being compared to the nearby Mississippi Delta region—was attributed to its "communal" approach. This communal approach was a tradition in Tupelo, a tradition that, I was told by Ann and others, originated in the activities of George A. McLean. Informed by a New Deal philosophy (called *socialist* by one of my more conservative informants) and working in conjunction with New Deal government programs, McLean started a variety of organizations aimed at providing basics such as food, clothing, shelter, and electricity.[2] Among those organizations was a Community Development Foundation, evidence of which appeared on street signs and buildings in the neighborhood of the newspaper, and the newspaper itself, which he reorganized as a nonprofit in 1972, "dedicated to the service of God and Mankind."[3] The role of nonprofits in articulating the social formation, as a "community," for capitalism, was explicit and embraced in Tupelo, even as the specter of "socialism" hovered nearby. But even while the emergence of the communal and nonprofit strategy in Tupelo is linked narratively to the Depression, to a crisis in capitalism, Tupelo's communal approach is cast as prior to and independent of capital. As a local tradition that differs from the tradition of the Delta region, "community" in Tupelo seems to be something cultural, something about values, not value (Figures 5 to 7).

To argue that nonprofits play a role in the supplementary relation between community and capitalism, and to attempt to specify that role, is to set for myself a complex and difficult task. To describe nonprofits as the mechanism that manages or facilitates a relation—supplementarity—

Figure 5. Community Warehouse Corporation, Tupelo, Mississippi.

that is not only about facilitation but also as much about displacement, is to describe a mechanism that is quite contradictory and multivalent. It would be much easier to argue that nonprofits are what Althusser calls ideological state apparatuses (ISAs), that they generate individual and communal subjectivity for capitalism. And to make that argument would be to tell an important part of the story of nonprofits; it is certainly the case that nonprofits have been deployed as ISAs, as I will show through readings of the dominant discourses (primarily the discourses of "civil society" and "development") in which nonprofits have been articulated.[4]

But to tell only that story would flatten the supplementary relation between community and capitalism, reducing community to an element of the capitalist structure, as if that structure were whole. My reading of the Romantic discourse of community suggests that community is not opposed to capitalism in the ways the discourse itself suggests that it is. However, the Romantic discourse of community does seem to express discontent, a longing for something missing from capitalism. In examining the discourse and practice of nonprofit organizations, I mean to take that expression of discontent seriously. Nonprofits often articulate desires not met by capitalism for specific goods—religion, education, health care, arts, social services, or social change—but also often for an alternative mode of production, namely, gift exchange. While economists

Figure 6. Community Drive, Tupelo, Mississippi.

read nonprofit production as complementary with for-profit production (it provides goods that for-profit production and the state do not provide [Hansmann, "Economic Theories"; Weisbrod, *Nonprofit Economy;* James, "Nonprofit Sector"]), insofar as the "good" provided by nonprofits is "community," nonprofits do not merely complement the market and the state but rather mark the absent center of capitalism.[5] Appearing at moments of capitalist expansion, instability, and crisis, nonprofits indicate that something, or rather someone—the subject of capital—is missing.

The common name, the fear-inspired name, for this absence of desire for, of consent to, the "free and fair" process by which capitalism distributes power and wealth to some while diminishing the power and wealth of others, an absence of subjects properly constituted as voluntary participants in capitalism, is, of course, Communism. Nonprofits make this absence present but they give it another name, the name Community. And more than that, by displacing communism, by offering another route for the desires for that which is not capital, they wed the missing subject, the subject who is not a subject of capital, to capitalism. To put this in more Gramscian terms, nonprofits function as a hegemonic apparatus, articulating the desire for community with a desire for capitalism.

But even as they mark an absence, as sites of performative production nonprofit practices make present multiple and multivalent individual

Figure 7. *Northeast Mississippi Daily Journal* building and Community Enterprises, Inc., Tupelo, Mississippi.

and communal subjects. They produce diverse and particular subjects and social formations. As Foley and Edwards note, "Voluntary associations, after all, are generally created to further some purpose beyond abstract social capital formation" ("Escape," 554). And these subjects and social formations may not necessarily, only, and immediately facilitate the circulation of capital; they may at times materialize the obstacles and resistances that capitalism needs to overcome as it expands. The extensive intentional deployment of nonprofit activity for hegemonic purposes is a crucial but not a complete account of the productivity of nonprofit organizations. Rather than inscribing participants as puppets, whose strings are pulled by a variety of structural ghosts, I would rather propose that participants are enabled in their projects, projects that are often important to the very survival of the people served by the organization, precisely because nonprofits are useful to capitalism. However, with Derrida, I would suggest that to deploy our abilities responsibly requires acknowledging and transforming our inheritances, a politics of memory and generation.

In order to articulate the relation between the performativity of nonprofit production and the supplementarity of community with capital, that is to say between the production of diverse particular subjects and the functionality (or failure) of those subjects as agents of capitalism and bearers of capital, I turn at various points in this chapter to ethnography, primarily my ethnographic study of one nonprofit organization, Theatre Rhinoceros. In this first ethnographic section, I draw on interviews I conducted with participants in order to illustrate the performative production of subjectivity. The narratives these participants offered might be understood as describing spatial or temporal trajectories, across which their subjectivities shift—shifted by, at least in part, their participation in the theater. Significantly, the subjectivities enacted through participation in the theater are quite complex and varied; and some of my interviewees raised critical questions about the identities and communities in which participation inscribed them.

The Performativity of Nonprofit Production and Consumption

I began to work at Theatre Rhinoceros shortly after moving to San Francisco; I migrated to the gay mecca after college precisely in order to be gay. I was already "out," but I wanted to participate in San Francisco's vibrant and extensive gay community and thus elaborate my own identity. At that time I thought I wanted to work in theater professionally and so working at the gay theater was the obvious choice. As it turns out, my story is quite common; for many of the people I spoke to, Theatre Rhinoceros played some significant role in their achievement of gay identity and community membership.[6] It was either, as for me, part of a coming-out process, or it was one of the places they found connection to the gay community when most of their lives took place at some distance from that community. Some were distanced geographically; many audience members lived in the suburbs and their Rhino subscription gave them occasion not only to come to a gay theater, but to have dinner in the gay Castro neighborhood or go out to a bar afterward. Some were distanced by their work or by their responsibilities as a parent.

Despite Theatre Rhinoceros's claim, in its marketing materials, that it was where "you" could "see yourself on stage," Donna did not feel that her life was represented on the Rhino stage. "I represent a very conservative lifestyle, compared to that community, I guess. I own a house; I live here in Berkeley. I have a kid; I'm very involved in her life. I'm a typical parent more than I am living the singles life in San Francisco... I mean relative to most of the people in Walnut Creek, I can be thrown in that population, but to myself, I think of myself as outside it. Going to Theatre Rhinoceros is almost the only thing I do that's strictly adult centered." Asked to characterize "that community," she said, "I love to just go walking down Castro. There is a certain creative energy that I appreciate. It's people alive and doing something, not just sitting back watching TV letting the world go by, rooting for Desert Storm.... As my daughter gets older and I get more involved, I'm getting to know a lot more gay men. And I enjoy it. They are people with a lot of discretionary income. They've been places, they do things, they're not dragged down by children.... There's just a lot more energy."

Robert Coffman moved to San Francisco with his partner of thirty years when, in 1978, he retired from his job for the City of New York. On arrival he joined a gay seniors group, called G40, with which he was still involved. A man he met in that group encouraged him to audition for a play at Rhino, which he did. Between 1980, when he first got involved, and 1991 when I interviewed him, he had performed in fifteen Theatre Rhinoceros productions.

When I asked Robert what difference it made to him that Rhino is a gay theater, he answered:

> Well, first of all, in New York I was—uhm—since I worked for the city, even in 1978, which isn't that long ago, and—uhm—I knew a man who produced gay theater there and he wanted me to come and be in his show . . . and I said John I really can't because you know I could be in a gay play and somebody could come and they'd fire me and they'd take away my pension and all these things were very real, at that time, even then. New York, despite what you might think, it's very closeted still . . . and I had that. And so when I came to San Francisco it was like coming home in a sense and I felt free and comfortable and became a member of G40 and then started acting in the plays and because of that and the difference and the first experience that I ever had of this freedom—since I grew up in a very repressive time as you can well imagine—it was, I just felt the warmth and the love, and the openness, and the opportunities and the fine things that Rhinoceros meant to gay people, its support of gay people. . . . I think any gay person must feel pride in knowing this represents us, that we have an identification with it. . . . And I have such wonderful friendships.

I then asked him with whom and he listed several people still active at Rhino, most of whom were involved in *The AIDS Show:*

> *The AIDS Show* was very important. It was such a satisfying experience because everybody responded wonderfully to it. It made us feel very good and that we were doing something groundbreaking. . . . We

travelled all over with it . . . I admire young people who are so forthright and able to stand up and say I'm gay because we just never dared to do that. Coming out used to mean coming out to yourself. Now it means making a public announcement. I never told my family or straight friends in New York—now these are intelligent people and I knew they knew . . . but we never talked about it. The first time I said anything about gaiety was when we took *The AIDS Show* to New York—I wanted my friends to come and see this show. So I wrote to all of them and I said, there are some very explicit things and it's about AIDS and you should know you don't have to come—I'd like for you to—but if you can't come I'll see you later, we'll get together and so on. All of them came, all of them loved the show and they all loved and hugged me and kissed me afterward and they just accepted it.

What has pleased me so much about Rhinoceros is that it has given me a good feeling of self-worth because I feel I'm making some kind of contribution, doing something, bringing pleasure to people, I hope, and enjoying it myself . . . and I have, to say a cliché, richness in the friends and the resources. That's why Rhinoceros has meant so much to me, because it's given me a life.

While Robert produced a whole gay life through his participation in Rhino, for Billy, participation at Rhino was an opportunity to dip into a gay community in relation to which he felt quite marginal. His sense of marginality was partly geographic (he lived in a suburb of Sacramento, about three hours from San Francisco) but, as for Donna, was also about his lifestyle. Billy explained that some of the things portrayed in the Rhino plays were foreign to his experience. "I've never been that sexually active . . . I don't have that sense of loss that some men do with AIDS and safe sex restrictions . . . I haven't tried drag or some of the fun stuff people do sometimes." Just in the last year he had joined two gay groups in Sacramento, a coming-out group and an AIDS support group. "I just know I need to start getting out and meeting people . . . I realize that there are things I have been missing out on, a sense of solidarity and support let alone the political part, changing the world." I asked him what it was like to see Rhino plays that were not about his experience. "It does fill me in. I was just reading the *BAR* [a gay newspaper], which is full of local politics and so on, to fill in . . . I'm not angry my life is not being represented—suburban home life—probably pretty boring." But later, after emphasizing the importance of Rhino showing gay lives in a way that is "affirming, supportive, and educational," he said, "I'm kind of concerned about Theatre Rhinoceros content being too specialized about gays and for gays . . . Gay people live in society and have to get along, want to get along with straight neighbors . . . This is my concern, but I told you about myself living mostly in straight society, without anybody knowing except my neighbors. It would be nice to see plays that integrate more people out in the world."

Billy, it seems, wants to join gay organizations and become knowledgeable about gay life but doesn't want to be trapped in an insular gay community; he seems to want Rhino, through integrated shows, to deliver him, more comfortable and secure, back into a broader world. Ann, who had stage managed a number of shows at Rhino and was at the time of our interview working in a part-time temporary staff position at the theater, echoes Billy's concerns about insularity, though her sense of Rhino as confining is not articulated in relation to a straight world but rather in relation to the gay community itself. Prior to working at Rhino she had worked at a women's music company and so, at first, because Rhino was coed, it seemed to her to be a relatively expansive environment. However, by the time I spoke to her, she had come to have a more critical view of the organization. She spoke of her participation at Rhino mostly in the past tense, suggesting that it was a piece of her life trajectory that she had moved through and beyond. I met with her at Josie's Cabaret and Juice Joint (the for-profit performance space that was Rhino's most direct competition for gay audiences and artists), where she was stage managing their current production, a series of plays dealing with gay male life from the 1920s through the 1980s.

Tell me about your first experience of Theatre Rhinoceros.
I first heard about Rhino when I was in college. A girlfriend of mine was working on a show . . . but I never actually got there to see a show until, god when was it, I think the first show I saw there was Queen of Swords *that Adele directed [in 1989].*

Did you buy tickets regularly?
No, because then I started working in theater in the area and I was usually too busy to go, but then I worked on Boys in the Band *at Theatre Rhinoceros . . . I was very excited about working there. It was my first involvement with gay men. I was the only woman involved in the whole show, which was a bit strange but now I'm a regular fag hag [laugh]. My life in the past three years is just totally different because I went from a women's environ-*

ment, and I got so disillusioned with that, and now I'm back in the theater communities, and I'm working with all these gay men... I feel a lot more comfortable and a lot happier. I don't understand separatists at all. Basically we're in the same boat, both oppressed... and gay men are involved in all the issues, fighting for gay rights, for domestic partners, gay teachers in the schools, every issue affects both of us in one way or another.

Tell me a little more about your experience working on "Boys in the Band."

First of all, I loved the show. Boys in the Band *is like a piece of gay history really. It's part of our past... I think it's important for us to learn about our past. The group of people we worked with were wonderful. I mean they were actors, there were sticky things here and there, but they were great fun to work with.... And I liked the idea of a gay theater...I think it's important to be involved in a community that you can identify with, that you have common interests with. I mean the straight world sure as hell isn't going to be very supportive and you know, do gay theater for me or have a parade for me... It was basically the only place you could see gay theater continually, not just like Eureka that does one or two, but it's a continuing growth process for gay/lesbian theater, where they had new and innovative theater. I think that has changed now, definitely. I think they are getting too cautious [laugh].*

In what sense cautious?

I'm involved in the community and yet you don't realize how many of us there are until you go to the gay and lesbian freedom day parade. My god! just the sheer number and the differences, I mean all the little contingents from different areas and different groups, so many and so diverse. Someone here at Josie's said that he thinks that every voice must be heard. That's something that Rhino has lost. They are too stuck on being politically correct and catering to white middle-class gays.

And what do they think those people want?

Something calm that doesn't make too many waves—very nice little pat stories about, oh, a couple running an inn like in Earl, Ollie. *.... I think when they get into that rut they are not making people think.*

Pam Peniston and I met for our interview at her (rented) house, a spacious Victorian on Potrero Hill, where she lived with her girlfriend and her girlfriend's daughter. Pam, a set designer, had a long history with Theatre Rhinoceros, spanning many years and many productions. Recently, Adele Prandini, the artistic director, had been advertising that Pam would be functioning as an assistant artistic director for the purpose of developing work by people of color and that, assuming funding could be found, she would be leading a playwriting workshop for lesbians of color. She was the theater's representative on the San Francisco Cultural Affairs Task Force. Only nominally on staff at the theater—she was not being paid and did not attend regular staff meetings—it was notable that she, an African American woman, was representing Rhino on the task force, when no regular member of the Rhino staff was "of color." Pam's narrative is quite complex, providing both a particularly rich example of the multiplicity and multivalence of identity and community enacted through participation in nonprofit production and a theorization of the relationship between the production of gay particularity, other particular identity communities, and what she calls "the mainstream."

I came out here in October of '84 or '85 and I started the next March at my day job. It's a law firm and my first day there there's this black guy sitting in the lunch room . . . Brian! Brian [Freeman] and I worked on a Negro Ensemble company piece in 1976 called Eden *in New York . . . We sort of re-formed a bond and became pretty good friends. He called me up the October after that . . . [he had joined the staff at Rhino] and said, "We had a designer slated to do* Poppies *and they just disappeared on us and we need somebody and you're in if you want it." Ummm, okay! I'd gone through a really ugly breakup but it was the right time. The worst part of the breakup was that my ex was so, as I put it, she was so far into the closet she couldn't see over the pumps [laugh]. It was pretty intense, being out here and not telling anybody—it was my first homosexual affair and I didn't know, I didn't know. It was so sick but I didn't know whether this was the norm or not.*

You didn't know other lesbians?
Not really. Because I was in theater and because I was in television I knew plenty of gay men. But the lesbians weren't out—same thing in theater at school. When I was in college there was the reemergence of civil rights and black power, and then there's the women's movement going on. So then you're dealing with two of those different things and now I have three

[laugh]. Did you see?—of course you saw Tongues Untied. *You know there is a great deal of truth to that—that there's a level of middle-class black that thinks that it's dangerous because you know the white man may then have just another thing against us... In high school I suppose it began to enter my brain that there's probably a women's version of this and then in college obviously. We were pretty naive back then in them old early sixties you know.*

So where were you? You were about to say yes to Brian and take that first job at Rhino, which sounds like something about coming out?
Yeah, it was. It was very much I think tied to that. I was ready to come out, was ready to accept the fact that yeah this wasn't a little minor league aberration—nowadays it's not as important it seems to declare one way or the other; there's a much larger bisexual community that is accepted now that I don't know that I would have made exactly the same choice. I wonder if I would have kept my options open. But I think I always have been, not more comfortable with women, but I think I definitely have always been more attracted to women.

How much did Brian know about your sexual preference?
He had actually assumed, he said, that I was a dyke when we had worked together in New York. I guess because the set designer is kind of a butch position you know [laugh]. But I wasn't. I was riotously heterosexual at the time and then when we first met again here I wasn't allowed to say anything to anyone—he teases me about that a lot. Everybody always seems to know before you do when you're a late bloomer [laugh].

So Brian said yeah come on over and work in this. And I met Adele and instantly had a crush on Adele; this is back in the time when if I knew you were a lesbian I immediately had a crush on you [laugh]. ... But it was a good show and I had a good time doing theater again. So Rhino kind of became the house theater for me. I did that show and I stuck around and kind of helped Brian a little bit on and off with other shows that he was working on and then Ken had just come aboard[7] and he asked Steph [a lighting designer] and I to do Going to Seed *... and the three of us really hit it, well the four of us actually, Ken but mostly Brian and Stephanie and I because we're all—my mother, Stephanie's mother and both sides of Brian's family were all New Englanders and New England blacks are a whole different matter [laugh] ... and it was nice 'cause ... as far as I knew from*

Rhino it was pretty much a white boy theater. I didn't know that much about it but just looking at what the run down had been I figured. Then Stephanie mentioned me to OET [Oakland Ensemble Theater, a black theater company]. They paid a lot better than Rhino [laugh]. And then OET became my house shop for a while.

Then I came back to Rhino for Queen of Swords, *which is the one I really wanted to do. It was everything that you think theater is going to be. It was the most sophisticated and most satisfying, "Hey kids, let's do a show!" experience I've ever probably had in theater. One of the best because it was so, "We're all in this together." It was very female, it was very lesbian, and it was just so satisfying. Adele has a very strong sensibility about crossing color lines and about wanting community in gay and lesbian theater, and of course even more in lesbian theater, to mean the* community *which crosses fifteen other communities. Because it's something you feel or add on, it's not something you're necessarily born with. We don't know that for sure but it's something you choose or could not choose. You might be lying to yourself but you don't have to do it. So, because we cross so many other political and economic and color lines, you know, it's—she wants it to be true, a true sense of community. And that show was, and that's one of the reasons I think it was so phenomenal. It was a really joyous place to be, a really nice working environment. Those girls were looking for dates for me for months [laugh].*

Were they all lesbians?

Not all lesbians but a good percentage and those who weren't were straight women with a wonderful sense of humor and great openness by and large. That's what I love about theater. The meetings and the getting together to make something whole, to make something bigger than all of the parts.

There should be no reason to do theater unless it does something, it's got to do something: enlighten, entertain, and if it does it to you nine times out of ten it's because the people putting it together as well have been able to have that experience.

But it was really difficult because we didn't get the support of the theater in terms of having posters available when we wanted them and flyers. . . . Leland was doing his show, The Balcony, *in the basement at the same time; he had press early, he had, he had, you know—we had Xeroxed flyers* and posters and he had gorgeous slick printed things and had them like two months before show time. It was really hard to take. Now a lot of that was Leland and Leland's own dollars and Leland's own agenda because he was dying and he knew it, I think, and he wanted to put everything into this show.

But it still—it was very much a his/her battle toward the end. And then there was the Bette Rhino awards [an in-house award ceremony put on by Rhino to celebrate its own best productions]. I can't remember but literally everything that won was one of the two boy plays you know... So there were a lot of bad feelings at the end of that—I was not sure that I would work there again.

And I didn't think Ken was doing anything to expand the multicultural aspect of the theater. I didn't see a lot more black people, Hispanic people, anyone of color but me and Steph going through that door. And I had thought that was why he was hired. I think Adele thought that that's why he was hired and I know that's why Brian thought he was hired. And he was never available, he was never around. We need to be a somewhat teaching organization. And I don't mean in the sense that we have classes but in that, if you wanted to come to Rhino eventually as a set designer, that I would have you assist me on a show, and then I would watch you work with another designer on another show, and then I would have you do a studio show on your own. And I would be there so if you wanted to ask a question you could ask a question and not feel like you were a fool 'cause we'd already have a working relationship.

So there is all this shit hit the fan and I see people just being eaten up and I was gettin' too many other job offers and I just said I really want to be part of this but I can't be part of this the way it is now. I don't like the feeling of traps. You know you can't be a minority quote unquote in this country and accept traps because we've been put in too many of them and there are too many people willing to trap us as one or another aspects of ourselves. I mean, in this task force, my favorite [heavy sarcasm] person on the task force went up to a gay man, an individual artist [and said], "Well, she certainly can understand the individual artists wanting to get money but the reason that none of the small and midsize theaters got any money is that they weren't very good." Now just for one year I'd like to put the Symphony or the Ballet or the Opera on our budget for the last ten years and see what they produce [laugh] and in our theater. You know, it's really *tough for Rhino and I kept coming back because I kept wanting to be, have a link with my people or my other people [laugh].*

So Rhino was your main gay/lesbian connection?
No, because as I came out and as I developed these friends and stuff, a gay and lesbian community began to happen around me.

So the theater wasn't your only access?
Yeah. Started out that way certainly, every time I would go there I would meet more lesbians and gays and a lot of—I began to find out that there was a pretty big reputation for Rhino. But then people started to appear with resumes. That's how I met B.B. . . . I got her a job as a carpenter at OET and she reciprocated by when she got a job at another theater and they needed a designer, she got me on and so that was the community that was starting—all these incredibly competent and wonderful women that I knew of who had worked in theater but a lot of them I met first [at Rhino]. I always teased Adele, how come you have the largest longest running gay and lesbian theater in San Francisco and I had to go to the Hispanic theater to meet a white girl [laugh]. . . . So I would meet a lot of people there but then we would stick together, we would hang together and that wasn't, it was first and foremost with the lesbians but I think it became just with women in general at that theater, even straight women who had worked there. . . . So it was great 'cause I would meet them and then I would put them in other places then they would bring in other gays and lesbians. It's kind of weird, because it can sometimes feel like you're weakening your central power base, because you're mainstreaming, you're going to work for these standard straight theaters and kind of co-opting them. We were all filling a lot of positions with ourselves and with people that we knew and stuff—expanding the women's community and the gay community to other theaters.
    But the backlash has hit in a lot of ways. Berkeley Rep [a mainstream nonprofit theater] is doing Spunk, *co-producing with Lorraine Hansberry [a black theater in San Francisco]. I bet all Lorraine Hansberry does is give 'em their mailing list, so now Berkeley Rep is multicultural, which is what they've been screaming and yelling about so that they can move into Oakland, into that brand-new space, and not be argued with for being a white theater. Now as you can tell I'm not real thrilled about that. And OET,*

which is a black theater, a professional theater, that has been doing terrific work and is in a hole of a place, can't get a new theater out of this—it boggles. It's a very irritating thing to see one of your other communities being co-opted into that kind of reaction.

Now how do you feel having the Eureka [a mainstream nonprofit theater] produce "Angels in America"—do you feel okay about that?
I would hope that there would be theaters that were theaters and produced anything the fuck that they wanted and because they had a diverse cultural representation would therefore use that as part of the reason that they chose a diverse cultural group of plays, directors—but hire those people, don't import those people. Why should we be the only one who does gay plays? That's ridiculous. You know, if there isn't room for five theaters to all of a sudden be doing a gay play or lesbian play in the midst of their season, we really screwed up. But there should always be a place especially for minorities who are not always getting the break and are sometimes only being co-opted and used and not absorbed. Especially in these times of so much smiling bullshit liberalism that is out there, so much hypocritical, "We need the grant so 'come on down,'" you know, "Minority of the week join us! Yeah hey, if you could injure yourself permanently we could get on three counts, you're black, you're a lesbian, couldya be crippled [laugh] and you're a woman. Come on!" Whew. I don't need to be used that way. I worked for companies because they've seen my design stuff or whatever and they're interested or I think the project is really interesting or I'd like to expand my horizons. . . . Every honest effort is going to run a fine line between tokenism and integration. You got to start somewhere.

So is that part of your role at Rhino now?
Yeah, that is.

Explain to me what your position is and what you're doing?
Okay, right at the moment my position is the unpaid position of assistant artistic director [laugh]. My job is to look for playwrights or people who have written interesting stuff who might want to learn to be playwrights and to help them develop works that would be done as readings in the studio and then hopefully boost them up to a mainstage production. This is back to my teaching role again; there are things you can ask a professional com-

pany that is a gay and lesbian company that you cannot ask a mainstream theater to do. Even though we are a professional theater, the black theater, the Hispanic theater, the Asian American theater, everyone of us multicul-turals [laugh], our theaters, that's our responsibility. We don't end, please god, with this generation and no one else out there is going to give us the leg up. You may choose to leave Rhino and you have our blessings, but if we've made the effort good for you, you'll come back. If we planted the seed there for you, if we've made it possible for you to be able to mainstream, for every mainstream you're going to come back.

So my charge is to bring us to the twentieth century, in a sense, bring us to the nineties, open us up so that we really do reflect the flag that we are, you know, we are all colors you know and we have all experiences, we can't stop with the gay white male experience, we cannot stop with the lesbian white experience. We mourned about AIDS, and there's still a lot more to deal with, but I also think that there are a whole bunch of other stories that really need to be told. There's a wealth of stories which will help us under-stand and begin to embrace truly our brothers and sisters. These are the things that can help you to cross that line and think, oh they're just the same, they feel just the same as me. They've had this unique problem and I can see a parallel in my life. And it can just go so far to breaking down in-ternal barriers, you know. We're always our own worst enemy and god knows that can be inside our own community.

The Unwilling Subject

The Specter of Communism

The history of the nonprofit sector in the United States is widely imag-ined in both popular and academic literature to be a story of voluntary associations welling up from the grass roots and evidencing the excep-tional American character. Quotations from Tocqueville attesting to the peculiarity to the United States of a widespread impulse to associate are featured in the introductions of many books and articles on nonprofits to show the historical depth of this exceptional characteristic.[8] Michael O'Neill narrates a four-hundred-year history of nonprofits in the United States, showing the emergence of the modern nonprofit sector from origins in diverse colonial religious organizations. And in 1986, in the preface to *The Nonprofit Sector,* an anthology claiming to represent the state of the art of nonprofit scholarship, Walter W. Powell writes: "The United States can be distinguished from all other societies (save, perhaps, for Israel) by the size of the work load it assigns to its voluntary nonprofit sector" (xii).[9] The two claims, that nonprofits are American and that they are an expression of the grass roots, are of course linked by an ideology that posits the United States as the model of democracy to which the rest of the world should aspire.

However, there is some academic scholarship on the history of private nonprofit organizations that provides the basis for a rather different perspective. Peter Dobkin Hall's essay "Inventing the Nonprofit Sector" narrates the history of the nonprofit sector in the United States as the story of a contest between private organizations and the state for control of public affairs—a contest ultimately won by private organizations when such private initiatives came to be seen as an alternative to socialism—but for Hall the agents of private initiative were not the grass roots but rather capitalists and corporations. Like Hall's story, Brian H. Smith's more global history of nonprofit, private voluntary, nongovernmental organizations (NPOs, PVOs, NGOs) links the development of such organizations to moments of particular expansion and/or crisis in capitalism. Smith, however, focuses on the instrumental encouragement of private voluntary organizations by states, rather than individual capitalists or corporations, as they colonized the world, contained communism, and then "developed" capitalism.

Neither the normative "bottom-up" Tocquevillian narrative of U.S. nonprofits as based in American grassroots entrepreneurialism nor Hall and Smith's top-down narratives of nonprofits as the instrument of capitalists or capitalist states are in themselves adequate; in fact, both accounts overstate the agency of the North (in one case "the people," in the other the capitalist individuals or governments) while erasing rather completely the agency of people in colonized and then "developing" regions. The value of Hall and Smith's narratives (the high points of which I will recount briefly) is not merely in providing a counternarrative to the narrative of grassroots voluntarism and American exceptionalism, but also in revealing the ongoing and explicit attention of both states and individual capitalists to the problem of subject formation; that is to say, they reveal individual and communal subject formation as an ongoing problem for capitalism, a problem for which nonprofits have been re-peatedly rediscovered by policymakers as *the* solution.

The global story begins with missionaries; in fact, churches and church-based (or, in the current terminology, "faith-based") organizations per-sist throughout the story as tremendously powerful actors in the elabo-ration of nongovernmental, nonprofit organizations (Chaves). In *More Than Altruism*, Smith argues that from the early sixteenth century on-ward, missionary organizations operated throughout the colonized world, not only proselytizing but also providing a variety of social services such as education and health care. Such organizations, he says, were subsi-dized by colonial regimes, which viewed them as important instruments of enculturation and social control: "Direct financial grants were made to both Protestant and Catholic overseas mission organizations by home governments . . . for the schools, clinics, orphanages, and other charita-ble works they administered," because, Smith says, "There can be no doubt that missionary groups served the interests of colonial adminis-trations by promoting Western culture and values" (28–29). According to Smith's narrative, in addition to subsidizing missionary work, North Atlantic states also subsidized and collaborated with a variety of other kinds of organizations that they saw as useful to colonial rule. He offers, by way of example, the case of the Tuskegee/Phelps-Stokes project:

> British missionaries from Africa in the years just prior to World War I
> visited the United States to study the network of vocational training for
> blacks developed by the Tuskegee Institute and supported by the Phelps-
> Stokes Fund. These missionaries helped convince the British Colonial
> Office, searching for a uniform educational strategy to support its policy
> of indirect rule in Africa, that the Tuskegee philosophy of restricted
> education for blacks was well suited for strengthening its control in
> various African territories. The Phelps-Stokes Fund—and later in more
> substantial terms, the Carnegie Foundation in the 1920s and 1930s—in
> turn contributed to British-sponsored vocational education in various
> territories in Africa. (31)

According to Smith, after WWI, missionary and other PVOs, with the support of the U.S. government and U.S.-based corporations, began to provide substantial amounts of "technical assistance" in the Middle East, Africa, and China as "a means of establishing more long-term U.S. in-fluence in these regions" (38). Smith argues that the substantial network of private organizations, often subsidized by states and almost always working in cooperation with states, were "in Simmel's terms, system-maintenance institutions, but now transposed from the domestic arena (where many had long been performing needed tasks governments could not, or would not) to the international realm where they began to complement foreign policy interests of their respective home governments" (31).

While Smith is principally concerned to point out that such organizations supported their governments' interests, he also makes it clear that governments saw the work of such organizations as useful to their interests. His use of Simmel's concept of "system-maintenance" belies a much too static view of the expansionist processes (colonization) in which these organizations were involved. The elaboration of nonprofit organizations might more accurately be read as contributing to the tremendously transformative process of primitive accumulation. Hall, for instance, argues that the creation of professional associations in the postrevolutionary United States was largely a technique deployed by "mercantilists" who pushed their sons into the professions in order to "disengage capital from familial and social obligations . . . for investment in expanding markets" (34–35).[10] The concept of system-maintenance does, however, recognize a defensiveness on the part of those deploying PVOs as hegemonic instruments in the face of real or imagined crises. In fact, the ongoing deployment of PVOs for capitalist expansion around the world is accompanied by an explicitly defensive—anticommunist—rhetoric from the late nineteenth century onward.

Well before the Cold War, both the U.S. government and U.S.-based capitalists identified PVOs as a technology that could be used to resist and contain impulses in the United States and Europe toward communism. Carnegie's manifesto of philanthropy frames philanthropy—and its use to create institutions such as libraries, universities, museums, and parks, which he imagined as creating equality of opportunity if not equality of outcomes for all—explicitly as a means to stave off the specter of socialism raised by the stark disparities in wealth that industrial capitalism had created in the nineteenth century. Hall argues that as a direct response to radical anticapitalist movements in Europe and the United States in the late nineteenth and early twentieth centuries, business elites created numerous new organizations for "economic cooperation" and diverse mechanisms (foundations, community chests, and so on) for supporting charitable initiatives ("Inventing the Nonprofit Sector," 41–57). Likewise, Smith points out that one of the first responses of the United States to the Russian Revolution was to support the activities of U.S.-based private relief agencies in the new Soviet Union (*More Than Altruism*, 33). But these early antisocialist and antisoviet efforts rather pale by comparison to the elaboration of nonprofits incited by the real (and not merely spectral) worldwide disarray in which capitalism found itself at the end of World War II.

Christina Klein argues that "haunted by the specter of the 1930s worldwide depression," U.S. policymakers during the Cold War period were focused at least as much on "reinforcing the 'interdependence of the free world' by strengthening the economic ties that bound [noncommunist] nations to the United States" (*Cold War Orientalism*, ch. 1), as they were on containing communism. But "winning the minds" of both Americans and the people of other nations for this project of economic integration and growth depended on what Klein calls an "ideological" project. Policymakers and intellectuals in the United States, such as Arthur M. Schlesinger Jr., explicitly articulated a need to offer a positive vision of community, "'solidarity with other human beings', if Americans hope to prevent people around the world from choosing Communism" (Klein, ch. 1, quoting Schlesinger's *The Vital Center*). Inside the United States, this ideological project took the form of a "sentimental education" of U.S. citizens "that would enable Americans to transcend the barriers of difference—of geography, nation, culture, race—that separated them from the people of Asia and Africa and to recognize the bonds that tied them to each other." In 1956, Eisenhower launched the People to People program, a government program that functioned as an umbrella to promote, coordinate, and partially fund an array of private efforts (from stamp collecting clubs, to cultural exchanges, to sister-city affiliations to professional associations) to facilitate contacts between U.S. citizens and people in other parts of the world. Some of these private organizations were new and some were ongoing; Klein argues that People to People drew on the prior traditions (and sometimes even appropriated the existing structures) of politically engaged cultural organizing, both the missionary tradition and the left internationalist Popular Front, for the project of "free world" integration. Nonprofits had been once again discovered as the means for closing the subjectivity gap at the heart of the capitalist project.

With regard to those outside the United States, this ideological project initially took the form of state-supported postwar reconstruction efforts such as the Marshall plan "to alleviate the conditions in the non-communist world that create a breeding ground for communism" (Klein, *Cold War Orientalism,* paraphrasing Schlesinger). Very quickly, however, the strategy shifted away from direct government programs and toward state-supported private organizations. Throughout the 1960s, the U.S. Congress regularly attached amendments to foreign aid bills directing the U.S. Agency for International Development (AID) to focus attention on PVOs operating at the grassroots level among the poor in developing countries: Smith cites the 1962 bill as saying, "emphasis shall be placed upon programs of community development which will promote stable and responsible governmental institutions at the local level" (*More than Altruism;* 59). Reasoning that "there is a close relationship between popular participation in the process of development and the effectiveness of that process," the 1966 foreign aid bill (known as Title 9) urged AID to foster "cooperatives, labor unions, trade and related associations, community action groups, and other organizations which provide the training ground for leadership and democratic processes" (quoted in Smith, 60). In 1973, the Congress passed what came to be called the New Directions initiative. This initiative directed U.S. foreign aid to and through U.S. NGOs, which were seen as the best conduits to Southern NGOs, which in turn were seen as the best conduit to the poor in developing countries who had not been benefiting from the large-scale projects of the development establishment (68–69).

From the late nineteenth century through the 1970s, the number of nonprofits in the United States and throughout the world grew exponentially as capitalists and capitalist states repeatedly deployed nonprofits, in moments of crisis or expansion, to hegemonize potentially anticapitalist populations. In the United States, "numbering only 12,500 in 1940, 50,000 in 1950, by 1967 there were 309,000, by 1977, 790,000 and by 1989, just under one million—an eightyfold increase in just forty years. By contrast the number of business corporations during the same period increased from 473,000 to three million—a mere sevenfold increase" (Hall, *Inventing,* 62). This extraordinary increase has continued unabated. And as Powell and Clemens report, "the expansion in the number of nonprofits is by no means confined to the United States" (*Private Action,* xv). Lester Salamon suggests that the enormous increase in the number of nonprofits since the seventies is due to the crisis of Fordist capitalism and the consequent dismantling of the welfare state ("Rise of the Nonprofit Sector"). A project currently sponsored by the Ford Foundation illustrates his argument as well as my own about the location of nonprofits at capitalism's subjectivity gap.

The Partners for Fragile Families project was presented in glowing terms at a forum organized by the Hauser Center for Nonprofit Organizations at Harvard's Kennedy School of Government (October 19, 1999).[11] This project and, in fact, the twenty projects funded by Ford through their Strengthening Fragile Families program are cast in the program literature (as they were in the Hauser Center forum) as a response to the Personal Responsibility Act of 1996—the act that ended welfare as we knew it in the United States by shifting responsibility for social welfare from the state and onto persons (Johnson, *Strengthening Fragile Families,* inside cover page; see also National Center for Strategic Nonprofit Planning and Community Leadership, *Annual Report,* 1). The program materials point out that the act "obliged" state governments to "encourage the formation and maintenance of two parent families." The speakers at the forum, following closely the script provided by the printed literature, noted that while great attention has been given to the attempts to force poor mothers into the workforce, the act also shifted a substantial part of the responsibility for dependent children from the state to fathers, requiring mothers to identify the biological fathers of their children in order to obtain benefits and requiring child-support enforcement agencies to pursue all fathers for support and not just those fathers with means to pay such support. However, the brochure argues, "it becomes increasingly clear that collecting significant amounts from the (3 million) most disadvantaged fathers in America and devising means of inducing them to enter into stable relations, including marriage, with the mothers of their children, would not be so easy" (Johnson, *Strengthening,* inside cover).

This is where Partners for Fragile Families comes in. The "partners" named in the project title are on one hand community-based organizations that are already working with poor young men and on the other the child support enforcement agencies seeking to extract money from these men on pain of imprisonment—two groups that had previously seen themselves as adversaries. The goal of the project is to change the cultures of both groups, to transform the enforcement agencies into gateways to social services and to transform the community-based organizations into organizations that bring men into the system rather than shielding them from it. A significant component of the project is a standardized training program offered through the community-based organizations that offers fathers not only job skills but also parenting and relationship skills so that they can fulfill responsibilities to their families—responsibilities that, according to the project literature, these fathers already accept and attempt to fulfill. The project, then, aims to function in what Charles Reilly calls the "local 'capillaries' of society" ("Public Policy," x), deploying and strengthening structures of communal obligation (parental and marital) to support the larger project of a state looking to get itself out of the way of the free market.

The Ghost

> The massive structures of the modern democracies, both as State organizations, and as complexes of associations in civil society, constitute for the art of politics, as it were, the "trenches" and the permanent fortifications of the front in the war of position. (Gramsci, *Prison Notebooks*, 243)

In the 1990s, "civil society," defined as the presence of private (nongovernmental) nonprofit associations,[12] has been explicitly invoked as a crucial fortification against communism, against the spectral present-absence of capitalist subjects in the former communist countries of Eastern Europe. In contemporary civil society discourse, communism is fully identified with totalitarianism, and markets (capitalist markets) thus appear as a precondition for civil society. John Keane, for instance, who is probably the preeminent theorist of civil society, examines a variety of Marxist and post-Marxist theories and decides that they all inevitably tend toward totalitarianism.[13] But the problem for civil society theorists is that the end of communism has not automatically produced civil subjects. In fact, postcommunist subjects don't seem to know how to do either capitalism or "democracy" right; their economies are rife with corruption and their political behavior with violence. Enacted uncivilly, capitalism doesn't look so appealing, doesn't seem free and fair, but rather appears too baldly as a system in which the powerful bully the weak.

And so rather than being the happy consequence of the end of communism, civil society (that is, voluntary associations) appears to be a precondition for capitalism.

According to Keane and Ernest Gellner, the subjectivity that postcommunist subjects fail to have appears at first to be simply that of the liberal individual, the subject who formulates choices as an individual. Released from the centralized power of the communist state, postcommunist subjects "regress" to premodern communal subjectivity, in which their behavior is determined by kinship, tradition, and awesome rituals (Gellner, "Importance of Being Modular"). Gellner evokes this (missing) liberal subject through the peculiar metaphor of modular furniture: "The point about such furniture is that it comes in bits which are so to speak agglutinative . . . you can combine and recombine the bits at will" (41). However, for the pieces of furniture—the people—to be simultaneously movable and able to fit together, more than abstract liberal subjectivity is required. Despite their insistence on the voluntarism of the associations that compose civil society, both Gellner and Keane acknowledge that the "fit" must be generated by a normative supplement: values must supplement the abstract value of pluralism and free association. These supplementary values must be of two sorts. There must be particularizing values that differentiate subjects from each other: "The substitution or replacement of one man by another only has a point if, precisely, they do differ" (43). But Gellner also argues that a substantial degree of "cultural homogeneity" is required and that this homogeneity will be supplied by a "learned nationalism" (43, 44–45); Keane calls this homogenizing supplement "national identity" (*Civil Society*, 87).[14] Thus, when America's nonprofits "give voice to our hearts," as the Independent Sector Web site says they do, what they express are our already "shared values." The (absent) subjects of a civil society, that is, subjects who participate in private nonprofit associations, voluntarily express their particular communal preferences by submitting to communal (national) norms.

In civil society theory, then, voluntary associations (which seem, along with the subjects for whom they would provide evidence, to have gone missing) would, if they existed, be the site at which community (traditional, primitive, or otherwise particularizing) is reduced to a private source of preferences. Such associations would be the site from which (individual, not communal) participants are launched into a public sphere, which, while ostensibly abstract and open to all, is in fact con-

stituted by particular norms and values that facilitate not only democracy but also capitalism. Civil society theorists tend to turn at this point
to listing the features of a "democratic" state (that looks a lot like the
United States) as the necessary condition for civil society and ultimately
throw up their hands at the problem of how to institute the "values"
supplement.

Meanwhile, those of a more practical bent have attempted to promote
the establishment of voluntary associations, taking them to be not merely
evidence of civil subjectivity but a means to produce willing subjects,
for whom participation in community (that is, both particular communities and a capitalist community) is not merely coerced by nature or culture but is voluntarily undertaken. George Soros's Open Society initiatives, an elaborate network of nonprofit foundations all over the
postcommunist countries, are a case in point. Tocqueville's description
of local associations as schools for citizenship is oft-echoed among
those taking this instrumental approach. Nonprofit, nongovernmental
organizations are touted as "veritable 'academies' of democratic learning" (Ewig, "Strengths and Limits," 76, quoting Reilly).

Capitalism in Crisis

Many observers of and participants in the development establishment
(the International Monetary Fund [IMF], the World Bank, the Inter-
America Foundation) claim that that establishment, influenced by the
events in Eastern Europe, has since 1989 shown an unprecedented interest in promoting civil society around the world. Feldman says, "In 1989,
an NGO discourse, infused with notions of public participation, greater
representation of the poor, and more equitable access to resources, gained
currency" ("NGOs and Civil Society," 48); and Edwards and Hulme write,
"In recent years, and especially since the end of the Cold War in 1989,
bilateral and multilateral donor agencies have pursued a 'New Policy
Agenda' which gives renewed prominence to the roles of nongovermental
organizations and grassroots organizations in poverty alleviation, social
welfare and the development of 'civil society'" ("Too Close for Comfort," 961). And certainly the spate of books describing and promoting
the deployment of NGOs in development processes suggests that NGOs
have been discovered again by those seeking to promote the expansion
of capitalism around the globe.[15] While references to Eastern Europe
bolster the development establishment's framing of their promotion of

NGOs as political, as a wedge against totalitarianisms of both left and right in Latin America and elsewhere, the embrace of nonprofits by the development establishment can and I think should be read as an attempt to deal with its own contradictions.[16]

While Feldman may be correct that the language of civil society and democratization was borrowed by the development establishment from the discussions of events in Eastern Europe in the late 1980s, the dramatic shift in development practice that has included a renewed embrace of NGOs as development instruments actually predates the fall of communism and can be better accounted for as an outcome of the history of development itself.[17] The key term in contemporary development strategies is *sustainability.* This term is often associated with the notion that development should sustain the lives of the poor and the health of the environment. It is also used with regard to the management of NGOs, suggesting that they should be if not actually profitable, then at least not ongoingly dependent on philanthropy. However, I would suggest that it is the sustainability of capitalism itself that is really at stake.

The debt crisis of the 1980s, during which many developing countries found themselves unable to repay huge loans from Northern banks— thus putting those banks at risk[18]—revealed what are now considered to be deep flaws in a dominant development model that was focused exclusively on gross domestic product growth, without any concern for the actual distribution of wealth (Clark, *Democratizing Development;* Phillips, *Third Wave*). In *Development: New Paradigms and Principles for the Twenty-First Century,* part of a series entitled "Rethinking Bretton Woods," Sixto Roxas, a development economist and banker, points out that the previous paradigm of development, which was largely controlled by multinational corporations and was focused on large-scale infrastructural projects to enable the construction of large-scale industrial production, created extraordinary wealth for elites around the world and, simultaneously, extraordinary poverty for the majority, as it displaced local populations to make room for capitalist enterprises. According to Roxas, this widespread immiseration has come to be a problem for capitalist enterprise itself since it excludes potential participants from the economy—they are placed beyond "economic recovery"—and provokes social instability and/or the "excessive" growth of government welfare programs (8–9). And so while one response to the debt crisis has been IMF-dictated structural adjustments—forcing a retreat of the state from welfare provision—another response has been to diagnose the crisis as based in the failure to develop human capital and, thus, to prescribe micro rather than macro adjustments (Clark, *Democratizing Development*).[19] Nongovernmental organizations have been identified as the primary substitute for the state and as the key instrument through which to perform these microadjustments, that is, to reach into impoverished populations and engage them in the development process. Roxas, stating a view that is reiterated throughout the development literature of the 1990s, says, "The imperatives of national and planetary sustainability, even survival, require business to place the concerns of communities and NGOs in the mainstream" (*Development*, 13).

Feldman, who identifies herself as a feminist poststructuralist critic of development, offers a more complex account of the renewed deployment of NGOs, suggesting that earlier development efforts did not simply create across-the-board impoverishment but also shifted the social dynamics within local communities. Taking up the case of Bangladesh, she argues that in addition to large-scale infrastructural projects, earlier development efforts included NGO initiatives aimed specifically at women, offering them education, health care, and credit; such efforts not only drew women into the market economy but produced a backlash among petty bourgeois men who had relied on women's labor for their incomes and status. The combination of generalized impoverishment and the particular disempowerment of petty bourgeois men has, according to Feldman, simultaneously created a market for further NGO activity, particularly the delivery of job training and credit to the poor, and generated resistance to Western development, framed in terms of religion and tradition. Feldman's narrative is interesting on two counts. First, and this is the relevant point here, she, like Roxas, shows how, for the development establishment, the promotion of NGOs is articulated as the answer to an absence of capitalist subjects, the means for discouraging the galvanization of anticapitalist movements (here Islamic rather than communist). But Feldman also raises the question of participant subjectivity; she describes NGOs as hegemonic instruments that have created modernized subjects and answered the desires of subjects who want to participate in capitalism. As I will discuss in the next section, this account of participant subjectivity is powerful but inadequate.

Given that the recent rediscovery of NGOs by the development establishment was provoked by the debt crisis, it is particularly notable that the most intensively encouraged and celebrated NGO activity has been the provision of microcredit.[20] While providers of microcredit are not always traditional nonprofits in the sense that they may be cooperative banks and nominally for-profit, they are distinct from commercial banks in a number of respects: their source of capital for the loans is generally philanthropic; they do not require financial collateral of the borrowers; they charge higher interest rates than commercial banks; and they generally strive for sustainability rather than profit. (The high premium placed on financial sustainability in microlending organizations is becoming a "best practice" model for NGOs in general.) Despite or, rather, because of this not-quite-nonprofit approach, I would propose that microlending epitomizes the supplementary enactment of communal and capitalist subjectivity at the site of the nonprofit.

The most widely known and imitated provider of microcredit is the Grameen Bank, which operates in Bangladesh. Both the celebrity of microcredit and the centrality of the Grameen Bank as the model for such programs is evidenced by the fact that the November 1999 issue of *Scientific American* featured an article about the bank by its founder, Muhammad Yunis. The key feature of the Grameen model is that, rather than requiring financial assets as collateral for loans, communal relationships function as collateral. Borrowers, who in the case of Grameen and many other lenders must be women,

> are required to join the bank in self-formed groups of five. The group members provide one another with peer support in the form of mutual assistance and advice. In addition they allow for peer discipline by evaluating business viability and ensuring repayment. If one member fails to repay a loan, all members risk having their line of credit suspended or reduced.
>
> Typically a new group submits loan proposals from two members, each requiring between $25 and $100. After these two borrowers successfully repay their first five installments the next two group members become eligible to apply for their own loans. Once they make five repayments, the final member of the group may apply. After 50 installments have been repaid a borrower pays her interest which is slightly [actually often drastically] above the commercial rate. The borrower is now eligible for a larger loan.
>
> The bank does not wait for borrowers to come to the bank; it brings the bank to the people. Loan payments are made in weekly meetings consisting of six to eight groups, held in the villages where the members

live. . . . Not all the benefits derive directly from credit. When joining the
bank, each member is required to memorize a list of 16 resolutions.
These include commonsense items about hygiene and health . . . as well
as social dictums such as refusing dowry and managing family size.
(Yunis, "The Grameen Bank," 117)

Not only do microcredit schemes mobilize local communal relations
among women as the mechanism for guaranteeing the loans, they also
deploy communal relations to supplement the flow of capital in their
very choice of women as the borrowers. A number of reasons are generally given for the selection of women as preferred borrowers: they are
more likely to repay; they are more needy and thus worthy; and they use
the loans better. Loans to women are thought to have a higher "impact"
than loans to men, improving the economic security and standard of living not only of the woman (whose "mobility" and power vis-à-vis patriarchal domination and violence are often increased) but of her house-
hold; men by contrast are seen as relatively irresponsible and more likely
to spend the money only on themselves (Vinelli, "Managing Microfinance
Organizations").[21] Women are preferable borrowers, relative to goals of
"modernization" and greater integration of the poor into a capitalist
economy, precisely because of their greater community-mindedness,
their greater sense of obligation to their families and communities. So,
while the modernization goals of microcredit, especially the goal of em-
powering women within their families, undermine "community," the
disciplinary strategies of microlending simultaneously depend on and
reinforce, even as they transform, just such communal hierarchies: "The
successful outcomes of micro-enterprises utilize the very same institutions that the NGOs consider to be oppressive and that their programs
seek to transform. Put another way, the NGO interventions have led to
legitimization of the very institutions that are considered to be an
obstacle to women's empowerment" (Fernando and Heston, "NGOs
between States," 8).

Microlenders such as Grameen often frame their loans as a replacement for indigenous moneylending (in relation to which the shock-
ingly high interest rates offered by microlenders appear low). In fact,
the quantities of credit made available through such programs are far
greater than the credit previously available at any interest rate to the
poor women borrowers. That is to say, microlending has produced huge

new amounts of debt among poor populations (Solomon, "Micro-Credit's Dark Underside"; Dorado, "Microfinance Organizations"). Yunis suggests that the loans empower the poor by enabling them to become independent entrepreneurs. However, in the context of a global economy that runs largely on finance capital, the production of new debtors might be better equated to the freeing of labor from the means of production that allowed capitalism to get off the ground in the first place, or the freeing of consumers to construct their identities through their choice of commodities in the twentieth century. The means of production being appropriated, transformed, and elaborated in this version of primitive accumulation, however, are not material means of production but rather the social relationships among the borrowers and between borrowers and their families and "communities."

Microcredit organizations, like nonprofits more generally, simultaneously deploy and transform communities, communities that function for, but also in excess of, the needs of capitalism. It is important to recognize the excess of community over capitalism: for instance, it would be extraordinarily reductive to say that the subjectivities generated at Theatre Rhinoceros are simply capitalist subjectivities, even though, as Ann and Pam Peniston began to point out in the interviews I presented earlier, the gay and other communal identities generated through participation in Theatre Rhinoceros are often co-opted for what Pam called "smiling bullshit liberalism." However, even where nonprofit activity is organized through discourses articulated as outside or in excess of capital, such as antimodern patriarchal structures or gift exchange (which I will discuss in the next section), that exteriority is still constitutive of capitalism, still drives the circuit of capital onward. In the next section, I draw again on my Theatre Rhinoceros ethnography to elaborate the paradoxical but constitutive role that is played by the very exteriority of community to capital.

Debt and the Gift

> The feeling of guilt, of personal obligation, had its origin in the oldest and most primitive personal relationship, that between buyer and seller, creditor and debtor: it was here that one person first encountered another, first measured himself against another...
> The community, too, stands to its members in that same vital basic relation, that of the creditor to his debtors...The aim now is to preclude pessimistically, once and for all, the prospect of a final

discharge . . . until at last the irredeemable debt gives rise to conception of irredeemable penance.
—Friedrich Nietzsche, *The Genealogy of Morals*

Though we laud charity as a Christian virtue we know that it wounds . . . There are no free gifts; gift cycles engage persons in permanent commitments that articulate the dominant institutions.
—Mary Douglas, Foreword to *The Gift*

Scott got the 1992 board-staff retreat started with an exercise in which the participants had to say why they had come to Theatre Rhinoceros and why they had stayed. In trying to explain what we were each supposed to do, Scott suggested that "you might, for instance, tell us that this was your opportunity to give something back to the community, that while you were a ruthless businessperson during the week, this was where you could be generous and giving." A number of the volunteer board members (especially men who had been on the board for several years) followed and enriched this model in interesting ways. Billy, for instance, said: "I love live theater. I wanted to give something back to the gay community. When I got involved I fell in love with the people at Rhino. In addition, I've stayed because I felt it was important." Edward explained that his voluntary communal participation only began after his business relationship with the theater ended: "Alan [Estes, the founding artistic director] approached me in 1980 about the Redstone building [the current residence of the theater], which my company owned at the time. In landlord-tenant capacity we got along well with Doug [Holsclaw] and Adele [Prandini, current associate artistic director and artistic director, respectively]. I attended productions over the years. When we sold the building I approached Ken Dixon [then artistic director] to join the board. I stay because I love drama. It is still a thrill each time I see a play that realistically portrays gay and lesbian life. I bring a group of six others. It's a good occasion to socialize. All seven of us, all men, enjoyed *Twice Over* [a women's play]. And certainly, I've gotten a lot out of the gay community and it's an opportunity to put something back."

As the exercise proceeded around the room, several participants identified which member of the Theatre Rhinoceros community had brought them onto the staff or board. The emphasis on personal relationships was quite central to the articulation of Rhino as a community and as a community-based, community-serving organization. What might elsewhere be called office politics, a focus on personalities and individuals above jobs and tasks, was a huge part of my own and others' experiences of participation at Rhino. One young woman board member complained to me about what she called the "wig-wars," personal, sexual, stylistic competition and power battling among and between staff and board. She characterized this behavior as particularly gay and in doing so made it into a signifier of the particular relation between this organization and the gay community. Professional attention to jobs and tasks, regardless of the individuals carrying out those tasks, connotes, by contrast, a more impersonal formation and a rejection of communal ties. For example, when a new board member, at a small committee meeting, voiced concern as to whether the current artistic and financial directors of the theater were competent to do their jobs, the question, which even to my ears had the ring of blasphemy, was answered in such a way as to protect the current occupants of the jobs.

The question of quality, the presumed outcome of professionalism, was a difficult one at the theater because it evoked an abandonment of "community" norms, such as personal and communal loyalty. At a retreat held approximately a year earlier (which I had not attended but was described to me by the same board member who complained about the wig-wars), an outside board trainer had elicited from this same group their beliefs about the mission of the theater; the crux of the discussion, as reported to me, was that people were very concerned that the theater be both community based *and* "professional" but they feared that these things were in contradiction. Staff members tended to reject this opposition between communality and professionalism. They framed their own presence at this gay theater, as paid employees, not in terms of voluntary gift exchange but rather as a coerced result of the homophobia of mainstream theater; they wanted Rhino to be professional so that their own work, and gay theater more generally, would be seen as worthy of mainstream recognition and not as merely "community theater."

Sitting at an outdoor cafe in San Francisco are four thirtyish, Jewish, highly educated lesbians, eating salads. One is a friend of mine, in from out of town, another a friend of hers I do not know, and the third a woman I have never met but know of: she is a well-respected and very popular performance artist in town. I've seen her perform many times. She turns to me:

So what do you do?
I'm a graduate student, working on my dissertation.

Oh really, what's it on?
Well, part of it is on Theatre Rhinoceros.

Theatre Rhinoceros? Why are you studying them? No one takes them seriously.
Well, I know some of the work they do isn't great but they have been an institution in the gay community for fifteen years and they do have a very loyal subscription audience. For my academic purpose—that is, to study community—they are worthy of some attention. I'm interested in looking at why people participate and what Rhino itself thinks it's doing and what gayness has to do with people's involvement.

Adele asked me to give them a script but I won't do it, maybe some work in progress in the studio or something, but I'm not going to be the one to bring their quality up. I want to take my work where I have artistic respect for the people who run it, like the Marsh or Intersection or New Langton. Those aren't gay places but I don't owe anything to the gay community.

Debt, duty, obligation: a bond to the gay community seen as constraining or even demeaning and refused in favor of artistic merit, an abstraction, a form of value, of evaluation, that allows her work to circulate beyond the gay community. If she were to give Rhino a script it would be a gift, a gift owed in reciprocity for something; so instead she takes her work elsewhere. Like the board members, she sees the circuit of gift exchange that bonds the gay community and the circuit through which artistic merit flows as mutually exclusive. But where the board members fear that emphasis on artistic evaluation will undermine communality, she articulates the gay gift-exchange circuit as a closed circuit, an entrapping circuit that would exclude her from the circuit of artistic value; gay particularity would weigh her down.

As Marcel Mauss pointed out in *The Gift*, the notion of the gift in western, modern economics—a notion he seeks to contest—depends on a set of oppositions, between "liberty and obligation; liberality, generosity, and luxury as against savings, interest, and utility" (73). The gift is supposed to be freely and generously given; the defining pretense of the gift is that it does not oblige reciprocation and is not motivated by self-interest. While commercial exchanges are likewise supposed to be free—freely entered contracts—they are accounted by economists as useful and self-interested; obligation to reciprocate is central to commercial exchange, an obligation freely undertaken and confined to the exchange itself. The gift becomes in this schema almost an excess of freedom, the willful display of the freedom to renounce self-interest and utility. In refusing to give her work to the gay theater, the performance artist might seem then to be lacking this freedom, to be lacking the excess of artistic capital that would enable her gift. A critique of the freedom, the voluntarism, of the gift goes to the very heart of the freedom supposedly subtending rational maximizing exchange.

Mary Douglas situates Mauss's *The Gift* as precisely such an intervention against Anglo-American utilitarian political economy. As Douglas characterizes it, the French critique of British utilitarianism was primarily a critique of individualism, of "an impoverished concept of the person as an independent individual instead of as a social being," a view that "did not explain the role of social norms in shaping individual intentions and in making social action possible" (foreword, x–xi). The brunt of Mauss's argument is precisely that gift giving is not in fact free from the constraints of self-interest and power, cannot be opposed to commercial exchange through notions of altruism and disinterestedness, but is an exchange system driven by and determining the whole hierarchical social formation within which it takes place. But Mauss also refuses to reduce the gift to what he calls cold economic exchange, noting that the kinds of obligation and self-interest involved in gift exchange exceed economic utility and include honor, social bonds and hierarchies, religious goals, and so on. "For him," Derrida says, "it is a matter of thinking the economic rationality of credit [exchanges in which reciprocation is deferred across time] on the basis of the gift and not the reverse" (*Given Time*, 44). Interpreting economic rationality on the basis of the gift, he implies that, like the gift, economic exchange must be understood as socially constituted and constitutive.

At the end of *The Gift*, when seeking to apply the lessons of his study of archaic and primitive societies to modern society, Mauss posits gift exchange as a complement to commercial exchange. Sounding rather like Andrew Carnegie, he writes, "The rich must come back to considering themselves—freely and also by obligation—as the financial guardians of their fellow citizens... However, the individual must work. He should be forced to rely upon himself rather than others" (69). But this notion of complementarity, which sustains an opposition between gift exchanges as socially implicated and commercial exchanges as narrowly utilitarian, contradicts the argument he has made up to that point in certain crucial ways. It contradicts his desire to articulate a form that blends the two, in which exchanges might be both free and obligatory (73). It contradicts his claim that gift exchange is the origin of economic exchange, of forms such as credit that are said to be advanced or modern but are, he says, very old and inherent in gift exchange. And most importantly, in reaffirming the utilitarian narrowness of commercial exchange, it contradicts his theory of the "total social phenomenona" (3), the action that is multivalent, in which "all kinds of institutions are given expression at one and the same time—religious, juridical, and moral, which relate to both politics and the family; [and] likewise economic ones" (3).[22] In his recourse to a complementarity between gift and exchange, Mauss closes the circuit of meanings and values that he had seemed to open (although the notion of total social phenomena, while an opening by comparison with a utilitarian view of exchange, is ultimately a closure as well).

In *Given Time,* Derrida works to reopen that circuit. Derrida argues that the gift, defined as that which is free from circuits of exchange, is impossible: insofar as a gift is even recognized as a gift, he says, it is annulled by a reciprocation of some sort; it redounds if nothing else to the subjectivity of the giver: "Someone *intends-to-give* something to someone.... a subject identical to itself and conscious of its identity, indeed seeking through the gesture of the gift to constitute its own unity and, precisely, to get its own identity recognized so that that identity comes back to it, so that it can reappropriate its identity: as its property" (11). Derrida insists on this definition, on the project of articulating the impossible, "even though," as he says, "all the anthropologies... have, quite rightly and justifiably, treated together as a system, the gift and the debt, the gift and the cycle of restitution, the gift and the loan, the gift and credit, the gift and counter gift" (13) precisely in order to point to the openings, the excesses beyond a particular economic circuit, that are implicit in the gift (and for that matter in exchange more generally) and further to point to the supplementarity of these excessive values to the circuit of exchange itself.

For finally, the overrunning of the circle by the gift, if there is any, does not lead to a simple ineffable exteriority that would be transcendent and without relation. It is this exteriority that sets the circle going, it is this exteriority that puts the economy in motion. It is this exteriority that *engages* in the circle and makes it turn. If one must *render an account* (to science, to reason, to philosophy, to the economy of meaning) of the circle effects in which a gift gets annulled, this account-rendering requires that one take into account that which, while not simply belonging to the circle, engages in it and sets off its motion. (30–31)

Derrida here articulates a supplementary relation between the circuits of gift exchange, based on complex and unaccountable social obligations that he elsewhere calls (after Bataille) the "general economy" (but which the performance artist would certainly see as a restricting economy), and those circuits of exchange of equivalents (money, artistic merit) that he calls "restricted" (but that, in the context of liberal capitalism, have a certain air of freedom). This supplementary relation between gift exchange and economic circuits was regularly deployed at Theatre Rhinoceros, much as it is in the context of microlending, where obligation to community members becomes collateral for obligations vis-à-vis capital. In other words, the staff tried to resolve the opposition between communality and professionalism by mobilizing communal obligation in support of the project of artistic equality.

The theater itself, by which I mean the artistic director and other staff members speaking for the theater in an official capacity, regularly articulated the project of the theater as a project of development. The development project involved the linked political and economic goals of forging a multicultural gay community and creating work of quality (and cost) that would be equivalent to that found in mainstream theater. These goals were linked through a series of programs that were intended to do both things at once. But such "development" depended on contributions from the gay community, contributions from artists of their work, and contributions from audience members through their subscriptions and financial donations. Adele thus cast the development programs as themselves gifts to the community in relation to which the community should reciprocate. For instance, at an open meeting with artists called by Adele to try to bring new talent into the theater, she particularly emphasized first that "we need to broaden gay and lesbian theater. The gay and lesbian community is a diverse community and we want to reflect that diversity on our stages." She then described what she called the "minimal production series ... opportunities for the development of work." She continued:

> As you/we all know, the problem with gay and lesbian theater is that it is considered less than professional, professional good art. We do have a commitment to produce polished work. We want to provide the opportunity to work on the work. We also offer the co-production option. Rhino began as a very white organization. Slowly we have been working to change that. We recently had a woman of color co-production—it was good to see that, to begin that opening.

And in her orientation lecture to the people who would be working as telemarketers, she said:

> Our contribution is to creating that sense of community. Theatre Rhinoceros provides a sense of community, a sense of safety, building bridges within the gay and lesbian community across diversity within that community. For the past ten years watching the AIDS crisis I have witnessed something—gays and lesbians leading, contributing to coping with that. We can make such a contribution on the artistic front. I take inspiration from the models created by gay and lesbian AIDS workers—the fact that they have been influential; we want to influence the world. We will use the studio to develop new works. We have an assistant artistic director to do outreach to peoples of color. We have a playwrights workshop and a comedy improv class free—this is something we give to the community. We are going to be doing shows in larger venues this season, "nothing is too good for the working class." We do a good job on our stage—which is the size and shape of a bus—but the mainstream needs to move over. Going into larger venues is part of that struggle. We can create Equity level work. Our audience deserves it, our performers deserve it. We as a people deserve it.

Adele's gift to me here is obviously her reference to Equity, the actors union, her shorthand for artistic quality, professionalism. In invoking Equity she argues that gifts contributed to the theater, as recompense for its gift of community to the community, would allow the theater to produce work that is not only particularly gay, that not only moves in the circuit of gay value, but also turns the circuit of artistic value.

The call to philanthropic duty in the service of this development project was answered quite happily by some members of the Rhino audience, and especially those white gay men who had been the primary addressees of the theater's productions over the years. I met with Jim and Thomas in their well-appointed home in a wealthy, semi-suburban section of San Francisco. Both nearing fifty years of age, they had been together almost twenty years, and they had been attending Theatre Rhinoceros since its inception in 1977. They took a season subscription and donated a substantial amount of money every year. But they explained that because they were busy with subscriptions to the opera and other social and cultural activities and spent many weekends away at their country house, they found that they could only attend about half the plays each season. I asked them what they thought of the plays they did see. They complained that the quality hadn't been consistent, that the acting is not very good, and they told me that they used to like it more in the early days—though they objected to the fact that every single one of those plays involved some attractive man stripping down to his "undies." They claimed to have equal interest in the men's and women's plays—their best friends are a lesbian couple—although they did feel that for a time the theater shifted the balance a bit too much toward women's plays. I wondered, given the mixed reviews they gave of the plays, why they were still so generous and committed to the theater.

JIM: The theater stands for something for us. . . . We're proud of who we are. We, we would like to see it get better and better. And we feel it needs to continue to be supported. . . .

THOMAS: We don't have very many congealing elements in the gay community . . . The community is very diverse, and lots of times it doesn't look like we have a unified front of any type, that we're so diverse we can't organize or we can't get it together in a way. The theater gets people to interact more and it breaks down the walls you have about being with a gay woman or about being with a gay man, because that's what tends to separate us is you don't have too much experience around certain types of people.

JIM: Those things do give us a sense of family, I think . . . and we, our friends are people like us, whether they're men or they're women, and we like both.

MIRANDA: What do you mean, "like us"?

JIM: I mean people that are culturally involved. We had dinner with two women couples last Saturday night. One of the women is a member of the San Francisco Conservatory of

> Music. She loves to sing, she loves to go to the movies. We
> love to go to the movies. She loves to eat, we love to eat. And
> I guess we're sort of middle-of-the-road people. Neither one
> of us is flamboyantly nellie or outrageously butch. The
> women friends that we have would be acceptable in any
> company.

Unlike the participants I interviewed who describe their involvement with Rhino as part of a trajectory of identity formation, Jim and Thomas articulate an already-achieved gay subjectivity. Speaking in a philanthropic voice, these wealthy white men seek to produce other subjects by helping Rhino do its work of drawing in, drawing together, creating a community. Fully reiterating the development discourse offered by the theater, they imagine the communal subjects they help to produce to be at the same time diverse and like them and, in fact, like any and everyone else, "acceptable in any company," that is, simultaneously particular and equivalent.

But it was not easy for the theater to sustain the linkage between producing gay particularity—a gay community articulated through reciprocal obligation—and producing mainstream equivalence. The specter of mainstream equivalence always posed the danger of undermining the project of producing a particularized community and thus the indebtedness that sustained the development project itself. At the public forum one artist, the author and star of a play (produced at Rhino) about her experience as a transgendered lesbian, accused the theater of being "assimilationist," of producing "plays that say that gay people are just like everyone else." Meanwhile, the ingratitude of artists who "made it" in mainstream theater sent Adele into a rage.

Sitting in the office of the theater one morning reading through copies of grant applications Rhino had submitted, I thought I'd have some quiet time to myself since the staff normally didn't arrive until afternoon (though all did full-time jobs, almost no one was on a full-time salary and so they worked when they wanted). But Adele walked in almost immediately, and announced, "Well I'm just pissed."

She had just read a local newspaper's interview with Tony Kushner, the author of *Angels in America: A Gay Fantasia on National Themes*, a play about Roy Cohen, AIDS, gay relationships, and the Reagan/Bush political climate, which was being presented at the Eureka Theater. The play was beginning to get the tremendous celebration that would carry it on to long runs in Los Angeles and New York.

Adele explained that the source of her outrage was that Kushner had trashed gay theater for being only about coming out and relationships. In the article he is quoted as saying, "I feel the scope of gay theater is very small, that the issues it addresses of sexuality and relationships are important, but they're not placed in the context of the ideology, politics and society in which they exist." Reading this inspired her to come in and get to work. She placed calls to the heads of a couple of local foundations. She called the publicist to tell her to try to get a Sunday arts section spread for Gay Pride Week on next season that would "explain what we really do." "I've been doing this for twenty years and twenty years ago we were doing plays about nuke bomb testing as part of lesbian theater." To a board member on the phone she said, "The work we do is really strong so I'm mad." When I suggested that the criticism had some validity, that even the theater staff complained that lesbians only wrote plays about their mothers, she said, "Yeah, but how many straight plays are about relationships or family?"

Wait a minute, I guess I don't understand, what really is the problem with this statement of Kushner's?

The problem is that it tells straight people that they can just ignore us, that it is not important for us to have visibility, to have our own voices, that we can just speak through them from time to time if we do it in their way. These white boys make it, assimilate, co-opt, are only out for their own success. We aren't in it for our own self-aggrandizement but for social change—but you can't say that. We need room, we need to have our own place to speak. All the minority groups: blacks, women, gays. Rhino is an established institution that deserves resources, and not just some fringe group.

She explained that in the 1980s minority arts organizations were being starved out, given just enough to fail. She said that a study had been done showing that the gay people in the city spent $4,000 per year on the performing arts while everyone else spent $1,000. Other theaters, she argued, weren't doing gay theater because of their political commitment but because it was financially sound.

Adele's anger here is largely directed at Kushner, the white boy who made it and who, in making it, betrays the gay community, neglects his duty, his debt, to the gay community. But her anger also turns to the "other" theaters, the mainstream, that deploy gayness to attract gay dollars. Seeing co-optation where others might see success—that is, in the inclusion, recognition, tolerance of gays in mainstream society—she, like Pam, offers a critique of the hegemony building strategy of the mainstream. She becomes precisely the absent subject of capitalism, a problematic resistant subject, the site of crisis that capitalism tries to address through the deployment of nonprofits. The dialectical process that Adele's anger signifies, in which the very success of the nonprofit strategy in producing communal subjects of capitalism also produces resistance to such subjection, has been discussed at length by development practitioners and critics who are, respectively, concerned with the perceived legitimacy or actual authenticity of NGOs in relation to the communities they are supposed to serve or represent. In the next (and last) section, I take up this question through a discussion of the voluntariness of voluntary associations.

The Willing Subject

The promotion of nonprofit nongovernmental organizations as instruments of hegemony-building depends on the notion that, despite the fact that these organizations are actively and instrumentally encouraged, participation in such organizations is voluntary, is an authentic expression of real "grassroots" communities and their interests. The literature, both popular and academic, on nonprofits in the United States is relentless in its insistence that nonprofits express the already-formed desires and relationships of willing subjects. Emphasizing the idea of expression, one page of the Independent Sector's Web site is titled "America's Nonprofit Sector Gives Voice to Our Hearts." Even Lester Salamon, in an article that primarily accounts for the recent growth of NGO activity around the world in terms of the crises of capitalism and the state, says, "The most basic force is that of ordinary people who decide to take matters into their own hands and organize to improve their conditions or seek basic rights" ("Rise of the Nonprofit Sector," 112). Daniel Levine presumes that associations reflect or express already-formed communities when he argues that the differences between the mutual aid societies formed by different ethnic groups at the turn of the twentieth century in the United States can be read for "what they tell us about how that group saw itself" ("Immigrant," 1). And likewise, a recent study entitled "Creating Communities: Giving and Volunteering by Gay, Lesbian, Bisexual and Transgender People," conducted by M. V. Lee Badgett and Nancy Cunningham, presumes that the gifts of time or money are a consequence of gay identity rather than productive of such identity.[23]

Ample evidence of the centrality of voluntarism to the dominant conceptualization of nonprofits is provided by the *Edited Proceedings of the April 1997 Inaugural Conference* of the Hauser Center for Nonprofit Organizations at Harvard University, a public relations document summarizing a conference that brought together heads of major foundations and nonprofits, philanthropists, business executives, and scholars to celebrate the opening of the center and the Hausers for their founding gift. In a passage tying together panelists' attempts to define the "nonprofit sector," this document defines nonprofit organizations against business and the government, highlighting the role of the willful but altruistic individual:

> The sector was like politics and government in that the sector seemed to be focused on defining and realizing public purposes—providing avenues for the expression of individually held views about what was good and right and just, and providing goods and services that would not ordinarily be supplied by market mechanisms.... Unlike the government, however, the nonprofit sector sought to produce those results by aggregating individual, voluntary contributions; not by relying on the coercive power of the state to mobilize collective efforts to deal with the problems.
>
> The sector seemed just like business in that it depended on voluntary individual transactions aggregated up into socially significant enterprises.... Unlike business, however, what animates the sector was not the desire for material goods for oneself, but instead a desire to serve others, or to bring about attractive social results which one could enjoy, but not necessarily profit from financially.
>
> So, it seemed that the nonprofit sector was that sector of society that sought to deal with social problems or exploit social opportunities through individual voluntary effort. (6)

In another section, this text again emphasizes individual subjectivity (and especially the subjectivity of those "with the financial capacity and public spiritedness" to make "large contributions"):

> The nonprofit sector can be legitimated not only as an instrument for achieving public purposes, but also as the natural expression of a right that all citizens of liberal democracies have: the right to express their views about what purposes should be publicly valued, and to associate with one another to accomplish those purposes. (9)

Given the instrumentalization of nonprofits and NGOs that I have described, this insistence on voluntarism might seem to be disingenuous at best. The rhetoric of voluntarism attributes to participants in nonprofits the (liberal) subjectivity that nonprofits are meant to construct, disavowing both the constructive work and the particularity that must supplement this liberal subjectivity. The discourse of voluntarism must be understood as part of the means for constituting liberal subjectivity at the site of the nonprofit.

However, rather than seeing it simply as a disavowal, the discourse of voluntarism can also be read as recognizing, even as it obscures, a division between two classes of nonprofit actors, attributing to all a volition available only to some. Speaking to the Hauser conference audience, Jeanne Noble, of the National Council of Negro Women, implies precisely such a distinction between those already willful individuals ("we") who "produce" and the objects of that production, subjects who "become":

> Changed individuals and society are what we nonprofit organizations can best contribute to society. . . . Perhaps the best contribution we make to society, is to produce inspired, enlightened, and trained volunteers. Indeed, the greatest challenge for nonprofits is to help the individual volunteer become a changed individual. (9)

While her speech clearly aims to stroke the egos of the wealthy donors in her audience, in doing so, it marks a crucial difference in the roles played—and power exercised—by various nonprofit actors.

The notion that the dominant account of nonprofit NGOs as voluntary masks a class division, in which nonprofits are a site of willful action only for some, while for others nonprofits are sites of a becoming and an incorporation they do not control, has been well articulated in critiques of the deployment of nonprofits in the context of development.[24] The basis for this critique, which comes from both left/feminist scholars and from members of the development establishment, is the recognition that inequities are operative in a capitalist civil society and that those inequities shape participation in NGOs. Many scholars find that NGOs are not "democratic" either in their internal decision-making structures or in their relationships with the social groups they serve and claim to represent. Individual NGOs and the NGO system as a whole[25] build on existing hierarchies, exacerbating existing differences in wealth and power at global, national, and local scales.[26] While liberal civil society discourse assumes that the only power one need worry about is the power of a totalitarian state, the development context enables observers of various political orientations not only to see inequities within civil society but also to recognize that liberal states support such inequities. Broadly, critics argue that the extraordinary increase in funds offered by Northern NGOs and official aid agencies to Southern NGOs (directly and through governments) over the past twenty years has co-opted existing organizations and fomented the creation of new organizations that must, because of their dependence on the funding, enact the agendas of the donor agencies (Hudock, *NGOs and Civil Society*).

Hashemi argues that in the wake of new state and international funding, "Now, rather than the poor organizing themselves, it is the groups within the civil society—lawyers, journalists, university professors—who will lead social change" (paraphrased in Fernando and Heston, "NGOs between States," 9). Edwards and Hulme point out that the articulation of populations as "clients" of NGOs rather than citizens that is concommitant with the shift of service provision from the state to NGOs may be a self-fulfilling strategy of disempowerment ("Too Close for Comfort," 967).[27] Ewig affirms this view in her essay on the feminist healthcare movement in Nicaragua, arguing that the successful NGOs are those run by professionals with prior political or business experience and that such professionally run organizations offer little opportunity for staff and target populations to participate in decision making.[28]

> Reaching out to women of the poor and working classes is not the same as allowing these women to participate in making decisions. This kind of relationship between the service provider and the clients risks reinforcing class hierarchies and paternalism. ("Strengths," 97)

Ewig points out that those organizations with more money are also the organizations that attract more money and tend to take a leadership role without the participation of smaller NGOs. The recent celebration of NGOs has only increased such disparities as NGO leaders are invited to participate in the policy discussions of states and international organizations, as if they really did represent "the people": "As might be expected, the larger and more professionalized NGOs tend to gain positions in the state and civil society institutions. . . . These NGOs 'represent' a constituency (women) that neither elected the organization nor has clear participatory channels for negotiating how that NGO represents its interests" (97).

Further, Feldman and others argue that the management ethos imposed by donor organizations, borrowed directly from business (which values short-term individualized measurable outcomes), has produced a loss of commitment to "the principles of reciprocity, obligation, and community solidarity" ("NGOs and Civil Society," 5). Edwards and Hulme argue that the deployment of NGOs as "efficient" conduits for development funds specifically undermines the stated agenda of democratization for which they were supposedly chosen, since "the standardized delivery systems and internal structures (often hierarchical) able to manage large amounts of external funding" are contradictory to the "qualities required to promote success in democratization," namely, "independence from external interests, closeness to poor people, longtime horizons for capacity building, and a willingness to confront those in power" ("Too Close for Comfort," 965). In *Intermediary NGOs*, Tom Carroll, writing as the head of the Inter-America Foundation, likewise acknowledges potential trade-offs between efficient service provision and "group capacity building"; trying to redeem the foundation's support of NGOs from the criticism that it undermines group capacity building, he argues that group capacity building is possible if the NGO is careful to facilitate rather than replace grassroots activity by requiring, as Andrew Carnegie suggests, that the recipients of NGO aid contribute to the project (whatever that may be).

These critiques of NGOs tend to oppose what they see as current distortions of such organizations to what they imagine to be more authentic and legitimate organizations that preexisted this new flood of funds or that might exist were development carried out differently. Left and feminist critics argue that NGO activity has shifted toward the incorporation of subjects into the state and capital, where it once, they claim, offered opposition or alternatives to both: "Increasingly, NGO programs are oriented toward facilitating the effective participation of the poor in the market economy, rather than providing alternatives to it" (Fernando and Heston, "NGOs between States," 7). And likewise, MacDonald argues, from an explicitly Gramscian perspective, that in the context of the recent increase in funding, many organizations have shifted their focus from political dissent and protest to depoliticized service provision; as contractors working for the state, she argues, many NGOs have submitted to state regulation and have literally become agents of the state. The critics from within the development establishment are not so much concerned that opposition or alternatives to capital have been eroded as that these failures of NGOs to embody the a priori needs, desires, and agency of individuals and communities compromise the "legitimacy" (of the NGOs among "the people") and the "effectiveness" (in democratization and poverty alleviation) of the "New Policy Agenda" as a whole. In a sense they suggest that their real concern is that such NGO practices might promote rather than ameliorate the exclusion of subjects from capitalism.[29]

What these critiques fail to account for, in positing a remainder of "real" grassroots desire and agency outside development processes and institutions, is the willingness of the poor and all sorts of not-so-poor individuals and communities to participate in and make use of NGO activity. In this account, NGO participation would seem to make sense only as coerced or as an act of false consciousness.

Feldman solves this problem by arguing that no such remainder exists, that participants in effect have no choice but to choose to participate. She argues that development and modernization efforts have created populations, which, in the absence of state-based programs, are vulnerable to NGOs that offer services aimed at integrating the poor and disempowered into a capitalist economy:

> With the demise of household forms of subsistence, for example, the privatization of rural production has reached new levels and is increasingly based on the individuation of production as well as consumption.... These conditions provide a ready market for NGOs able to generate employment and income sources, provide skills training, and support the privatization of small-scale production and petty trade. ("NGOs and Civil Society," 4)

"Modernization" she says, "is a process of intervention with the explicit goal of reorganizing constituent interests, generating new economic and political alliances, and reorganizing resource control and distribution in the move toward the commodification and privatization of all social relations" (3). Echoing Escobar's assertion that development has operated as a dominant discourse that makes desire for development that only possible desire, she suggests that NGOs have become the only practical and imaginable means for acting in one's own interests, which are thus constructed as the interests of the modernized individual.

Feldman is quite right to argue that NGOs are both a consequence of and a technology for the reconstitution of subjectivity. However, neither participants nor the philanthropists, states, or development agencies that undertake nonprofit activity want only to produce individuated and equivalent subjects of capital, nor do they only produce such subjectivity. As Inderpal Grewal points out, grassroots groups and NGOs "have complex positionings as well as problematic power relations inscribed in their efforts. These have to be carefully scrutinized . . . not with the view that they may not be authentically grassroots, but with the belief that complex subjectivities, positions and power relations are endemic to all groups, whether in the north or south, First World or Third" ("New Global Feminism," 523).

The performativity of nonprofit production and its location at the site of the absence of capitalist subjects tends against a reductive assessment of nonprofits, an assessment that measures their productivity only in terms of a "restricted" economy. The sheer multiplicity of identities and social relations performatively generated by participants at Theatre Rhinoceros, which include not only gay community membership but also gender, race, adulthood, professional status, friendship, social equality, and political resistance, among others, indicates that more than the production of equivalence is at stake. The Partners for Fragile Families project simultaneously produces and fulfills not only the desire of poor young men for marketable job skills but also for fatherhood, and while fatherhood might be accounted in some part as a form of individualized and privatized capitalist subjectivity, it also carries connotations of communal obligation, especially where it is capitalism that has apparently prevented them from being "fathers" in the first place. Jim and Thomas support Theatre Rhinoceros in order to produce gayness both as difference and sameness. If nonprofits are haunted by the specter of communism insofar as they are sites at which agents of capitalist expansion seek to engage subjects as bearers and producers of capital, they are also haunted by the specter of communism insofar as they are sites where participants enact their Romantic longing for for something other than capitalism, for collectivity based in gift exchange, "cultural" identity or interest, and where they get help in fulfilling their communal obligations.

Feldman points out that the desire for capitalism may come as much from participants as from development agencies; conversely, the desire for community would seem to be quite central for philanthropists and development agencies. According to development practitioners, NGOs fail when they fail to manage adequately the paradox of enlisting for capitalism that which is other than capitalist, the very communality that Feldman's narrative of modernization as individuation would suggest is destroyed by development. The common articulation, in the United States, of both nonprofit participation and philanthropy as "giving something back to the community" marks a crucial indistinction between the philanthropist and the participant, the capitalist, and the would-be community member.[30] In noting this indistinction, I don't mean to erase the power differences between nonprofit actors that the development critics so eloquently elaborate, but rather to trace the transaction at the site of the nonprofit between general and restricted economies. Nonprofits mobilize for capital—but not only for capital—subjectivities that are not (only) of it—are in fact its absent center—and yet set it in motion.

CHAPTER FOUR

The Perfect Moment: Gays, Christians, and the National Endowment for the Arts

> I want them to know they don't have to be gay.
> —Michael Cooney, "Set Free" Ministry[1]

Beginning in 1989 and continuing through the early 1990s, a public controversy took place over the funding practices of the National Endowment for the Arts (NEA). Christian conservatives attacked the NEA for funding the creation and exhibition of artworks by gay and feminist artists, works that they deemed obscene. Arts, gay/lesbian, and civil liberties organizations all joined the battle in defense of the NEA.[2] At various points in the controversy Congress imposed content restrictions on NEA funding,[3] but the most significant outcome of the battle has been a dramatic reduction in the funds allocated to the NEA.

I did ethnographic research on this controversy.[4] The form of this research differed in many ways from the work I did on Theatre Rhinoceros. While, as in the Rhino study, I conducted interviews and sat in on meetings, for the NEA study the interviews and meetings took place all over the country, and more importantly, a significant part of my research involved collecting an extraordinary amount of paper. In the offices of arts and civil liberties activists in San Francisco, New York, and Washington, I not only interviewed executive directors and public policy directors, but I also copied file drawers full of faxed "calls for action"; the direct mail of both sides; press releases; "talking points"; newspaper and magazine articles (usually partisan opinion pieces) written by, published by, or merely collected by the file keeper; drafts of legislation; legal briefs;

handwritten notes from phone calls and meetings; lobbyists' letters to Congress; and "dear colleague" letters written by anti-NEA Congress members. All the while, I was building my own file full of newspaper and magazine clippings, transcripts of talk radio shows, direct mail solicitations, and notes from meetings.

This controversy was grist for a huge organizational and information-technology mill; it involved relatively little (but not none) of the face-to-face communication that is so frequently taken to indicate the existence of community. And yet the discourse of community ran rampant through it: those attacking the NEA's funding practices spoke of the religious community that was offended by the NEA's funding of artworks by members of the homosexual community, which, they said, was trying to gain an unwarranted legitimacy vis-à-vis the American nation, the communal nature of which was thought to be threatened by homosexual legitimacy; those supporting the NEA's funding of gay expression spoke of attacks on the gay community and of the artists' constructive role within their communities and the national community.

I was initially drawn to explore this controversy because, at the time, it was the main site for a mutual obsession of gays with Christians and Christians with gays. Although, from the perspective of Washington bureaucrats and arts administrators, it was the budgets of arts organizations that were most at risk and it was arts organizations that were most active (along with a variety of religious right organizations) in lobbying in Washington, outside the Beltway, these events served to focus the attention of gays on Christians and Christians on gays.

Gay/lesbian, arts, and civil liberties organizations all responded to the attacks on the NEA launched by conservative Christians. However, their roles in the battle were quite different. The arts industry responded by working on congressional authorization and appropriations legislation pertaining to the NEA. Gays and lesbians and those arts organizations representing individual artists (which tended to have a significant gay constituency) felt that the arts lobby was willing to compromise in the wrong places, allowing restrictions on content in order to save dollars, in effect sacrificing gay and lesbian expression. No one in the arts community was willing to admit to such a sacrifice, although, as arts advocates acknowledged, many in the arts world were slow to see the attack on gay artwork as "my issue." Civil liberties groups and, in particular, People for the American Way, worked with the arts groups in Washington and helped to mount a national public relations campaign for arts funding; they framed the attack on the NEA as an attack on free speech and thus on American values. Gays and lesbians, by contrast, were peripheral to the legislative process; their response took place in gay newspapers, on gay stages, and in a shift in self-understanding that would produce a campaign entitled "Fight the Right" by an organization originally formed to fight for rights, the National Gay and Lesbian Task Force (NGLTF). Of course, the Fight the Right campaign, primarily a tool used in relation to antigay rights ballot initiatives, was a campaign for rights. But in this campaign the enemy was not framed as a homophobic society at large. Instead, it was a specific right-wing religious community.

The NGLTF's Fight the Right Action Kit is a compilation of articles, essays, speeches, resource lists, and instructional materials on how to organize, build coalitions, and "talk the talk." It begins by introducing the reader to what is variously called the "New Right," the "Christian Right," and the "Far Right." A historical article locates the birth of the movement in a mobilization of conservative Christians by right-wing political strategists in the 1970s and 1980s (Mozzochi et al., "New Right"). While this cynical treatment of the Christian right as a political construction denies them authenticity as an organic community, the article also constructs them as a community by describing particular cultural and historical parameters and origins: blue collar, southern white, Christian, reaction against the civil rights movements. The article is likewise ambivalent about the claims of the movement to being "of the people," suggesting on the one hand that its populist and democratic claims are false, but on the other that it is the product of a mass mobilization, and thus has a large and powerful, if hoodwinked and manipulated, constituency; the Christian right is not then the "true minority" it claims to be, even while simultaneously claiming to be the moral majority and naming its opposition as "radical extremists." According to NGLTF, the Christian right is somehow both large and marginal, popular but not populist.[5]

The newspapers, newsletters, and direct mail of organizations affiliated with both gays and Christians were filled with articles tracking the activities and "agenda" of the other. Quite a number of articles in gay journals cast their essays on the Christian right as "undercover reports," as revealing an otherwise inaccessible and dangerous other. The ruses and costumes undertaken to do these stories, described in some detail and displayed in photographs, seemed intended both to give the reporter entrée, as "one of them," to an otherwise closed and conspiratorial world, and to protect the reporter, as if her person would be in danger were she discovered.[6] Likewise, many of the Christian reports on gays claim to be uncovering a secret world, spied on covertly, as if video footage of that most public of events, the gay pride parade, were footage of a cell meeting obtained by a hidden camera. Such reports were frequently structured in a myth versus fact format intended to debunk the supposed lies perpetrated by gay people that might lead one to think gay existence was benign rather than the threat to society and to salvation that it truly is.[7] In these articles, the authoritative testimony of the expert is generally accompanied by the personal testimony of an individual who has given up that degrading lifestyle in favor of Christ, marriage, and children. In my own research process, I produced a notable number of testimonials to conversion in the opposite direction, from Christian to gay. These conversion narratives suggest the mutual incompatibility, if symmetry, of gayness and Christianity.

The direct mail solicitations of the American Family Association (AFA), the Christian organization that initiated the attack on the NEA, describe the "anti-Christian bigotry" funded by the NEA, the "forced taxpayer funding of prohomosexual, anti-Christian pornography."[8] These pieces often incorporated gay-themed or authored "anti-Christian" art—and there was for a while a great deal of art produced that targeted antigay figures such as Jesse Helms[9]—consuming and reproducing the configuration of gays and Christians as symmetrically opposed communities.

The gay versus Christian battle, which certainly began before the NEA controversy—with arguments over AIDS being predominant in the 1980s—escalated after the arts controversy to include explicit battles over civil rights: in several states and many more municipalities initiatives have been placed on the ballot by the religious right that aim to overturn existing and outlaw additional gay rights ordinances.[10] Huge nationally monitored campaigns have been waged over these initiatives, in a sense referendums on gay citizenship, gay subjecthood. These campaigns have been accompanied by relatively high levels of antigay violence.

It has seemed to me that the obsession of gays with Christians is counterproductive politically: we feed their organizing efforts by attacking them and fail to intervene in the larger social processes that generate homophobia. In this chapter, I deconstruct the gay/Christian opposition by reading the arts controversy as a renegotiation of the roles and relations between community, nation, and state in the context of the emerging discourse of globalization. In analyzing globalization as a discourse rather than an empirical fact, I treat it as a process of articulating social formations at a moment of economic and political crisis and transformation. The discourse of globalization suggests that nation-states are no longer the optimal units of economic activity and that in fact they have lost their power to control the global flow of capital. It suggests that nonnational communities are emerging as more appropriate sites for production and consumption, while control over capital flows has shifted to international trade organizations and to the global market itself. The NEA controversy engaged this discourse, generating new communal economic sites and dismantling the nation-state by separating nation from state, but it also enacted a certain resistance to globalization, marking the costs and benefits of particular transformations for various constituencies.

All of the activism, for and against the NEA, other than that of the government itself and the for-profit media, was undertaken by non-profits—some newly formed for this purpose, many already in existence—most organized as 501c3 charitable, educational organizations, a few as 501c4 lobbying groups. (Organizations operating under one name are often actually a pair of organizations: People for the American Way [PFAW] and PFAW Action Fund, for instance, are the 501c3 and 501c4 counterparts of each other.) These organizations operate through an array of common techniques for raising funds, mobilizing grassroots support, and engaging in direct lobbying. One of the most prevalent techniques in this battle was direct mail (or fax or phone) campaigns, one of the more potent forms of niche marketing, aimed at carefully selected potential constituents/consumers, employing rhetorics of community—gay, religious, arts, and American community—to realize those constituents.

The NEA, founded in the 1960s, precisely the moment of an extraordinary explosion in the number of nonprofits (Hall, "Inventing the Nonprofit Sector"; Weisbrod, *Nonprofit Economy*) and of a very high level of social strife in the United States, is itself a mechanism for generating and supporting nonprofits. With the exception of relatively minor individual fellowship programs, at the time of the controversy, the NEA funded only formally incorporated nonprofit organizations. These organizations were usually members of local or state field specific arts service organizations, and these local and state service organizations were generally members of national service organizations, which were again field specific, the artistic fields matching precisely the funding categories of the NEA. Artists and arts organizations around the country were thus tied through the hierarchy of organizations to the national state. The NEA controversy reanimated these hierarchies of organizations and developed new ones.

As I argued in the previous chapter, participation in nonprofit organizations serves to articulate liberal political and economic subjects. And the inscription of arts activism in nonprofits did produce all participants in this battle as analogous subjects of capitalism and the liberal nation-state. However, the various participants also took up substantively different positions, elaborating quite distinct subjectivities. The direct mail of Christian organizations addresses a very different subject than that of civil liberties groups. The Christian letters are highly personalized; "Beverly" [LaHaye] or "Don" [Wildmon] write to say: "Today I'm asking you to help." Their letters include stories of their personal or organizational trials and tribulations and of personal experiences that illustrate some principle of righteous living. In other words, these are witnessing letters, from one situated, gendered, familied subject to another.

The direct mail of PFAW is very different in style and substance from that of the Christian organizations. For one thing, their letters are very, very long (four to six pages), single-spaced as-if-typed documents explaining the details of the legislative process and rehearsing a large number of issues or aspects of an issue. The PFAW letters do not come from an individual with any personal characteristics but from the president, speaking for the organization ("We've told you who we are—and what we stand for") or they come from a famous person who has allowed his name to be used but has not managed to inject any personality into the text itself. To give the text authority, a copy of an article in the *New York Times* will sometimes be included in the package. One abstract rational mind addresses another, who will respond because he has been persuaded: "Now, it's time for you to act." The urgent actions to be taken— write to your congressional representative; send money to PFAW—are overwhelmed with information.

Enacting their opposition in a battle over *national* arts funding, these differently articulated subjects articulated very different notions of the proper boundaries and functions of the nation-state. Gays, arts organizations, and civil libertarians imagined the state as the neutral site of rights and as the active promoter of Enlightened secular culture; Christians meanwhile articulated the nation as a particular cultural and political entity, not as an abstract and endlessly capacious provider of rights. In struggling over the NEA, speakers of Enlightenment and nationalist discourses attempted to preserve their privileges and the (liberal) state or (Christian) nation that might provide them while simultaneously attacking the nation (as Christian) and state (as liberal), respectively, and thus in different ways undermined the linkage of nation with state.

The Parable of Christina

While in Washington in the spring of 1992 for a meeting of the National Council on the Arts, the appointed board of famous people that makes policy for the NEA and gives final approval to their grants, I met a woman who occupied an extraordinarily complex position in the controversy. Christina was the head of a national arts advocacy agency. As such, she participated actively in efforts to preserve NEA funding and to prevent the implementation of content restrictions. When I spoke with her she talked at length about the many gay men she had befriended through her work in the arts. With regard to her own sexuality she said that she was "primarily interested in men," leaving the details to my imagination. I sought her out for an interview, however, because I had been told by a mutual acquaintance, in whispered tones, that she was also a Christian.

Christina understood herself to adhere to what she considered "the basic principles that were taught by Christ and that you can lift out of the Bible." And what are these? She answered carefully and sincerely:

> There is a higher being who is in some way responsible for what exists. And secondly, that being has some kind of an entity that allows a personal interaction with what has been created or what has occurred. . . . (I'm trying to use words that aren't buzzwords that evangelicals would be happy with me using.) . . . The notion of sin: A result of free will was the separation that occurred between the communion of God and the human, that put the human soul into dire jeopardy [laughs]. And the whole notion of Christianity is built around the idea that Jesus, who was God incarnate, came to earth to live a life that was perfect and exemplary and die on behalf of all people, in other words to take all of that separation . . . to act as a kind of sacrifice for all of that . . . Placing your faith in Christ

has to do with trusting that in that act you're no longer separated from God . . . the notion of grace, which is, if you put your faith in Christ, what you experience in the eyes of God is unmerited favor. . . . The other thing, and this gives people the willies, but a real Christian believes that in some way Christ is going to come back.

She said that she could honestly answer yes to the question, "Do you know Christ as your own personal savior?" though she would not normally describe her faith in that way. As if to prove a cultural affiliation with what she called "the evangelical subculture," she asserted "a very deeply painful difficulty with promiscuity. . . . I don't care whether it's two gay men or two gay women or two straight heterosexual people." Likewise, she said that she had chosen not to go to the Mapplethorpe exhibit: "I didn't want to see it. I'd seen pictures of the pictures and I didn't like it."

Given the mutually exclusive and antagonistic postures of gays (and arts advocates) with Christians, I wondered how this woman made sense of her life. She did posit as personal problems the issues of her own geographic and communal locations. She lived in Virginia, where she grew up, trying to "prove that you can go home again," while she worked in Washington, D.C.; she spent, she said, 30 to 50 percent of her time traveling; and she told me that her best friends were to be found in New York and San Francisco. She described maintaining a certain discretion with the people she worked with in the arts, viewing her relationship with Christ as a private family matter that she did not need to share, except with those who became close friends. She used this public/private distinction to reconcile her work and her beliefs, what she called her "role as a citizen" and her "role as a Christian," though she believed she acted on her Christian values in her work life, pointing to her efforts to raise the consciousness of the organizations that comprised the membership of her organization about workplace policies for people with AIDS.

As indicated in her avoidance of "buzzwords," she distanced herself from the evangelical community as well. She specifically said that she did not consider herself any longer a member of that community, though she took with her "the best" of what she had grown up with: "to be really grounded in the Bible and to really understand the significance of a personal relationship with God." She had traded in the Baptist church of her childhood for an Episcopalian church that professed a less proscriptive version of Christianity, one that makes much more room for symbol and sacrament (which she equated with art) than the Baptist tradition does. She did maintain friendships and relationships with evangelicals. Her greatest sense of community, she said, came from the relationships she had with people, now geographically scattered, with whom she had attended Wheaton College, an evangelical institution in Illinois—the site of her realization that arts and Christ were not mutually incompatible but that, in fact, arts could be "one of God's great gifts to humanity."

She claimed for herself and her organization what she called a "middle ground" in the arts-funding debate. She felt it was wiser not to focus on the freedom of expression aspect of the issue, even while she was clear that she did not support the content restrictions proposed by congressional representatives of the Christian right such as Jesse Helms. Her so-called middle ground involved focusing on the level and pattern of funding distribution. She was on the liberal side of this middle, arguing against shifts in the distribution of arts moneys toward the states, proposed by congressional "moderates," the conservative middle, that would ostensibly have allowed more local control and thus sensitivity to "community" concerns, but that amounted to a shift of funds away from national urban arts centers like New York and Los Angeles and from individual artists to organizations.[11] And she was against proposed shifts away from the support of artists and arts organizations and toward "arts in education" programs, a proposal again from congressional moderates looking to preserve the NEA by shifting support away from what were marked as decadent or elite or politicized adults and toward innocent children. This administrative middle ground, consisting of a focus on the details of funding policy, effectively effaced both gays and Christians from the debate, even while claiming to take both into account.

In this managerial discourse, gays and Christians become structurally analogous, if different, constituents with equally valid claims, consumers with different tastes. Christina asked, "Is it possible to fund the arts in a democratic society? . . . Is there a way to have a policy when multiple points of view is a fundamental idea?" The Fordist answer was to create the NEA, which offers funding and, even as the site of battles, encourages incorporation, incorporation into nonprofits and thus into the nation-state and capitalism. This battle over the NEA questioned and renegotiated that Fordist strategy, promoting a new regime of social formations even as it enacted the old one. Christina's claim to a middle ground was enabled by the marking of gays and Christians as extremes, but it does not do justice to the comprehensiveness of the administrative production of "community" in which she was engaged. At the same time, the upshot of the NEA controversy was not the expansion of the NEA and its incorporative powers but rather the reduction of its budget by half, and thus the reduction of its community constructing abilities. The attacks by Christians, rather than increasing their control over the subject-forming apparatus of the state, served to delegitimate the activities of the state altogether.

The Enlightenment/Nationalist Binary

The NEA controversy was enabled by, invoked and reworked, a familiar discursive battleground. Pastor Allen of Walnut Grove Baptist Church, Christina's father's pastor, articulated the NEA controversy as an opposition between nationalist and Enlightenment discourses. During a group interview I conducted with Christina, her father, Pastor Allen, and his wife, Pastor Allen attempted to explain Christian activism on the NEA issue, to explain why he cared:

> The place I would retreat with other Christians is to go back to the foundations of our country and the Judeo-Christian ethic that . . . made our country great. I don't like the eroding away of those traditions in the name of well, . . . we're kinda beyond that narrow-minded thinking of our founders and we're in a new enlightened age.
>
> Throughout the history of our country we have defined what a family is. There are strong forces now that want to throw that out and pretend that our history didn't matter, that we were kinda in the dark ages then and now . . . family means just two people living in the same place, whether you're homosexuals, you're lesbians . . . That has tremendous social implications . . . That is the beginning of a nation collapsing. History proves it over and over again. When there is broad tolerance, when cultures have that attitude where this is modern . . . then they all waltz to destruction.

A bit startled that his response to the NEA controversy made so little reference to salvation, I said, "You're talking about what makes a nation great . . . What's the significance of a nation for a Christian?"

> Well, that's another set of values. You know, nationalism is going out; internationalism, global world is coming in. That's another set of values that helped build our country that's being thrown out and replaced by

new. I think we should be global-minded, and as Christians especially we're to reach the whole world and appreciate all cultures, but not to the extreme that you throw out patriotism and you throw out allegiance to your nation.

The opposition Pastor Allen articulates between nationalism and modernity or Enlightenment is certainly tied to what he called the "historical modern-fundamentalist debate." The terms *modern* and *fundamentalist,* Susan Harding argues, were cemented as oppositional through the Scopes trial ("Representing Fundamentalism," 390). They describe sides in a battle that took place both within religious denominations between liberal and conservative factions, and between a secular society and religious traditions. These terms have been used by academics to describe the situation of religious conservatives: James Davidson Hunter, in *American Evangelicalism,* casts the emergence and evolution of fundamentalism as driven by the struggle of an already existing conservative religious ideology with modernity (11–19). Harding, criticizing the uncritical participation in the modern view that scholars like Hunter evidence, suggests that fundamentalism is an invention of the modern imagination, projected to define its boundaries, serving as its necessary other ("Representing Fundamentalism," 392). Her suggestion that these discourses are already inside each other, that the modern is implicated in the construction of the fundamentalist, is borne out by the discourse of each, insofar as it defines itself by opposition to the other. In renaming the opposition "Enlightenment vs. nationalist," I want to emphasize the historical specificity of the NEA controversy in the moment of "globalization" and evoke a somewhat different discursive legacy.

As many writers have noted, the "nation" entails a central ambivalence, an ambivalence highlighted by the very notion that there could be an antagonism between Enlightenment and nationalist discourses (Bhabha, *Nation and Narration,* 1–3, 292–294). The usual history of the nation is as modern, as a product of the Enlightenment, leaving behind, if growing out of, religion and dynasty as forms of social organization, instantiating a liberal, fraternal, horizontal, rational imagination of social space (Anderson, *Imagined Communities*). However, as Habermas argues, emerging from the French (and U.S.) Revolution as a standardized and increasingly pervasive form for the exercise of sovereignty and rights, the territorial boundaries of constitutional states would be utterly arbitrary save for particularistic (not to mention hierarchical and oppositional) notions of culture, language, and blood. These notions frequently ground the nation in re-membered histories of religion and blood or race (Habermas, "European Nation State"). Fundamentalist and nationalist movements have the function of generating patriotic enthusiasm, the willingness on the part of citizens to promote national/imperial economic interests.

The ambivalence of the nation-state has been fully evident in the United States. Historical and cultural particularity in the United States has meant that Christianity has actively articulated many aspects of contemporary policy and politics.[12] The Supreme Court's decision on the Georgia sodomy law, *Bowers v. Hardwick* (478 Sup. Ct. 186 [U.S. 1986]), does so explicitly; and *Miller v. California* (113 Sup. Ct. 2360 [U.S. 1973]), the decision that defines obscenity by referring to "community standards," is another obvious instance. As Christina's self-explication demonstrates, the liberal public/private distinction actually allows (dominant) private beliefs to be deployed in public life. On the other hand, Enlightenment liberation movements, civil rights movements, have been central to, if sometimes the unintended consequence of, the construction of the liberal subject. Such movements have at times worked against the particularity of the nation, pushing it to fulfill the promise of abstraction, of neutrality toward "private" difference.

Pastor Allen's nationalist reaction to globalization reiterates the Romantic anticapitalism of the Burkean reaction to the French Revolution and the fascist reaction to capitalist-modernization (Carlston, *Thinking Fascism*). Many of the terms—the city, the homosexual—epitomizing the "decline" posited in that Romantic discourse recur in Christian nationalist rhetoric.[13] The opposition between Enlightenment and nationalist discourses in this controversy, while deploying available discursive resources, was not inevitable but rather seems to have been provoked by economic and political transformations. Its appearance suggests a crisis in the complicity between the particular culture and history of the nation and the modern state. It is a cliché to say that the right, in its loss of the communist enemy, turned to internal enemies, such as gays and lesbians, for their sense of purpose and definition,[14] but I suspect that the reappearance of the opposition between Enlightenment and nationalist discourses at this moment did have a significant relationship with the expansion of capitalist hegemony.

The joining of modern and in a sense premodern discourses in the construction of the nation-state is possible so long as the nation is actually the unit of modern economic and political life. But to the extent that modernity, especially in the form of capitalism, begins to articulate other geographic sites and scales—and the discourse of globalization does seem to refigure the globe in nonnational units—a particularistic nationalism may work at cross purposes with the Enlightenment discourses of modernization and progress that articulate and are articulated by the state. Culturally defined national formations, including identity movements such as that of gays and lesbians, may remain or become important units of production and consumption, but they are delinked from the state as a regulator of capital flows and subject formation. In its role as an apparatus of capital, the state, separated from the nation, is freed from the task of producing a coherent national citizenry and enabled to promote international alliances while allowing the elaboration of internal difference, disparities of wealth and power that benefit multinational corporations rather than national bourgeoisies.

Space and Time

In the context of the NEA controversy, Enlightenment and nationalist discourses were organized as oppositional around common points of reference. At each common site the discourses articulated matching but reversed binary evaluations. As the attempts to rearrange the regional distribution of NEA funds suggests, spatial claims are central: in the Enlightenment discourse the urban is the site of civilization, sophistication, and urbanity, while the rural home of the fundamentalist is a bastion of ignorance and incivility; the urban is the site at which diverse cultures meet to learn from and fertilize one another, while the rural is the site of backwardness. As Holly, the person responsible for arts issues for a gay and lesbian lobbying group, said:

> [Sadomasochistic imagery is] not something that somebody from Buffalo, New York, is going to find acceptable.... The Moral Majority sends out mindless stuff. They are just playing on fears. Because education is not out there, because people have not allowed different points of view to be brought into education, you can just play on their ignorance. These people might not even understand or know about Michelangelo, or DaVinci, or know that Goya might be controversial.

For the nationalist discourse, by contrast, the heartland is the root, the foundation, the origin of a communal life with its own organic integrity, while the urban is the site of overrefinement, decadence, the rootlessness and impurity—the pollution, penetration, cultural miscegenation—that harkens the fall of a civilization. As one pastor explained, using a Biblical example, "Corinth was a center of trade and so different cultures were constantly meeting there and so all kinds of sin broke out: thievery, incest, homosexuality."[15] There have been a variety of figures for this rootless, decadent pollution at different times and in different places: Jews are a traditional figure; in the 1980s gays and people with AIDS were salient figures; and in the 1990s immigrants of color were vilified.[16]

The temporal dimension of Enlightenment discourse is the discourse of progress and emancipation—the future is open-ended and improving. The narrative trajectories in this discourse trace stories of development and perfectibility with reference to individuals and groups, describing the sequential granting of rights to women, African Americans, gays, and lesbians. The individual is freed by a society organized on the basis of rights, procedural rights, civil rights, to fulfill his own desires and abilities, to express himself. But as Holly points out, for Christians, the connection of expression with civil rights works in reverse; rights are not meant to enable self-development and expression, but rather, the expression of the subject is used to measure their worthiness for citizenship and civil rights:

> If you can't convince people that the art work and the images that your artists create . . . are not obscene . . . because . . . it's a representation or an expression of a group of people that are always seen as a certain type of sexual entity, then you're not going to be able to convince them that we are legitimate enough to have our civil rights, because they see that all our actions, all our words, all our depictions are obscene, then, therefore, we are obscene people.[17]

The granting of civil rights—the rights to expression, self-elaboration, and development—depends on a basic optimism about those to whom the rights are granted. Christians did not seem to share this Enlightenment optimism.

The temporal trajectory in the nationalist story is one of destiny or decline, the fall of civilization, the apocalypse. While it is certainly individuals who will ultimately be saved by Christ from the apocalypse, it is not through the exercise of rights to individual expression but rather through freely willed obedience to a set of moral absolutes, through "discretion." *Discretion* was the term used repeatedly by Christians I interviewed in Washington to describe the change they wanted to see in the operation of the NEA; they didn't want to see the whole agency sacrificed, they just wanted it to show some discretion. They wanted it to show that it had internalized a set of external standards. And what standards should those be? Well, as a man I met in the gym in Tupelo, Mississippi, suggested, "The Bible would be a good guide." "Discretion," here as for Christina, is the site at which the boundary between public and private is porous, at which the openness of the liberal state can be limited by cultural and communal particularity. Run by experts, as a supposedly value-neutral meritocracy, the NEA had ostensibly refused to use discretion.

In addition to their matching but inverted spatial and temporal schemas, the Enlightenment and nationalist discourses each make high culture–low culture distinctions. In the Enlightenment discourse, reason, education, expertise, experience, empirical exploration, and representation both of the world and the psyche (the source of that much debated "expression"), as well as the familiarity with and tolerance of difference that come with such knowledge, are marked as positive terms against ignorance, fear, bigotry, and "narrow-mindedness" (PFAW membership pamphlet, 1992). Christina and many other arts advocates defended the peer review process of grant selection, the selection of grantees by experts in the particular artistic field of specialization.

Conservatives, on the other hand, lobbied for the introduction of lay people onto the selection committees. In the nationalist discourse sophistication and expertise are cast as the signs of elitism—the highness of the culture is negatively marked—and are thus contrasted with the common sense of the common man—the low gets a positive valence. Sophistication and expertise are signs of hubris, of humans thinking they can act on their own authority instead of following the rules of God: as "heartland" displaces "rural backwater" when we shift from Enlightenment to nationalist discourse, the positively valenced willingness to take a moral stance displaces the derogatory attribution of narrow-mindedness. Pastor Allen again expressed this reversal of valence by critiquing the Enlightenment discourse:

What I read between the lines . . . was that there seemed to be a homosexual agenda in some of this, and a way to go along with their agenda
that this is just another group that's being discriminated against, and
they should have a right to display their art . . . and if you're offended,
you're a narrow-minded, bigoted person . . . And that's what I resented,
that it was being used as another way to promote that broad-minded
approach that says it's just another alternate lifestyle, there's no problem,
you should be tolerant . . . it's trying to categorize anybody that comes up
with moral stances as some kind of "you're out of it."

Mrs. Allen argued that the arts issue "is almost used as a hammer, it's
a very political issue. . . . Conservatives are using it to make points with
their constituency and the so-called liberal side is using it to create an
image, or cast an image on the conservatives." Even more importantly,
framed as an opposition between Enlightenment and nationalist discourses, the arts issue was a site for a debate over the very nature of the
nation. Though in financial terms, the NEA is a trivial part of the state
apparatus, the controversy over it enabled a clear articulation of national cultural particularity (the limits set through moral stances) in
opposition to the boundariless abstract neutrality of the liberal "modern" state. In the context of this opposition, it is no surprise that the
Christian criticism of the NEA did not primarily result in discretion,
the deployment of Christian beliefs through the mechanisms of the state
(through, for instance, congressional imposition of content restrictions)
but rather worked most effectively to support the dismantling of the
state apparatus itself.

Traveling

The spatial and cultural oppositions articulated in the controversy shaped
my own research. As a lesbian and an academic, born and raised in New
York City, living in San Francisco, I lived amid the gay community and
had easy access to the arts world. I started my research at the arts service
organization for which my mother served as a board member, which
happened to be centrally involved in the legislative games over the NEA.
Through my connections there I was introduced to many other arts administrators. Arts administrators recognized me as one of their own,
opened their file drawers, and invited me to meetings; when we all camped
out in Washington for the quarterly meetings of the National Council, I

was able to join in on lunches and dinners. Through another route, an old friend, I made acquaintance with Tim Miller and attended court hearings of the NEA Four. To the extent that I wished to pursue these avenues, they were available to me.

By contrast, my arrival on the Christian scene felt much more difficult and indirect. I knew no one who could give me a free pass to the heads of Christian organizations. I contacted a few independently and conducted a few awkward interviews, aware that I could not even begin to know how I appeared to them, what questions to ask, presumptions to make. I decided to back up and try to learn more generally about conservative Christian perspectives, beliefs, and culture. I assumed that to find "real" Christian conservatives I would have to travel away from my own world. Although all I really had to do was turn on my television or walk across the street to the Christian bookstore, I enacted my presumption that Christians were "other" by going elsewhere.

I went first to a church in San Jose, one of the new "megachurches," as they have been called. Anything but backward, this church, located on Disk Drive (as in computer disk), looked like an eighties restaurant, spacious and airy, pale pink with green trim and wall-to-wall carpets. The first half of the service at this church "in the Pentecostal tradition" was a rousing rock and soul concert performed by a large band with lead and backup singers. The sermon explicitly addressed the concerns and interests (drug addiction, Lexus automobiles, the desire for economic prosperity) of its impressively multiracial (are they really multicultural if they are all members of this church?) Silicon Valley clientele. This church put together a Spiritual Warfare conference, bringing in an international array of speakers, in preparation for mounting a campaign against the Satanic forces to the north (San Francisco). Susan Harding explained this effort as part of a new theological innovation: she had heard quite a bit of talk lately of "regional demons," which appeared to justify local political activism—take over the school board to exorcise the demons.

Meanwhile I did also attend a church in San Francisco, a Baptist church that substantially fulfilled my stereotypes. I entered this church with the same kind of cover used by gay reporters at Christian conventions. I concocted a story about visiting from Stanford and being new to the area, feeling that I needed to disguise and distance myself from the urban gay culture I assumed San Francisco represented. I was greeted at the door by older women dressed in pastels and took my place in the starched and sparsely populated narrow sanctuary where I listened to a middle-aged, heavy-set, double-breasted, pink-faced preacher threatening damnation as the consequence of ecumenism and praying for "this country to be on the right path." Vehicle references here were to Fords, Chevrolets, and camels. However, despite the fact that this church seemed to match the image of Baptist churches I had seen in movies, it too, as a member of the Traditional Values Coalition headed by Lou Sheldon, was in some ways on the cutting edge politically. Sometime after my staid Sunday morning attendance, Sheldon and his following of gay protesters paid a much more raucous visit to this church (Levy).

In the spring of 1993, I took a driving trip through the south, organized primarily around stops in Tupelo, Mississippi, the home of Donald Wildmon and the American Family Association (Figure 8), and Nashville, Tennessee. My contact in Tupelo was at the newspaper: a magazine writer I knew who had done an article on Wildmon put me in touch with a local reporter. Ann, along with her friend, Tim, also a writer for the paper, were identified to me as the most progressive clique on the staff, though the paper as a whole was considered liberal for Tupelo (notwithstanding the fact that its editorial policy was explicitly antigay). I was welcomed with open arms. Files were opened, lunches and dinners were arranged, tours of town were provided. Clearly there was some hunger for what another reporter, Wayne, called an "exotic" visitor, which he translated as someone from the coasts; he said that exotics only turned up in search of Wildmon.

When Wayne and I met for dinner after his Lions Club meeting, he told me the story of the various versions of Christianity he had participated in through his life, Baptist, Methodist, Catholic, and through his current girlfriend, Church of God. He explained that while he doesn't believe every word of the Bible, he goes to church because it makes him feel good: he thinks of himself as a good person, honest and generous, a community-minded person, giving to the community by doing volunteer work with a church-affiliated charity group and by participating in the community theater. Despite Wayne's church-hopping, it was also clear that church membership was constrained by, and constituted, social hierarchies that were not quite so flexible; the old First Methodist Church, for instance, was described to me as the high-society church that the upper echelon of the newspaper management patronized (Figure

Figure 8. American Family Association, Tupelo, Mississippi.

9). No one I met at the newspaper had ever attended Donald Wildmon's church, which was located in a relatively new tract-house development (Figure 10).

While I was welcomed at the newspaper, I found that I could not, at least not in the course of a week, get any closer to Donald Wildmon than I would have been if I had stayed in San Francisco. I spoke with his brother Allen a couple of times on the phone: once from San Francisco during which call he told me not to bother to come to Tupelo, and once while I was in Tupelo, during which he submitted to a five-minute interview, interrupted by his asking me repeatedly what magazine I worked for; I had mailed him substantial documentation of my university affiliation and on this occasion explained again that I was a student working on a dissertation. His reply was to ask moments later if I was a freelancer. People in Tupelo suggested two possible explanations for this: either he doesn't know what a dissertation is, or he is just paranoid. Both ignorance of dissertations and paranoia suggest low culture habitation. I think he was sophisticated enough to know that I could not possibly be of use to him if I was not from the media and that, if I was from the media, he needed to carefully control our interaction. Being a media-watch organization, the AFA is highly conscious of media portrayals of Christians. For instance, Donald Wildmon did grant an interview

Figure 9. First Methodist Church, Tupelo, Mississippi.

to the local paper, but this interview was accompanied by an elaborate contract with regard to the format of publication and was followed by plausible threats of a lawsuit. (AFA has a legal branch and did in fact sue to stop distribution of a film about the organization called *Damned in the USA*.)

My stop in Nashville was hosted by my partner's close old friend from their days together in New York. She had become a Church of Christ Christian and had moved to Nashville (which she called the buckle on the Bible Belt, a belt with lots of buckles—Memphis, Dallas, Atlanta— if all claims are to be believed) in order to be with other Christians. She spoke of her move much the way I speak of my own relocation to the gay mecca, as San Francisco is often called: she described a sense of liberty and support in being able to say to a coworker, as she walked into a tough meeting, "Pray for me." I stayed at a hotel that was literally right next door to the headquarters of the Southern Baptist Convention, stopped in their extensive bookstore, and attended services at three different churches. This tourist approach to church-going certainly did not yield a sense of understanding; I left Nashville with the realization that I did not know what Christianity meant to the participants; I did not know how church-going structured their lives or articulated their politics. But at the same time, Christians and church attendance were

Figure 10. Lee Acres United Methodist Church, Tupelo, Mississippi.

starting to feel more familiar to me. I felt less and less that I was about to be discovered as the evil other. Attacks on gays were not a central part of any of these services and, appearing in these churches as a friend of one of the regular congregants, my presence provoked little discussion of the political controversies that motivated my attendance. But the normalization of church-going also defamiliarized my relation to the gay "community."

The last stop on my tour was Washington, D.C. I met my partner and several friends from San Francisco there. We assembled to participate in the March on Washington for Lesbian, Gay, and Bi Equal Rights and Liberty. Milling and marching amid hundreds of thousands of gays and lesbians, I found that I felt oddly "other" and awkward as I participated in the requisite performances of gay identity.

Reversal

The notion that communities are economic units, that the bonding produced by particular values serves the abstract needs of the circulation of capital, is an argument that I have been making throughout this book. But the debate over the NEA seemed to disrupt the supplementary relation between the particularity of the nation and the abstraction of the liberal state as an apparatus for the facilitation of capital flows. While I would suggest that in part this allowed the constitution of nonnational social formations for capital—gays and Christians as niche markets—the separation of nation and state through the opposition of Enlightenment and nationalist discourses was also experienced as a lack. The insufficiency of each discourse to stand on its own led both sets of speakers to make recourse to the discourse of the other. Enlightenment speakers cast themselves as nationalists and nationalist speakers cast themselves as Enlightened and as subjects of rights.

Rebecca, yet another executive director of yet another (in this case regional) nonprofit arts service organization, gave a passionate, tearfully patriotic explanation for her engagement with this issue:

> If any organization in the country gave us a feeling of national identity it was the National Endowment for the Arts. If there was any one institution that gave us pride as artists with a capital A and not theatre workers, dancers, curators, yabadee yabadee ya, it was the National Endowment for the Arts. It put us on the map, it put us on a par—I'm getting emotional [tears]—with other industries. And the fact that those political opportunists and those from the far right chose that agency to attack—they attacked its right to exist—it was emotionally devastating. They were pushing us away from the table. They were saying you do not belong in the ecosystem of the American economy and in the social structure of our nation . . . you do not belong, you do not do work that is significant to the health of our nation or our nation's children.

Obviously, she doesn't sound much like Pastor Allen. Her nation is a different one, an ecosystem, a society, an economy, rather than a community, but she does have nation and she does have family.

Although she clearly speaks her patriotism in an impassioned way, she also casts nationalist rhetoric as a deliberate strategy:

> One of our frustrations was that it was so easy for the conservatives to make a case against freedom of expression. Who is going to argue with "Why should public dollars go for a photograph that shows a man with his fist up somebody else's anal orifice?" I mean really, honestly, even here [a liberal urban area] . . . In the same 60 seconds how can you explain to someone who is a construction worker or someone who typically you wouldn't think generally goes to the symphony all the time, how can you explain to the taxi driver, in 60 seconds, the value of art. Finally, we came to the place where we realized that if we were going to be politically smart, we had to be more American than they were. And that's when People for the American Way got on board. We had to reframe the issue, not "I'm for pornography," but "I'm for freedom."

As even its name suggests, the strategy of PFAW was to promote abstract rights such as free expression as values on a par with the moral values promoted by the Christian right.

In the face of accusations of elitism, arts advocates frequently spoke of the communal value of the arts, but also of the need to instill in artists a greater commitment to and engagement with their communities, if they were to earn the popular support necessary for continued funding. One prominent Washington, D.C., arts lobbyist, Jane, for instance, envisioned a new advocacy organization that would do a public relations campaign

> to help the middle ["the American people out there, people in the square"] realize what their investment is . . . that art and cultural diversity help us understand each other the way nothing else will . . . We are a country that is based on communities and linkages of communities.

This campaign was necessary because

> As the debate grew both sides became more arrogant . . . artists felt that they were entitled to this money. The arts community from the very beginning didn't even know they were under siege, because they feel they are right and rightness of course will win. And artists by their nature are individuals: they don't cook together and they don't get together for cause.

Some arts organizations attempted to remedy the arrogance and individualism of the artists, to instill in artists the sense of commitment to and engagement with community, necessary to earn popular support for the arts. Dance/USA, the national advocacy organization for the field of dance, an organization "linked" via coalition to Jane's organization, had its 1992 national conference on "The Dance Community Working in Communities." The conference featured talks on topics such as "The New Community Paradigm," "Community Leadership," and "Presenters in Communities: Making Partnerships Work," which aimed to articulate partnerships with for-profit companies, audience development, and the development of grassroots activism for the arts in terms of community service.

There are certainly important differences between this pluralist nationalism, which founds the nation in a "linkage of communities" and that assimilates difference through a balancing of individualism and community, and the exclusionary national narrative of the one true and original organic national community deployed by conservative Christians.[18]

142 The Perfect Moment

However, in claiming "community" for artists, arts advocates rely on the nationalist notion that the nation is epitomized by the heartland, the locus of the real American community. In its own defense, NEA itself often trumpeted its "Folk Arts" program.

The most interesting appropriation, though, was of the arts and "expression," by conservative Christians. Mrs. Allen and other D.C. Christian conservatives claimed the cultural terrain as one that Christians ought not yield to "liberals," who, they asserted, had until then controlled it. In Washington I was relentlessly confronted with arts-appreciative Christians. Mrs. Allen taught art appreciation classes and had recently given a lecture on the National Cathedral that Christina's father, himself a jazz musician, had found particularly enlightening. Andrea Sheldon, Lou's daughter and a Washington lobbyist, also went on at some length about her appreciation of beautiful and uplifting artwork and especially recommended to me the National Cathedral.

Jim Ross, a staff person for a famously conservative senator, told me about his wife the artist, who had dragged him around to more galleries than he really cared to go to before they were married. (Since their children were born she had given up her artistic pursuits.) It was through her that he had learned of the narrow and prejudicial funding practices of the NEA: they only fund the avant-garde works of a small clique. Ross elaborated for me a conservative ideology of art: in his view, art should be anchored in fundamentals, such as skills in figurative representation, rather than in the "self-expression" favored by liberals. The *Heritage Foundation Backgrounder* on "The National Endowment for the Arts: Misusing Taxpayers' Money," by Robert Knight, draws out a very similar position. Like Ross, Knight lends legitimacy to this type of art by naming experts and art schools who represent, study, and teach it, and asserts that even though this is a developed and legitimate approach, artists working within this ideology are systematically rejected by the NEA.

Mrs. Allen seemed a couple of steps ahead of Ross and Knight, appropriating not only arts but "expression" for Christians:

I think for so long conservatives and Christians haven't had any sense of a cultural mandate.... And I think because there has been such a vacuum in the cultural arena these other agendas have had possession without any contest. Maybe what Christians really need to do is involve themselves in the arts and through artistic media make their contribution in such a good way that it communicates . . . express[es] our worldview, our perspective.

Displacement

Mrs. Allen recognized that, in fighting over federal arts funding, Christians had appropriated the Enlightenment discourse of rights. Anti-NEA activists were extremely successful with the rhetoric of taxpayers' rights not to be offended by government-funded art. Jesse Helms used the formula of antidiscrimination law in his legislation aimed at limiting the content of funded works. He would have prohibited the funding of "material which denigrates the object or beliefs or the adherents of a particular religion or non-religion or which denigrates, debases or reviles a person or group or class of citizens on the basis of race, creed, sex, handicap, age, or national origin." But Mrs. Allen wasn't sure that this was such a good idea:

> I feel that maybe Christians in their tactic of talking in terms of rights, my right as a Christian to have this or that, I don't know how productive that's going to be in the long run. . . . I mean we do need political involvement to say what we think. But in, in terms of saying my right, I wonder if we're just adopting the other side's tactic of "my rights."

Though she didn't explain herself, it seems clear that deployment of rights discourse by Christians would be too likely to legitimate the claims of gays and lesbians as well.

In his book on the gay market, Grant Lukenbill says, "The gay and lesbian consumer revolution is at once both Madisonian and Jeffersonian in its textbook defense of free enterprise and simultaneous call for federal government to uphold their rights in housing and employment based on sexual identity" (*Untold Millions*, 83). Lukenbill here casts rights as a form of nationalism, as the enactment by the state of the particular valuing of gays and lesbians, and this nationalism as necessary to correct and uphold the neutrality of the market. This formulation applies as well to the participants in the NEA controversy, who all seemed to need to link the powers of the state, the rights of abstract citizens within the state, to some particular conceptualization of the values embodied by the nation. So while the opposition of nationalist and Enlightenment discourses works to undermine the linkage of the two in the constitution of the nation-state, the recourse to nationalist discourse by Enlightenment speakers and to Enlightenment discourse by nationalist speakers suggests that this separation involves losses and reveals weaknesses in each discourse.

If the nation is separated from the state, the nation becomes merely another site of production and consumption; Christians are merely a market niche equivalent in many ways to gays. Although conservatives arguing against the NEA often suggested that the arts ought to be subject to free market forces, it is precisely Christians who stand to lose through the separation of their values from the power of the state. Meanwhile, if the state is separated from the nation, gays would seem to lose the protection afforded by abstraction, by the indifference of the state to communal particularity. The linkage of nation and state would seem to protect both groups in different ways from the vagaries of the market. It protects gays precisely by subjecting them to citizenship and capital, affording them certain limited kinds of recognition. It protects Christians by producing a particularized hierarchy of citizenship through its attention to the particularity of communal values. While globalized capital also attends to particular communal difference, it is not so clear that it will pick out Christians for the dominant role.

The opposition of Enlightenment and nationalist discourses clears a path for the new social formations of globalization. Christian attacks on the NEA are fundamentalist/nationalist assertions against the promotion of difference, but they are also part of a neoconservative clearing away of regulatory and distributional barriers at the site of the nation. Gay and arts community arguments for the NEA look like retrograde modernist attempts to hold onto a coherent nation-state that is the site of rights, but they are also an attempt to inhabit the state as it regulates capital flows for the production of queer communities that exceed the nation. As enthusiastic participants in a capitalism that is superseding the nation-state, gays help to undermine the structure that could support their claims to rights and Christians undermine the nation in which they cast themselves as privileged members.

In articulating the structural similarities of gays and Christians as communities organized through nonprofits and their complicity in producing a transformation of social and political structures for globalization, I hope that I have unsettled our complacent participation in articulating the binary opposition between them. The discourses each articulates are remarkably ambivalent, simultaneously promoting and obstructing the power of the nation-state and thus the expansion of capital. Linked to each other through the discourse of globalization that simultaneously produces them as autonomous, in speaking against each other for their own legitimacy as authentic communities, both miss the real site of political and economic struggle, that is, the processes of production and consumption through which they are constituted as communities.

CHAPTER FIVE

Kinship and the Culturalization of Capitalism: The Discourse of Global/Localization

In a talk presented at the CLAGS (Center for Lesbian and Gay Studies at the Graduate Center of the City University of New York) conference on Homo Economics and now published in *A Queer World*, Michael Piore argues that since the 1970s capitalism has become much more tolerant of diversity. He notes that there are more and more businesses catering to the gay market and he claims that "we are developing an entrepreneurial class, a capitalist class of our own." He says that "it is hardly in the interest of these businesses to assimilate to the dominant culture" and that "our" capitalist class "has an interest in preserving a distinctive gay culture and niche markets" ("Economic Identity," 505). Piore attributes this increased tolerance to a transformation in the organization of capitalism, from mass production, which required and produced conformity, to what he elsewhere calls "flexible specialization," which can cater profitably to niche markets.

His account of a transformation in capitalism is just one version of a story we hear relentlessly these days. The transformation is narrated in popular and business media as the emergence of "globalization" and "flexibility."[1] Within the academy, it is recounted as a transition to post-Fordism or flexible specialization or flexible accumulation or disorganized capital.[2] The popular media casts globalization as inevitable progress, as the post-Soviet world triumph of capitalism; Merrill Lynch advertisements placed in the *New York Times* in 1999, for instance, claimed, "the world is 10 years old," thus dating the birth of the world to the fall of the Berlin Wall. The academic story, only somewhat less triumphalist, is that at some point in the late 1960s or early 1970s the world economy based on Keynesian strategies of national economic management and Fordist modes of mass production and consumption went into crisis. In response to this crisis, the story goes, capitalism has had to innovate by undoing the rigidities of national economic regulation and mass production. Globalization has been one response; localization has been the other. Even as capital (and information and people) flows ever more unfettered across the boundaries of nations, traveling great distances instantaneously,[3] capitalism, we are told, attends ever more precisely to place and culture and depends ever more profoundly on the extra-economic bonds of community and kinship.

While *localization* sometimes connotes places—industrial districts, towns, regions, and even nations (as sites of culture, but not as regulatory states)—against the imagined placelessness of global capital, more often *the local* is, like the term *community*, used much more broadly to invoke particularity of identity, social relationships, and values against the abstraction of capital. The emphasis on localization in the discourse of globalization implies that capitalism is and should be aligning itself with a more organic or authentic set of social formations, formations posited in opposition to the nation, the site of the old Fordist organization of production. Where capitalism once appeared to produce homogeneity—an identity of the particular with the abstract—it is now explicitly articulated as thriving on heterogeneity.

The notion that capitalism now addresses us in our diversity and particularity has been quite seductive. For popular promoters of capitalism, who are concerned not with the emancipation of oppressed groups but rather simply with the health of capitalism, this global/local rescaling is a movement toward a more thoroughly free market. In Kenichi Ohmae's formulation, "regionalism" rationalizes the global flow of capital, liberating it from national constraints, which consist of protectionism and other irrational economic behaviors provoked by the conflictual diversity within nations, allowing it instead to accommodate (and take advantage of) the variety of local circumstances.[4] In the new "borderless" world, the unequal economic participation of diverse (internally harmonious) regions and localities will be guided by a global invisible hand that will lift the boat for all. And as globalization frees capital from the constraints of the nation, it is also celebrated for freeing individuals from the constraints of local culture to pursue the best jobs and commodities (Ohmae, *End of the Nation State*; Stanley, "For Ambitious Entrepreneurs").

The global/local rescaling is valued as well, however, by those whose claimed interest is the emancipation of oppressed groups. While noting class-based limitations on its liberatory reach, Piore claims that capitalism is now directly emancipatory of "diverse cultures." And as Avery Gordon's discussion of the business school and consulting literature on diversity management reveals, this view is enthusiastically proclaimed within corporate culture itself ("Work of Corporate Cuture"). Meanwhile, in articles in *The Post-Fordism Reader,* both Margit Mayer and Green Party activist Alain Lipietz suggest that localized economic development implies an increase in local power and autonomy and that this is good because the local is a more democratic space than larger social units (Lipietz, "Post-Fordism and Democracy"; Mayer, "Post Fordist City Politics").

Left cultural studies scholars tend to offer a more dialectical account, viewing the localization and differentiation that characterize globalization as simultaneously an increase in the power of capitalism to exploit and an opportunity for resistance. Lisa Lowe and David Lloyd, for instance, state, "Our interest is not in identifying what lies 'outside' of capitalism, but in what arises historically, in contestation, and 'in difference' to it" (*Politics of Culture,* 2). And in fact, for them, it is "the differentiating process of advanced globalizing capital" (2) itself that enables a strategy of "local and heterogeneous" (1), "'indigenous'" (13)[5] and, most importantly, "cultural" resistance, which they see as an improvement, surpassing the impossible and homogenizing class-based modes of opposition offered, they say, by Marxism (2). They contend

> that transnational or *neo-colonial* capitalism, like colonialist capitalism before it, continues to produce sites of contradiction that are effects of its always uneven expansion but that cannot be subsumed by the logic of commodification. We suggest that 'culture' obtains a 'political' force when culture comes into contradiction with economic or political logics that try to refunction it for exploitation or domination. (1)

While they imply here a greater continuity between contemporary globalized capitalism and previous forms of capitalism than the other scholars I have cited, their claim that "relatively autonomous"(4) sites of contradiction "have the potential to rework the conception of politics in the era of transnational capital" (2) depends on "a recognition of the heterogeneity of the contemporary capitalist mode of production" (2–3).[6]

In all of these cases, the moment of political optimism depends on and affirms some version of the narrative of a transformation in the nature of capitalism. And it is on this point that I want to offer a caution. In the discourse of globalization, as in the Romantic discourse of community that I described in chapter 1, a temporal narrative, a narrative of historical rupture, supplements a spatial narrative that renders community, here *the local,* autonomous from capital and from other communities or localities. While I don't doubt that capital's penetration and saturation of the globe is both more extensive and intensive, nor that corporations use innovative as well as tried and true strategies to promote that extension and intensification, the crucial change as I see it is in the story capitalism is telling about itself, or rather in capitalism as a story, a discourse.

Crucially, where the Romantic narrative, the Fordist narrative, was articulated in terms of binary oppositions—between community and society, between us (our nation) and them (competitor nations), and, I propose later in this chapter, between heterosexuality and homosexuality—this new story operates through analogic inclusion, narrating all social formations, all communities, cultures, and kinship arrangements, as equivalent but by no means equal sites of production and consumption. In this chapter, then, I explore not globalization, but accounts of globalization. I argue that the narrated discovery of the local and communal by contemporary capitalism, like prior discourses of community as the "other" of capitalism, serves to legitimate hierarchies within and among cultures, localities, and communities, even as it reincorporates precisely those communal formations that have been "othered" by capitalism. In shifting from, but building on, the binary narratives through which previous moments of capitalism were articulated, this analogic narrative enables the hegemonization of diverse social formations as capitalist formations. I will propose, in particular, that it rearticulates "the family" as a site of value and that it does so, at least in part, by inscribing gays and lesbians as families.

My examination of this discourse has been substantially inspired and informed by the recent work of J. K. Gibson-Graham and David Harvey, which has called for critical analyses of the discourse of globalization.

Gibson-Graham argues that the universal acceptance of an account of "globalization" as a new, rapid, and inevitable transformation toward a telos of the total global penetration of capital operates as a "'regulatory fiction'" (*End of Capitalism*, 2, quoting Butler). Harvey rightly points out that capital has always operated globally: "In my more cynical moments I find myself thinking that it was the financial press that conned us all (myself included) into believing in 'globalization' as something new when it was nothing more than a promotional gimmick to make the best of a necessary adjustment in the system of international finance" ("Globalization in Question," 8; hereafter referred to as GIQ). He argues that we have to view the advent of the term *globalization* as having particular political purposes and effects, especially that of deterring local and national working class and political movements (GIQ, 1).

Harvey and Gibson-Graham attempt to disrupt the proclaimed totality and inevitability of globalization by disrupting the narrative.[7] They propose to analytically break apart the capitalist monolith, with its supposedly homogenizing effects, thereby opening the space in which to imagine and thus potentially enact various resistances. Harvey suggests a shift in terminology from globalization to "a process of production of uneven temporal and geographic development" (GIQ, 8).[8] And certainly there is much ground for contesting the accuracy of a narrative of a totalizing and homogenizing global capital. Within the economic and geographic literature there is great debate over the extent to which Fordist mass production was ever hegemonic and the extent to which it has actually broken down now; many argue that Fordist productive regimes have simply been displaced from more to less developed economic locations.[9] It would be more appropriate to talk about capitalisms than capitalism. But the recognition of the global diversity of capitalism is not, I think, quite as optimistic a discovery as Harvey and Gibson-Graham would seem to suggest.

Local heterogeneity does not necessarily imply resistance to globalization, at least not based on externality to globalization either in the form of authentic original otherness or excess. Numerous specific studies show the weakness and dependence of the local within globalization. Amin and Robins question the notion that localization is a coherent or salient tendency within the current economic restructuring. They suggest we are witnessing not the end of mass production but merely increased product differentiation ("Re-emergence of Regional Economies,"

12). They argue that the phenomenon of localization is itself diverse and is contradicted by countervailing tendencies toward "transnational networks" (8). They cite Manuel Castells to argue that the most important effect of the new international economy for localities is their loss of autonomy (28). Jamie Peck and Adam Tickell mark the dependence and vulnerability of the local in relation to the global by describing the competition between, and the internal conflict within, localities that each hope to attract global capital ("Searching"). Neil Brenner and Arif Dirlik both draw on Lefebvre's work to argue that globalization and localization (fragmentation) are corollary symptoms of the same process of capitalist evolution (Brenner, "Global"; Dirlik, "Global in the Local"). Dirlik specifically criticizes the celebrations of heterogeneity and local culture found in "postmodern" and "postcolonial" cultural studies. In "The Global in the Local," he argues that "to the extent that postmodern criticism fails to account for the totality that is its context, its ideological criticism becomes indistinguishable from an ideological legitimation of the social forms that are the creation of global capitalism" (36; see also his essay, "The Postcolonial Aura").[10]

Brenner and Dirlik offer important analyses of the supplementary role that locality plays within globalization. And Harvey and Gibson-Graham usefully contest the notion that globalization is actually totalizing and homogenizing. But what is peculiar about these critiques is that they find little opposition from the dominant discourse of globalization. There do remain a few antiglobalization critics who assume that globalization implies the production of equivalence and homogeneity, a McDonaldization of the globe. Accounts such as those collected in Mander and Goldsmith's *The Case Against the Global Economy* reiterate an opposition between the local and the global, articulating local communities as threatened by and the site of resistance to globalization. And some, for instance, Russell Berman, resort to a romanticized view of the liberal nation-state, as though in the face of globalization out of control, the nation could act as the preserver simultaneously of communal history and of democratic agency. But the dominant global/localization discourse is striking precisely because it seems to acknowledge the crucial role of particular communities for and within capitalism. In fact, the focus on the interdependence of capital and culture (or community or kinship) in many popular and academic representations of globalization at first seemed to me a congenial insight. Making this interdependence of culture and capital explicit has also been a central project of left cultural studies in general and is a central project of this book.

However, the particular role of the local and communal in the discourse of economic transformation is not unproblematic. Even among those who recognize that globalization actually depends on localization, or in Storper's terms, that deterritorialization is paired with territorialization, localization is seen as the silver lining of the current transformation ("Territories"). Part of the seductiveness of the global/localization story (by contrast with the globalization as totalizing story) is that it seems such a precise answer to the yearning for community produced in the Romantic narrative. But it is too perfect an answer; it reiterates the very terms of the Romantic discourse of community. In a blatant disavowal of the transformation process it describes, most iterations once again constitute community as autonomous from capitalism and modernity.

Michael Piore is primarily known not for his contributions to lesbian/gay studies but as the author, with Charles Sabel, of *The Second Industrial Divide,* one of the most influential accounts of the current economic transformation. In that text, Piore does not articulate flexible specialization as opening spaces for diverse subcultural niche markets associated with progressive social change as he did in his CLAGS talk. Rather, the spaces within which prosperity might be created are (actual or fictive) kinship-based communities. This text has been roundly criticized on a number of fronts, for its technological determinism, for its reductive characterization and differentiation of historical periods, for lumping together very different regional economic formations, and for its overly optimistic assessment of industrial districts as a means for local or regional economic development (Amin and Robins, "Re-emergence"). I take it up not to reiterate these criticisms per se, but rather because it is elaborately symptomatic of the discourse of community that structures much of the optimistic literature on post-Fordism and globalization across the political spectrum.

Piore and Sabel make two moves in their book. The first is to claim that at this historical moment, due to a crisis in capitalism, there is an opportunity for a form of production they call flexible specialization to supersede mass production, which they claim has been dominant since the nineteenth century, when it superseded an earlier version of flexible specialization. Their second claim is that flexible specialization is politically and socially preferable to mass production precisely because it depends on and facilitates communal, local, and regional economic development.

Within flexible specialization, workers with flexible craft skills use general purpose machines to produce small batches of diverse products; this is contrasted with mass production in which deskilled workers deploy specialized machines to produce long runs of one commodity. Flexible specialization and the production of diverse short runs of products require not only skilled workers but a high degree of cooperation among firms, between suppliers and producers and distributors. Further, the success of such firms often requires what Piore and Sabel call self-exploitation. They argue that the extraeconomic communal ties that they presume can be found in the regional specificities of kinship, ethnicity, culture, and history will promote the necessary skill sharing, cooperation among firms, and voluntary contributions to the common project of economic growth. While other narrators of the postcrisis transformation of capital offer alternative causal accounts, the notion that capitalism is now more dependent on extraeconomic cultural values and relationships is quite typical. Nigel Thrift, for instance, attributes this increased dependence on personal relationships to the increased quantity and anonymity of information flowing across the globe, information that must be sorted and interpreted ("A Phantom State?").

In *Trust,* Francis Fukuyama argues that kinship ideology, as the key to trust, is crucial to the success or failure of various nations and regions within globalizing capital. He writes:

> If the ["modern"] institutions of democracy and capitalism are to work properly, they must coexist with certain premodern cultural habits that ensure their proper functioning. Law, contract, and economic rationality must . . . be leavened with reciprocity, moral obligation, duty toward community, and trust, which are based in habit[s, customs, and ethics] rather than calculation. (11, [5])
>
> Liberal political and economic institutions depend on a healthy and dynamic civil society for their vitality. "Civil society". . . builds, in turn, on the family, the primary instrument by which people are socialized. (4–5)

Fukuyama distinguishes between low-trust societies (China, France, Italy, South Korea), in which he suggests that literal kinship is overvalued and thus it is difficult for people to engage in trusting business relations on a global scale, and high-trust societies (Japan and Germany), in which the family instills values that allow trust beyond the literal family and thus allow easier participation in global capital. (The United States is a problem case for him—not categorizable as either high or low—because of a failure of family to socialize people at all.) It is notable that he describes nation-states as "societies," to which he then attributes the features of "culture," that is to say, a common set of values, practices, history. This reimagination of the nation as a culture rather than as a political-economic administrative entity is the opening move of Robert B. Reich's *The Work of Nations* as well.

The notion that the intimate relationship between community (or kinship or culture) and capital is or should be new implies that there is some prior autonomy of those spheres. The Romantic story relied on a historical discontinuity between the era of community and the era of society to establish the autonomy of community; the narrative of a reconciliation between community and society presupposes this autonomy and reproduces it. In the articulation of a historical break between Fordism and post-Fordism, the cultural communities and localities with which capital interacts are hypostatized: our production of our social formations through our participation in production and consumption is erased; both capitalism and social formations appear inevitable. Appadurai calls this phenomenon "production fetishism . . . an illusion created by contemporary transnational production loci, which masks translocal capital, transnational earning-flows, global management and often faraway workers . . . in the idiom and spectacle of local (sometimes even worker) control, national productivity and terrritorial sovereignty" ("Disjuncture," 16).

The suggestion that global/localization is new implies that globalization produces a "first contact" between capitalism and culture. Such an implication elides the effects of the first-contact narratives articulated in the anthropology of colonialism and in postcolonial development discourses, even as it builds on those effects and redeploys their discursive techniques. Colonial anthropology treated its objects of study—"primitive" cultures—as timeless, as outside of the progressive history of the west, but also suggested that they could and must join history through a process of modernization, through the salutory, if simultaneously destructive, effects of colonization. As Johannes Fabian argues, "It promoted a scheme in terms of which not only past cultures but all living societies were irrevocably placed on a temporal slope, a stream of Time—some upstream, others downstream" (17). Each "primitive culture" contacted by the more civilized west would begin its own history, moving independently across a common trajectory of development. Each culture would be at a different stage of the process but its course would be analogous to that of others.

Development discourses seemed to discover anew these autonomous differentially developed cultures and reiterated both their temporal and spatial autonomy and hierarchy, finding "the causes of underdevelopment in the Third World nations themselves" (Smith, "Satanic Geographies," 170) rather than in the history of colonialism. "Specifically, the lack of development in Third World countries was variously attributed to inadequate technology, cultural backwardness, and inappropriate and inefficient political and economic institutions" (170). And it once again offered "modernization" as the solution: "Modernization theory... argued that all modern industrial societies had undergone an established sequence of stages.... The development of Third World economies means learning lessons from the advanced industrial economies and following their lead" (172).

Despite its own claims to the contrary, "the language of globalization," as Smith argues, "represents a trenchant continuity" with both colonialism and development discourse (170). In *The End of the Nation State,* Kenichi Ohmae, for instance, proposes that regions, defined as units that are internally coherent and analogous with each other based on per capita gross national product (GNP), will follow "a fairly predictable trajectory along which priorities shift as economic areas move through successive phases of development" (21).

> This notional GNP ladder... does apply, across dividing lines defined by culture, to all developing economies.... The pull of the global economy, coupled with a growing ability to use that connection to move up along the ladder's various stages, is universal—and universally attractive. (24)

The ladder applies across cultures and yet culture does seem to correlate with the stage of a particular region on the ladder, becoming the organic source of inequality. Globalization appears merely to respond to these culturalized economic differences rather than being seen as a product of the history of colonialism or development projects.

Across the continuous history of the discourses of colonialism, development, and globalization, narratives of temporal discontinuity have been supplemented with a spatial discontinuity; in the articulation of a proliferating series of comparable—analogous—social formations, each location is rendered not only independent of historical processes but also of its present interactions with other locations. Analogy compares relationships and not objects themselves, so, as Amy Robinson points out, the SAT analogy test takes this form: A is to A's domain as X is to X's domain ("Ethics of Analogy"). Analogy serves as a particularly useful tool in the ongoing process of naturalizing the changing social formations necessary to capitalism both because it isolates each term in its own domain and because of its extraordinary power to articulate any social formation as a site of production and consumption. As Foucault says of the use of analogy in the sixteenth century, "Its power is immense, for the similitudes of which it treats are not the visible, substantial ones between things themselves; they need only be the more subtle resemblance of relations. Disencumbered thus, it can extend, from a single given point, to an endless number of relationships" (*Order of Things,* 21).

Piore and Sabel are particularly promiscuous in their deployment of analogy. They analogize their vision of local/communal economic development with historical industrial districts organized through a guild structure, with the Jewish- and Italian-dominated garment industry of the early twentieth century in New York and with craft unions in the construction trades. As Piore and Sabel describe them, entry into the craft unions is quite difficult and often based on ethnicity or kinship, but once accepted the worker has a great deal of job security because jobs are distributed through a collaboration between unions and firms. They offer as key contemporary analogues the networks of family firms in the textile-producing areas of Italy and the Japanese zaibatsu—federations of family firms (like the Korean chaebols and Indonesian "cronies" we heard so much about during the Asian economic crisis of 1997–98)— but also the Japanese kanban just-in-time inventory system, which ties a select group of subcontracting firms to a multinational corporation in a system of outsourcing tightly controlled by the multinational. Though industrial agglomerations run by multinationals might at first seem quite different from networks of family firms, Piore and Sabel explicitly compare these outsourcing arrangements with familial or ethnic groups in the structures of authority, allegiance, and exclusion through which they are organized. The biggest stretch for them is to include the regions based on new high-tech industries such as Silicon Valley; but again they manage to make the analogy by focusing on the collaborative relations between firms and universities and among the entrepreneurs who went to school together. The rearticulation of nations as cultures in Fukuyama and Reich's work would seem to make the nation yet another social formation potentially analogous to localities, regions, identity-based niches, that is, yet another in the series of sites that might be exploited by capitalism, without having regulatory power over capitalism.

The deployment of analogy in the context of global/localization discourse is not only continuous with its deployment in the discourses of colonialism and development but also with its deployment in the context of the nation-state, as Piore and Sabel's discussion of U.S. ethnic groups makes clear. Liberal pluralism has played a central role in constituting the communities now exploited by post-Fordist capitalism. And, although the global/localization discourse explicitly excludes the nation as the mediator between capital and social formations, a number of critiques of the liberal pluralist deployment of analogy, especially its deployment in the context of contemporary identity political civil rights movements in the United States, have much to offer in understanding its effectivity in globalization discourse.

As Janet Jakobsen has pointed out, analogy can function as a powerful political tool by which, as Laclau and Mouffe argue in *Hegemony and Socialist Strategy*, the articulation of equivalence among social struggles makes those struggles recognizable on the mainstream political landscape and potential allies for each other. However, Jakobsen argues, analogy also separates such movements and elides their connections with each other.[11] As Spivak argues in her discussion of Jean-Joseph Goux's analogy between the idealist predication of the subject (the subject of consciousness) and the materialist predication of the subject (the subject of labor-power), the use of analogy renders these two modes of determination independent of each other (as "exclusive predications") and complete unto themselves (each is posited as an internal continuity) ("Scattered Speculations," 154). It "excludes the fields of force that make [each of] them heterogeneous, indeed discontinuous," in itself, and "those relationships between the[m] that are attributive and supportive and not analogical" (156). It is precisely this presupposition of internal continuity and external discreteness that makes analogy problematic both in the context of contemporary social movements and in the global/localization discourse.

In "The Ethics of Analogy," Robinson takes up the common deployment of an analogy between race and sexuality. She points out that the use of the analogy "segregates race and sexuality as objects of analytic and political attention" and "presumes the normative whiteness of the gay subject." Similarly, in "Against Proper Objects," Butler examines the deployment of an analogy between feminist studies and lesbian/gay studies in the "Introduction" to *The Lesbian and Gay Studies Reader*. She argues that the analogy is used there to establish lesbian/gay studies as an autonomous field. According to Butler, the "Introduction" to the *Reader* asserts that the proper object of lesbian and gay studies is sexuality, while the proper object of feminist studies is gender. It thus suggests that sexuality and gender are discrete domains. As Butler points out, this account of feminist scholarship is certainly a slight to the extensive work on sexuality that has been done under the rubric of feminism, even while it would seem to suggest that sexual difference is not a crucial issue for the study of sexuality. Simultaneously, the analogy constitutes women's studies and lesbian/gay studies, falsely, as each internally continuous, to use Spivak's term, eliding the heterogenous "fields of force"—sexuality in women's studies, gender in lesbian/gay studies, race and class in each—and as somehow complete in itself, which it cannot be if, as Gayle Rubin and so many others have argued, gender and sexuality operate as a sex/gender system ("Traffic in Women").

The analogy articulated among various sites of production and consumption in the global/localization discourse, similarly, posits those sites as autonomous, as externally unrelated and internally continuous. Thus, when companies assess the advantage of moving factories from the United States to Mexico or Indonesia, where labor is cheaper, the use of analogy legitimates the differences between labor costs here and there. Just as Ricardo naturalized differences of national wealth in soil quality, differences in wage rates are now situated in cultural differences (their wage is to their culture as our wage is to our culture) *(On the Principles)*.

The authenticity and legitimacy of various analogized sites is often guaranteed by explicit recourse to extraeconomic ties of community and kinship. For instance, while Piore and Sabel do acknowledge that communality and kinship are often authoritarian and hierarchical, they claim that family-based community operates as a social safety net because members of a community will not allow others to fall completely out of the community. They are quite clear that the production of exclusion is as important to their communal regionalism as inclusion—they acknowledge that such a safety net can only extend to those who are already members of the community or the system would not work at all—but for community members they suggest a kind of trickle-down theory: the economic prosperity produced through a regime of flexible accumulation should mitigate the social hierarchies that these kinship- or culture-defined regions entail.

There is, however, a large body of scholarship that suggests that far from being mitigated by economic prosperity, kinship relations actively define and elaborate economic hierarchies. In her ethnographic study of Italian family firms, Sylvia Yanagisako argues that the ideologies of kinship organizing the ownership and management of the firms as well as the transmission of wealth across generations are complex hierarchies and processes that punish as well as protect various members of the kin network *(Culture and Capital)*. Sabel and Piore's "self-exploitation" often turns out to mean the exploitation of women and children. And kinship ties among firm owners position as labor those who are not members of the kin group but rather immigrants from southern Italy. Regional or local kinship networks and communities establish not one community of common welfare but rather the boundaries between classes, races, and nations.

Meanwhile, even as the deployment of analogy offers legitimating autonomy to these different classes, races, and nations, the differences among them are actively elaborated by economic processes. Scott and Storper point out that the development of high-tech industries in particular regions has depended on the availability of a highly polarized and nonunionized work force of highly trained engineers on the one hand, and on the other, impoverished new immigrants ("High Technology Industry"). But the "availability" of such communities of immigrant labor is hardly natural; as Saskia Sassen argues in *The Mobility of Labor and Capital,* the presence of exploitable immigrants is produced by the pushing of labor out of its previous locations by new investments of capital in some regions and the pull of work opportunities in others. Likewise, Melissa Wright argues that the gender hierarchies that are deployed by managers of maquiladoras are in fact discursively produced by those managers, even as they disavow their constructive role: Wright cites one maquila manager as stating, simply, "It's a cultural thing down here" ("Dialectics," 463). According to Wright, the managers differentiate women as "untrainable" (463), disposable workers whose declining value as variable capital is opposed to Mexican men, who are constructed as trainable and therefore of increasing value. This discursive differentiation is used to explain not only the high turnover rates of women in the factories—women who are employed in the lowest paying, least skilled, most physically draining and destructive work, women who are used up in their work and are ultimately seen by the managers as waste—but also the recent epidemic of murders of women workers. The women are said to be killed because they are not "good girls" and have thus exposed themselves to the "macho" behavior that is to be expected of Mexican men; the women are rendered as murdered by their own culture. The deployment of "culture," analogically constituted as autonomous in time and space, elides the fact that both the patriarchal binary gender construction and the violations of "good girl" norms by young women are incited by the presence of the maquilas (469, 471).

These deployments of kinship, race, and culture to naturalize localities are remarkable because these are the very terms that have previously been used to naturalize national formations. Adam Smith and David Ricardo articulate the nation as a social body and thus an organic, natural unit of wealth (Smith, *Wealth of Nations* and *Theory of Moral Sentiments,* Ricardo, *Principles*). Within such social bodies various participants have various specified roles to play, roles articulated and legitimated precisely by kinship. In the *Wealth of Nations,* Smith is quite clear about the necessity of what he calls "the distinction of ranks," or sometimes "race," to the economic prosperity of all (76). And, in *The Theory of Moral Sentiments,* he argues that "the peace and order of society" depend on distinctions that are wisely, naturally, based on birth and fortune rather than wisdom and virtue, the one being easy to see, the other more difficult for the "undistinguishing eyes of the great mob of mankind" to perceive (226). Smith proposes that our natural respect for wealth and power and our natural distaste, but also compassion, for poverty and wretchedness serve to maintain this "peace and order," as does our natural desire to maintain at least the existing powers and privileges of our particular subsegment of society (226, 230). Smith suggests that kinship not only provides the legitimation for necessary distinctions within the nation, but also provides the basis for our ties to the nation, for our economic patriotism, claiming that we naturally care most about those nearest and dearest, beginning with ourselves, extending to our families and immediate face-to-face communities and then by analogy to those we can imagine as like ourselves. He suggests that the natural limits of our sympathy are the limits of our nation.

For Smith, capitalist productive regimes reiterate the premodern social order. In the *Wealth of Nations,* Smith articulates his vision of the relation between various groups within society through his theory of value. He proposes a labor theory of value, arguing that what one is willing to pay for an object is the equivalent in money of the labor it would take to produce such an object. Labor for him, however, is not, or does not remain throughout the text, primarily the physical labor of the worker who produces the object; rather it is the labor of capital, which deploys a variety of means—"stock," land, and wage labor—to produce various objects, to which he credits production: "Those whose capitals are employed in any of these four ways ["cultivation of land, mines, or fisheries," "master manufacturers," "wholesale merchants," "retailers"] are themselves productive laborers" (*Wealth,* 303, [301]). Value "resolves itself" into the sum of rent, wages, and the profits of stock (*Wealth,* 51). "The whole annual produce of the labour of every country" is composed of rent, the profits of stock, and wages—each element distributed to one of the "three great, original and constituent orders of every civilized society" (*Wealth,* 217, see also 55); landlords must own land and collect rent, capitalists must deploy stock and collect profit, the working class must labor and collect wages. Capital and the capitalist subsume both land and labor, landlords and wage laborers, within a single self-regulating body. Differences between capitalists and wage laborers are either erased through the abstraction of national statistics, or naturalized, the poor being seen as organs of or parasites on the national body, as nonhuman means of production, or as a distinct race with intrinsically different, and lesser, material needs (Poovey, "Production").

While Smith and Ricardo's texts work to legitimate the nation as the unit of economic activity, when particular national formations have been inadequate to the task of assimilating and naturalizing the class differences that national (really colonialist) capitalism has produced, strategies of geographic and political reformulation are inevitably proposed or enacted. As David Kazanjian argues, Jefferson imagined the end of slavery as requiring the freed slaves to be exported to their own geographic and governmental space, a nation that would become a colony of the white United States. Spatial dispersal was also an economic and political strategy in twentieth-century United States. As I discussed in chapter 1, David Harvey and others have argued that ethnic and class conflict in urban areas was dealt with through the building of suburbs. Suburbanization not only absorbed overaccumulation but allowed various "communities" to elaborate themselves without experiencing the direct conflicts between and within themselves.

In the global/localization discourse, localities and regions are promoted as a solution to the obstacles to capitalism presented by "traditional nation states [which] have become unnatural, even impossible, business units" (Ohmae, *End of the Nation State*, 5). Localities and regions are, however, described in ways that are quite similar to Smith and Ricardo's nations. Successful capital accumulation is both the goal and defining feature of a region. Ohmae's use of GNP in addition to culture to delineate the boundaries of regions reiterates the use of statistical abstraction to assimilate the interests of all to that of capital. For both Sabel and Piore and Ohmae, firms rather than labor are the producers of wealth. Class difference is acknowledged but not seen as a problem; as Ohmae explicitly argues, economic success requires that all contribute to the production of wealth, not that all share equally in its distribution (53). Social conflict that might disrupt the flow of capital will be quieted by the rising tide of economic well-being. (In making this point, Ohmae specifically refers to "Southern blacks" in the United States, claiming that it was not civil rights legislation but rather the growth of the Southern economy that brought them social justice and economic opportunity [120].) Social difference is again abstracted, appearing only in the market as the idiosyncratic desire of individual sovereign consumers.

Even as contemporary global/localization discourse seems to be itself analogous to the discourse of economic nationalism articulated by Smith and Ricardo, in evaluating the prominent deployment of analogy in global/localization discourse, it is important not only to mark its continuity with prior deployments of analogy, but also to note its complicity with the binary logic that was a particularly prominent narrative structure in the era of Fordist nation-based mass production and consumption. Butler suggests that the analogic pairing of feminist studies and gay/lesbian studies, "a binary frame" ("Against Proper Objects," 6), excludes from consideration other relevant issues such as race and class. I think she is actually wrong here. While analogy and binary logics do work in complicity, she conflates the two much too quickly. Binary logic is a discourse of exclusion, a simple determination of us and them, a mode of self-definition by abjection. Analogics works in precisely the opposite fashion; it includes, making the other known. As Robinson argues, the analogy between race and sexuality implies that race is the known term by which we come to know, make familiar, a second, unfamiliar term. It "renders the struggle for racial justice to the past"—race is figured as a "solution (not a problem) in the American landscape" ("Ethics of Analogy"). It moves the inchoate subject (gays and lesbians) to the grounds of the (supposedly) known, choate, object; it positions the unseemly in relation to the seemly. The trace of a prior binary exclusion persists even as the formerly abject is analogically included, authorizing a hierarchy among the terms being compared.

The liberal nation-state has operated through the relentless sequencing of binary boundary making and cultural pluralist analogic inclusion of others who are then subject to oppression within the state. Nayan Shah describes a shift in the early twentieth century with regard to the construction of San Francisco's Chinatown (*Contagious Divides*). While it was at first imagined as the site of otherness, a classed, raced, sexualized, opium-infused culture that embodied the forbidden desires of a consolidating white bourgeoisie, it was later transformed into a version of that bourgeoisie itself. Likewise, as I described in chapter 1, exclusionary definitions of the nation-state articulated by conservatives operated in complicity with pluralist inclusionary strategies of liberals in the congressional debate over the National Endowment for the Arts (NEA). In arguing against the conservatives who saw the funding of gay art by the NEA as the legitimation of a homosexuality (and through AIDS-related work, a racial underclass) that should be excluded from the nation, Senator Moynihan makes an analogy between those artists now being subject to censorship and the white ethnic groups, now included, who were once upon a time subject to similar censorship (*Cong. Rec.* 26 July 1989 S 8815). In urging the inclusion by analogy of a new set of groups, he also legitimates the hierarchical positioning of those newcomers as available for exploitation; they are cast as offering, through their difference (their difference being their experience of suffering) an enrichment to the lives of the normative white, straight bourgeois subjects who are implicitly addressed in Moynihan's speech.

While the interplay of binary opposition and analogic inclusion is hardly new,[12] the shift from opposition to inclusion in contemporary globalization discourse performs a particularly potent and interesting set of transformations to the relationships between capitalism, kinship, and sexuality. The story about the relationship of kinship structures to capitalism that is familiar to us from the popular culture of Fordism is that productive extended family forms have been undermined by the emergence of capitalism and replaced by a much weaker nuclear family. The Marxist version of this story suggests that capitalism freed laboring subjects from the bonds of hierarchical family structures, allowing the formation of communities that are potentially more freely chosen. This is Marx's story of the shift from feudalism to capitalism. It is also Marx's response, in *Capital*, volume 1, to nineteenth-century concerns that child labor laws were destroying male control over family members; he suggests that this transformation will lead to a "higher" form of familial relations. This account is taken up by feminists who describe the liberation of young women from their patriarchal families as they left the family farm to go work in factories (Tilly and Scott, *Women, Work, and the Family*). And it recurs in D'Emilio's account of the formation of gay identity, which likewise involves the liberation of individuals from their kinship structures when they moved to urban centers created by/for capitalist production. D'Emilio's essay, which leans hard on Zaretsky's work, marks a return of kinship even as it describes its eclipse: Zaretsky argues that as the family was emptied of its productive role it took on instead a compensatory role as the site of reprieve from the public workplace. D'Emilio's essay would suggest this shift of production from domestic to public spheres as the moment of the creation of the ideology of "traditional family" (D'Emilio, "Capitalism"; Zaretsky, *Capitalism*).

Zaretsky and D'Emilio account for an ideological investment in "family" as a consequence of the abstraction of production from the family and the relocation of production in the newly distinct public sphere. However, the public space of capital is neither as impersonal as their accounts suggest, nor is the family the nonproductive space it appears in the ideology that Zaretsky and D'Emilio simultaneously describe and ascribe to. I would hardly be the first to suggest that kinship formations are an important site of capital: they produce variable capital, that is, labor power embodied in particular laborers; they are the site at which value leaves the circulation process, allowing surplus value to be realized, through the consumption of commodities. And the bourgeois family, at least, is the site of capital formation. On the other hand, while we may think of multinational corporations as highly abstract impersonal entities with little regard for the particularities of kinship and culture, a number of journalistic and ethnographic studies of capitalist firms large and small suggest just the reverse, that even the largest are often family businesses or businesses owned and managed by a closely knit group of people with multiplex social relationships to each other (Barnet and Cavanagh). The fetishization of family—our ability to forget that our attachments to our families are economic—occurs only in very particular political/ideological moments.

In the D'Emilio/Zaretsky narrative, the production of homosexuality through the freeing of labor seems to situate homosexuality in the public and constructed realm of capitalism, while the family would seem to represent the (ethical, religious, national) values that seem to lie outside of capitalism, to be prior to it. The homo/hetero binary places the heterosexual family on the side of use value, a use value that appears to lie outside of capital, operating as a fetish that, like the use value aspect of the commodity, hides its value, its role as a bearer of economic value (capital), by appearing to have an inherent value. Gays, freed from the family, like money-lending Jews, then seem to represent abstract value, abstract capital, itself, and become the scapegoats in a romantic or populist anticapitalism where only the abstractness of money and the impersonal corporation are seen as evil (Postone, "Anti-Semitism").

The opposition between gay identity and family that D'Emilio assumes may seem quite dated. Christians seem to have won the ideological battle over "family values" in the sense that gays have entirely given up the fight against family as an oppressive form and have instead joined it, claiming that they too enact family. And gays are addressed as a form of family in the consumer marketplace (Ikea and Volkswagen try to sell their products to bourgeois gay couples). This incorporation of gay kinship into capitalist marketing evidences an expanded notion of kinship, where the binary opposition of homo and hetero that subtended a binary opposition between capitalism/value and community/culture/values has been displaced by an analogic discourse articulating all social formations as potential sites of capitalist activity. The principle effect of rearticulating gays as family is to rearticulate the family as value rather than use value, as within rather than against capital.

However, as I have suggested, family plays a particularly central role in legitimating the localities to be included in capitalism. The task of promoting kinship as the legitimating basis for local and communal economic units, while keeping it flexible and expansive, is a delicate one, resulting in rather ambivalent and contradictory articulations in the global/localization literature. Piore and Sabel view family-proper as the positive model on which the various social arrangements analogized to it should be based. The positives are the loyalty and obedience of workers who view their employers as patriarchs and an easy flow of information among related firm owners. But they do not limit themselves to "real" families, moving by analogy to all sorts of other collectivities. Ohmae by contrast finds family too conservative, constraining the development of desires for a range of consumer goods, and seeks to replace it by the miscegenated kinship of a global melting pot. Crucial to his story of transformation from nationalism to a globalism mediated by regions is the freeing of the next generation of consumers from their familial bonds; the family, he says, is the site at which people are attached to their nations. He describes the experience of Japan, where a breakdown of family values has been happily brought on by capitalism. However, in order to achieve economies of scope, regions, though primarily defined by level of GNP, must also be coherent racially and culturally—race and culture are just the things he says find their home in the family. Fukuyama wants family values but not family itself: while he posits family as the site of socialization in trust, a trust necessary to doing business with nonfamily members, he says that an overinvestment in family will train people to not trust those who are not family members and thus overly constrain potential business relationships.

The resort to kinship is not altogether surprising in this moment in which it is a commonplace if not fully accurate claim that nation-states have been or are being disempowered as actors in global capital. In political theory and anthropology the common story—a story iterated in classic form by Engels—is that kinship provides the social structure in societies that do not yet have a state *(Origin of the Family)*. This is a developmental narrative in which modern state formations are seen as surpassing kinship as the technology for social and political cohesion.

However, as my reading of Smith and Ricardo suggested, kinship is quite central to nation formation. Alys Weinbaum has argued that even Engels recurs to an anachronistic "barbarism" as the source of the positive aspects of German nationality, which is to say he gives kinship a role in what was for him a contemporary state-centered social formation ("Engels' originary Ruse"). And Foucault's work, while with one hand suggesting that sexuality displaces kinship as the basis for social organization, with the other (and a little help from Stoler) more persuasively suggests that discourses of sexuality and kinship actually operate together to produce white European national bourgeoisies in relation to raced colonial others *(History of Sexuality)*. However, in the global/localization literature, nations do not appear as modern but rather as premodern obstacles to development and so the discursive link between kinship and nation, which seemed to provide such a nice model for the naturalization of new social formations turns out to be quite problematic.

The troublesome connection of kinship to nationalism provokes a particularly exquisite ambivalence about kinship and family in the representations of the success and failure of the Asian economies. In fact, I suspect that the focus on kinship may well have been motivated by the "Asian miracle." In these texts, all written prior to the "crash," the virtues of Asian family values form an important reference point in an attempt to make the rapid "development" of a number of Asian economies into a model that the already "developed" West might learn from. The crash has provoked a reassessment in the business press. As an article in *The Economist* says,

> Now some of the sins laid at the doors of the region's economic systems look suspiciously like Asian values gone wrong. The attachment to family becomes nepotism. The importance of personal relationships rather than formal legality becomes cronyism. Consensus becomes wheel-greasing and corrupt politics. Conservatism and respect for authority become rigidity and inability to innovate. Much vaunted educational achievements become rote-learning and a refusal to question authority. ("Asian Valves Revisited," 25 July 1998, 23)

This article goes beyond the critique of Asian values that it cites, criticizing the notion that there really are particularly Asian values; it suggests that the promotion of such an idea by Asian leaders was partly a postcolonial backlash against the West and partly an attempt to produce collaboration among Asian nations in an economic and political competition with the West. And certainly Suharto's reference to family values during Indonesia's negotiations with the International Monetary Fund seems an instrumental nationalist ploy. (According to the *New York Times,* he cited Indonesia's 1945 constitution, which says, "The economy shall be organized as a common endeavor based upon the principle of the family system" [Mydans, "Crisis Aside"].) Whether portrayed as sincere or instrumental, the representation of family values as a form of nationalist resistance to "open" financial and commodity markets (or as resistance to cutbacks in the social welfare practices that these Asians mistakenly think are owed to workers who enact obedience and loyalty based on their understanding of employers as kin) suggests that the Western business press is not so sure that family values are good for globalization after all. An article in the *New York Times Magazine* interprets Asian values as "traditional values":

> These Asian values aren't unique to Asia. When I was a kid growing up in the American South, I used to hear constant paeans to "Southern values." Our families were bigger and warmer than those of the cold dreary Yankees. We were more deferential and polite... European immigrants used to say many of the same things... What united all these traditional cultures was their relative lack of experience with a modern market economy... Asia, for reasons that have nothing to do with Western imperialism and everything to do with its own social and economic development, will look more and more like western Europe and North America.... It's called progress, and it is, despite many shortcomings, a good thing. (Mead, "Asia Devalued," 38–39)

While contemporary global/localization discourse is critical of family values where it implies nationalism or an inflexible valuing of a particular set of relationships, I have shown that these authors do like the idea of kinship as an organic force constituting—naturalizing—the boundaries and internal coherence of political-economic formations, and they redeploy it to legitimate the communal (regional, local) economic units they promote. The slippage from family to kinship to various fictive kin relations or modern substitutes for kinship serves to legitimate a broad array of exclusive and hierarchical economic communities; through the analogy with kinship, they are posited as expressions of authentic human relationships.

In marking a slippage from kinship to fictive kin I am in some sense making a false distinction. As Gayle Rubin points out in her classic essay entitled "The Traffic in Women," "A kinship system is not a list of biological relatives. It is a system of categories and statuses that often contradict actual genetic relationships" (169). She goes on to use Lévi-Strauss to argue that kinship systems not only organize relations within but also between social groups. The global/localization texts, which simultaneously center and decenter family, working by analogy from family to a wide array of fictive kinship arrangements, invest in the discourse of family/kinship as a powerful mechanism for generating social relationships that facilitate the flow of capital but simultaneously keep the nature of those relations quite flexible. The ambivalence, or flexibility, about family and kinship articulated through this use of analogy is an expression of the fundamental contradiction between use value and value—between the need for value to be embodied in particular concrete use values and its need to move freely among such embodiments. The discourse of global/localization mobilizes family as a mechanism simultaneously vigorous enough to motivate stable adherence to particular social formations and particular practices of production, consumption, and capital formation and flexible enough to allow those formations and practices to vary as needed.

Kinship relations, which lie at the heart of global/localization discourse, are discursively constituted and constrained performances of and for production and consumption. And it is clear that in relation to the flexible discourse of flexibility, that is, the global/localization discourse, no one particular kinship strategy—be it a homophobic family values movement or a gay marriage movement—will necessarily provide a space of contestation against the predations of capitalism. On the other hand, what the deployment of kinship by capitalism makes clear is that, as Gayatri Spivak has bluntly stated, "The complicity between cultural and economic value-systems is acted out in almost every decision we make" (Spivak, "Scattered Speculations," 166). In contesting capitalist exploitation, then, we must trace this complicity and evaluate our cultural practices, our communal practices, for the complex ways they simultaneously enable but can also be enacted to disable the circulation and expansion of capitalism. Such tracings and evaluations can enable us to imagine new opportunities for political and economic intervention and to articulate effective alliances.

EPILOGUE

What Is to Be Done?

At the University of Arizona, where I currently teach in women's studies and serve as the head of the Committee on Lesbian/Gay/Bisexual Studies, the gay "community" is highly organized: in addition to the academic unit, in which I am primarily involved, there are organizations for undergraduates, graduate students, staff, librarians, and law students. Most of these groups have e-mail listservs; the staff list is the most active and reaches the widest audience, with participation not only of staff but also faculty and students. Quite frequently, postings circulate on these lists that ask us to call Budweiser or some other corporation in support of their gay advertising campaign or announce that some airline has instituted domestic partner benefits (for its U.S. employees). Such postings generally produce no response beyond extensive recirculation (which appears to indicate support). On the other hand, when I post notices about the activities of our campus Students Against Sweatshops group or notices about anti-World Trade Organization protests convened by the Coalition to Organize Graduate Students, someone will inevitably complain about the posting of "irrelevant" or, worse, "politically correct" materials on the list. When members of the Committee on LGB Studies signed a resolution offered by Students Against Sweatshops, the president of the university responded that while he could understand some of us supporting the resolution as individuals, he could not understand and was dismayed that we would identify ourselves on this issue with the gay community, which he feels he has supported. And he has in fact had friendly meetings with some of the gay organizations on

campus, has explicitly affirmed his support for the university nondiscrim-
ination policy, and has agreed to consider domestic partnership benefits. So, while the recognition of gay people in advertising, nondiscrim-
ination policies, employee associations, or "studies" programs is sensible
for liberal university administrators and widely appreciated by GLBT
people, the assertion—one that I hope this book has substantiated—
that sexuality or even, specifically, gays and lesbians in the United States
are implicated in sweatshop labor or world trade policy violates common sense.

This common sense might simply be read as commodity fetishism:
gay commodities and consumers are visible and valued while producers
and the social relations of production are not. But the replies on the
listserv and by the university president go beyond a failure to recognize
the pertinence of the international division of labor to the constitution
of U.S. gay identity. And they are not merely correct in presuming shared
appreciation of the recognition of gays as consumers, employees, or objects of knowledge, while criticizing the identity-political presumption
that gay people would share "political" goals or views or interests. In de-
lineating the "political" (and the economic) as that which is not shared,
the replies oppose a gay public culture to the "private" political and economic views of gay individuals. They thus reproduce an opposition between gayness as a cultural category and economics or politics as indifferent to sexuality. The opposition between culture and economy, against
which I have been arguing throughout the book, reappears—mobilized
quite specifically to quiet anticapitalist activism—in the practices and
opinions of the individuals with whom I share a listserv or sit in meetings and in the presumptions of administrators who run a university
that favors and is familiar with the development of programs and de-
partments based on identity and discipline.

I opened this book with the hope that it might clear a space for creative thinking about the constitution of collective action, that it might
contribute to movements for social change. Between that opening and
this conclusion, I have told what might be taken to be a very depressing
story, one that might seem to close off spaces of activism by implicating
community, so often the imagined basis for activism, in capitalism. Over
the course of the book, I have identified numerous technologies by which
community is constituted as the site of values, of fetishized identities, of
culture: temporal narratives of the supersession of community by society,

spatial narratives that locate communities as discrete from each other, structural narratives of binary opposition and analogic inclusion. I have argued that these constitutions of community as precisely autonomous from capital enable community to operate as a supplement to capital, and that community thus enables exploitation. In light of this reading it would certainly seem that the two primary strategies of resistance offered to date—investment in particular local or identity-based communities and the proliferation and celebration of heterogeneity—are inadequate insofar as they participate in the constitution of community as autonomous from capital and aid capitalism in the elaboration of the differences it needs.

However, in describing the relation between community and capital as supplementary and in describing capitalist production and consumption as performative, I have also held out the possibility that productive participation in collective action need not only facilitate capitalism but might also be articulated as resistance or even opposition to the flows of capital. As a supplement, community is potentially disruptive and displacing, as the examples, scattered throughout the book, of conservative, nationalist, patriarchal communities make clear. It is this potential that drives capitalism to work so relentlessly and so explicitly to constitute community. The performativity of production, of the production of communities, means that a great deal of agency resides with the producers of community to make our collectivities more disruptive rather than less. In order to do so we must read the social relationships in which our communities are imbricated and assess the implications of our political goals and strategies, of the actions we do in fact all take all the time; and we must then reshape those goals, strategies, and actions with this, inevitably partial, awareness in mind. Over the course of this book I hope to have offered some useful particular readings as well as reading strategies that might be usefully appropriated in diverse contexts.

Deployed as what used to be called "an analysis," the kind of critical theoretical work offered here is a resource for imagining, articulating, and constituting disruptive or displacing social formations, active collectivities, that do not depend or insist on the closures and oppressions of community or pretend that difference in itself is resistance. Depressing as my story may be, it is a powerful tool for just such imaginative acts. Articulating connections among different sites, the analysis I offer here is meant to be expansive, generative, and open rather than totalizing or reductive. It can enable us to imagine ourselves as living in a large interconnected world and breathe some air into our identities and communities, allowing their definitions to shift. It can, for instance, be deployed to counter the quietistic commonsense delimitations of the "interests" of gays and lesbians at the University of Arizona.

I still feel the need, as I did when I worked at Theatre Rhinoceros, to carve out institutional and representational space for queers. But my strategy, my sense of what this means, has changed; I now work to build a queer studies program that is not analogous to Women's Studies or the various ethnic studies and area studies programs but is instead articulated with such programs through projects ("Sex, Race, and Globalization"; "Mexican and Chicano Masculinities"; "Labor in the Americas") that, in placing production at the center of their analyses, require collaborations across identities and disciplines. As I participate in gay communal spaces made possible by the university, I use my intellectual and institutional resources to encourage gay participation in Students Against Sweatshops protests, not only by posting e-mail announcements but by making the effort to articulate our dependence on sweatshop labor, our implication in sweatshop labor, as we constitute our gay community through consumption. Likewise, I deploy but also work to transform gay identity and community in arguments for queer participation in graduate student organizing efforts and in protests against the World Trade Organization, the International Monetary Fund, and the World Bank. Recognizing that sexual freedom is constrained by structural adjustment policies that undermine health care and welfare provision in the United States and elsewhere—policies pursued through both ideological elaborations and repressive enforcements of normalized family values and marriage—I explain our complicity in these policies as we pursue marriage rights and domestic partner benefits, eagerly accepting private responsibility for social welfare. But at the same time, I note that the cost of neoliberal economic policies is that gay people need the access to health care that domestic partnership benefits would provide (at least to those of us who have been adequately domesticated) and that those domestic partner benefits we might gain locally—for instance, through ordinances in San Francisco, Los Angeles, and Seattle that require businesses that do business with those cities to offer domestic partner benefits—could be voided if the WTO restricted for municipalities, as it already does for nations, such constraints on government procurement contracts. And so, while I have argued for queer participation in protests against the agents of such policies, I have also suggested that the gay staff organization on my campus might gain leverage for domestic partner benefits by collaborating with the Coalition to Organize Graduate Students.

None of these efforts is pure or perfectly oppositional to capital flow and none involve a complete abandonment of identity or community. Rather, they are highly contingent efforts, responsive to particular constraints and opportunities, to recognize and articulate identity and community differently, to act on a new sense of how I and my communities come to be, on whom we depend and who depends on us. Progressive appropriations of our complicity in capital—that is, efforts to contest "common sense" for justice—involve not only "a politics of memory and generation" that would remember "those no longer" and "not yet *there*," as Derrida calls for, but also a politics of scale and space that would refigure our understandings of *here,* of who is here with us. Such a politics involves strategic decisions to scale up or down, seeking what seem to be highly particular personal or cultural freedoms by contesting world trade policy or by addressing what seem to be larger or distant issues such as the exploitation of workers in sweatshops through local identity-based protests. But, more importantly, such a politics requires transforming the very meanings of scales and spaces, redefining what counts as local, what counts as global, what we understand to be the boundaries and contents of our bodies, communities, and nations.

I do not want to make overly optimistic claims for local action, as too many scholars have done. Nonetheless, I would argue that in tracing the complicity, the relationships, among communities, between local and global, between particularity and abstraction, I have shown not that there are no sites of potential resistance but a great proliferation of sites of weakness, of contradiction and crisis, in the circuits of capital and that those sites are us, in our desires and discontents. In the face of globalization the most important work that we can do—and it is work we can all do—is to mobilize such desires and discontents for social change by evaluating the personal and institutional practices in which we are each inevitably engaged, bring our abstract analyses to bear on the particular relations by which we are constrained and which our own performative actions produce, and struggle to rearticulate those relations and practices.

Acknowledgments

My first and most profound thanks are due to my parents, Ellen R. Joseph and Lawrence M. Joseph. This book argues for the inextricability of materiality and signification. Their tremendous financial generosity is inseparable for me from their emotional generosity, their fundamental faith that if I was doing it, it must be worth doing. Their support enabled me to have the self-confidence as well as the material means necessary to carry through this project, which took many more years to complete than any of us anticipated.

My work on this book has also been supported by a Rockefeller Fellowship at the Center for Lesbian and Gay Studies at the Graduate Center of the City University of New York; by a residency at the Bunting Fellowship Program at the Radcliffe Institute for Advanced Study at Harvard; and by a Junior Faculty Professional Development Sabbatical from the College of Social and Behavioral Sciences at the University of Arizona.

This book has been in process for more than ten years. The final product is a collaborative one, shaped by intensive and extended interlocution with a shifting but also remarkably persistent array of intellectual comrades. During my first five years of work on this project, when it was still becoming a dissertation, Leerom Medovoi and Marcia Klotz offered me the gift of sincere enthusiasm; in a very visceral and immediate way, the dissertation was written, chapter by chapter, and draft after draft, for them. Their contribution was matched only by that of Alexandra Chasin; Alex's relentless encouragement, radiant mind, great command of the craft of writing, and ability to make a sensible plan of action are among her array of contributions. Also crucial in those years was the labor of my colleagues in the Modern Thought and Literature Program at Stanford: Benjamin Robinson, Shaleen Brawn, Anahid Kassabian, Erin Carlston, and Kelly Mays (honorary MoTho member). Jane Goldman provided the love and stability that allowed me to finish the dissertation.

I first thought through Marx with Eric Schocket. We worked together in a reading group led by Regenia Gagnier, who was, throughout my years at Stanford, a great inspiration and a mentor. My essay, here chapter 2, on the performativity of production is in large part a product of the fortuitous simultaneity of that Marx reading group with a reading group on Judith Butler's *Bodies That Matter* organized by Morris Kaplan; I am very grateful to all of the members of both groups. I am also indebted to Neil Smith and the *Social Text* collective, which originally published the essay, for their wise suggestions.

There is no adequate way to thank Russell Berman, my principal dissertation adviser, who engaged me over the course of many years in the serious, persistent, and respectful debate that provided the basic questions motivating this project. Mary Louise Pratt guided me through graduate school with wisdom and care. It has been a privilege to have Alice Rayner as a teacher, editor, sounding-board, colleague, and friend. Sylvia Yanagisako helped me to plan and prepare for my ethnographic undertakings, but also pushed my thinking to the next level by regularly reminding me that the great new discoveries of those of us in Modern Thought were the oldest of hats for anthropologists. Susan Harding, with great charm and wit, offered a bridge to the study of Christian fundamentalism, sharing her deep understanding not only of Christians but also of the fieldwork experience.

This kind of book would not have been possible without the great generosity of the people who populated the "fields" in which I did ethnographic research. Very busy people spent substantial amounts of time with me. People with important agendas at risk trusted me with information and shared with me that most valuable of resources, their people— friends, colleagues, and family members. For reasons of confidentiality most cannot be thanked by name, but I want them to know that I do deeply appreciate their help. There are, however, a few that I can and would like to mention. Adele Prandini not only provided me with vast swaths of her own valuable time and wisdom, not only gave me complete access to the goings-on, the files, the human resources of Theatre Rhinoceros, she also took me in with great warmth and caring as a friend. Elliot Figman, Jim Sitter, and Jane Hill opened many doors for me and welcomed me into their worlds, ensuring that my travels were both productive and pleasurable. Sarah Rosen opened her home and thus Washington, D.C., for me.

The journey from dissertation to book has been a long and substantial period of intellectual and professional development. Janet Jakobsen has been crucial on both fronts: many of the ideas offered here were thought with her and I'm not sure how I would have either survived these years or gotten this book done without her. While in New York, I had the extraordinary pleasure and privilege of studying Marx with David Kazanjian and Alys Wienbaum; the reading of Marx's theory of value, presented here in chapter 1, is due to their intelligence but is not their fault. In Boston, David and Josie Saldaña saw me through the final thinking and writing of this book. David, Josie, and Alys have provided me not only with their very different kinds of brilliance and knowledge but also with a crucial sense of shared intellectual and political goals and orientations.

My sanity (such as it is) as well as my thinking has been profoundly enhanced through long and important friendships with Ira Livingston, Amy Robinson, Molly McGarry, Elizabeth Freeman, and Sallie Marston. Galen Joseph has turned out to be a worthy and generous colleague as well as a loving sister and friend. The beautiful and intelligent artwork of Gillian Brown was a crucial inspiration for the structure of chapter 3, and a timely dinner conversation with Geeta Patel and Kath Weston gave me the courage to do right by my ethnographic materials. Zoe Hammer-Tomizuka and Caren Zimmerman, my students at the University of Arizona, have offered great insight, enthusiasm, and, most importantly, friendship. During the last year of writing Dereka Rushbrook was a wise consultant, offering knowledge, a patient ear, and great editing advice. As a reviewer for University of Minnesota Press, Geraldine Pratt offered crucial feedback and support. And I am grateful to Julia DuSablon for the light touch and perceptiveness of her copyediting.

Thank you.

Notes

Introduction

1. Edward is a pseudonym. When I use full names I am using the person's real name; when I use first names only, those names are pseudonyms. While all the people I spoke to were proud of their sexuality and of their participation in Theatre Rhinoceros—and in fact some expressed an explicit desire to have their real names used—I have nonetheless chosen in most cases to protect my ethnographic subjects from my own sometimes critical portrayals with pseudonyms and vagueness about other potentially identifying features. I have used full real names only for those individuals whose public leadership roles at the theater would make them extremely difficult to disguise.

2. *The AIDS Show* was actually the second show produced by Rhino dealing with AIDS. A collection of skits and scenes, it was first produced in 1983 and then again in a revised version in 1984. The first version toured and was the topic of a public television program. The show was a tremendously important moment for all who participated as well as for many audience members; it was described to me as the first frank discussion of AIDS that the participants had experienced and was a remarkably upbeat and positive response to the crisis. The show brought to the theater many artists who then became regular participants in other shows over the next few years.

3. The fact that this meeting included no people of color and that no one discussed this fact at all, let alone treated it as an emergency, is rather notable for 1992 in San Francisco.

4. In a play by Doug Holsclaw produced a couple of years later, one character says to a man who is dating a younger man: "It'll never work out. You're gay and he's queer."

5. The literature on the modernity of the nation is a rich and extensive one. I have found Homi Bhabha's introduction to *Nation and Narration* particularly helpful in understanding the relationship of the nation-state to modernity, an issue I address further in chapter 4.

6. See, among others, Sylvia Walby's *Theorizing Patriarchy; Woman-Nation-State,* edited by Nira Yuval-Davis and Floya Anthias; *Between Woman and Nation,*

edited by Caren Kaplan, Norma Alarcon, and Minou Moallem; Deniz Kandiyoti's "Identity and Its Discontents: Women and the Nation"; and Ann Laura Stoler's *Race and the Education of Desire.*

7. Arjun Appadurai calls this conceptualization of community, and specifically, of ethnicity, "the primordialist thesis." He contests this thesis, arguing that contemporary ethnicity is "a historically constituted form of social classification that is regularly misrecognized and naturalized as a prime mover in social life" (*Modernity at Large,* 140). He argues that "Western models of polical participation, education, mobilization, and economic growth, which were calculated to distance the new nations from their most retrograde primordialisms, have had just the opposite effect" (141).

8. I am obviously using the term *liberalism* quite broadly here, including the full range of liberalisms from classic formulations (Locke), to all sides in the contemporary debates that have occurred in the wake of John Rawls's work between (procedural) liberals and communitarians, to Habermas. While some participants in the communitarian/liberalism debate and some Habermasians would object to my characterization of them as liberal, it seems to me that they share many fundamental presuppositions. Most importantly, while they disagree about where the public/private line should be drawn, they all agree that such a line should be drawn somewhere. That is, while they disagree over whether individual rights or the common good should take precedence, they all accept the fundamental opposition between these categories. In a sense, given the assessment of even classical liberalism as implicitly communitarian, it seems to me that the key difference between them is that communitarians explicitly acknowledge and positively value the normativity that is implicit and disavowed in procedural liberalism. I find this debate frustratingly repetitive; the two positions endlessly evoke each other, presenting, as they do, two unacceptable options. And as Iris Marion Young argues, both positions rely on a logic of identity, a metaphysics of presence (*Justice,* 229). (While some communitarians articulate a notion of social construction of subjects, they tend, as Young points out, to posit these subjects as constructed in common or symmetrical and stable ways that enable transparent intersubjective communication. Craig Calhoun also makes this point in his critique of communitarianism ["The Public Good"].) The way out of this cyclical debate is through a Marxist poststructuralist theory of social processes as ongoingly productive of differentiated and dynamic subjects. This is the view that I will develop throughout the book. Wendy Brown also develops such a position in *States of Injury* (see especially "Rights and Losses"). And likewise Chantal Mouffe's work, which I will discuss later, develops such a position, though she remains more within the frame of liberal theory than either Brown or I do, and in fact explicitly argues for the positive value of the public/private distinction.

9. See, for instance, Carole Pateman's "Fraternal Social Contract."

10. Habermas weds liberalism to critical theory, embedding his argument for a public sphere of communicative consensus-producing rationality in a narrative of modernization in which the life-world of communicative-rationality stands in opposition to the encroaching instrumental-rationality of the systems (capital and state) of modernity. He also recognizes the "linguistic turn" in philosophy, a turn away from Enlightenment notions of subjectivity as presocial and truth as singular and transparent. He thus posits the conditions for consensus (as well as consensus itself) as an achievement and not as the natural product of human nature or rational communication (*Theory of Communicative Action*).

11. Related critiques of Habermas have also been offered by Jakobsen ("Deconstructing the Paradox of Modernity") and Samantrai *(Alternatives)*. Fraser counters the universalization of particularity implicit in Habermas's version of the liberal public sphere by offering instead a prospect of an array of counterhegemonic publics ("Rethinking the Public Sphere"). Seyla Benhabib (in *Situating the Self*) has likewise tried to redeem the Habermasian approach while taking these feminist critiques into account. The limits of such a project have been articulated by Judith Butler in "Contingent Foundations" and elsewhere.

12. Thanks are due to Mary Louise Pratt for reminding me of the positive accomplishments of identity politics in a moment when my own view had narrowed to the negative.

13. In "A Manifesto for Cyborgs," Donna Haraway narrates the impact of this literature on (white) academic feminism. Christina Crosby also offers an account of the transformation of feminism and feminist theory in "Dealing with Differences."

14. This kind of inquiry has been theorized as "strategic essentialism" by Gayatri Spivak.

15. This sentence and my introduction more generally are indebted to Sedgwick's introduction to *Epistemology of the Closet*, in which she presents a set of "axioms," which, as it turns out, are all statements of what it is not possible or preferable to know in advance.

16. For various versions and interpretations of the argument over the value of poststructuralism for feminism and other progressive movements see (among others): Kirstie McClure's "On the Subject of Rights: Pluralism, Plurality and Political Identity"; Seyla Benhabib's "Feminism and Postmodernism: An Uneasy Alliance" in *Praxis International*; Judith Butler's "Contingent Foundations" published as a counter to Benhabib in *Praxis International*; Linda J. Nicholson's collection *Feminism/Postmodernism,* which includes essays by Benhabib, Fraser, and Butler among others; the essays collected in *Feminists Theorize the Political,* edited by Butler and Joan W. Scott, which individually and collectively make an argument for the usefulness of poststructuralism for feminism; and most recently the debate between Butler and Fraser in *Social Text.*

17. Jakobsen offers a useful critical reading of Young and a comparison of Young with Laclau and Mouffe (*Working Alliances,* 156–63).

18. I explore the problems with the deployment of analogy at length in chapter 5. Jakobsen has also offered a critique of Laclau and Mouffe's theorization of equivalence (*Working Alliances,* 159–60).

19. In fact, communitarian discourse seems to have displaced real leftist critique. I'm thinking here of Cornel West, the gay marriage movement, etc. West's defection from Marxism to communitarianism is widely recognized. For an excellent critique of West's communitarianism, see Nicholas De Genova's reading of West's *Race Matters* ("Gangster Rap and Nihilism in Black America").

1. The Supplementarity of Community with Capital

1. I will take up the spatial account and the interrelation of temporal and spatial accounts in chapters 4 and 5.

2. I am not alone in remarking on the relentless invocation of Tocqueville. Barber, for instance, comments that "few political speeches can come to an end nowadays without a reference to Tocqueville and his affection for civil society and local institutions" (Barber, *A Plan for Us*, 13).

3. For a relatively benign localist argument, see Barber (45), who uses Tocqueville to promote the development of public spaces that would support a public sphere of conversation among citizens. Rather more perniciously and typically, in "All Community Is Local," William A. Schambra uses a Tocquevillian image of a small town to argue against national social welfare programs.

4. Foley and Edwards make a similar argument. They note that Tocqueville has been "selectively misappropriated" by neo-Tocquevillians such as Robert Putnam, whose work they critique and I will discuss below ("Escape from Politics?" 550–51). They argue that "Tocqueville's argument is not about the 'political culture' of American democracy, as some have assumed, nor is it about a national genius for creating civil associations, as many have argued. On the contrary, Tocqueville argues that America's associational life springs from the twin social and political conditions of the new nation." Those conditions, they say, are "the relatively egalitarian character of American society" and "political freedoms" and that Tocqueville viewed these conditions as problematic ("Escape," 554).

5. While, for Tocqueville, the tendency to associate promoted by democracy can lead to factions and to political destabilization, that potential for destabilization is corrected by the equal freedom of all to associate and thus contain those factions that would cause trouble (Foley and Edwards, "Escape," 555).

6. There are, of course, significant differences among these texts: they are positioned differently on the political spectrum; and they are divided between earlier texts, in which the principle problems of modern society are said to be conformism and alienation, and later texts, in which the central problems are insufficient conformity to social norms, as evidenced by crime, drug use, single parenthood, and even poverty. What they share, or rather, what these texts as a group construct and evidence is a particular way of moving from a temporal account of the relation between community and society to a structural account of that relation applied to the present.

7. See also articles by Alan Wolfe ("Is Civil Society Obsolete?") and Jean Bethke Elshtain ("Not a Cure All") in Dionne's *Community Works*.

8. Williams begins *The Country and the City* with an amusing account of what he characterizes as an "escalator": from the perspective of the early 1970s, community was destroyed sometime after WWI, but from the perspective of the 1930s, organic community seemed to have disappeared just before WWI, but then earlier authors trace the ending of community to the 1860s, and moving further back in time, Williams points out that Hardy locates a lost community in the 1830s and so on, back to the Greeks (see especially chapter 2, "A Problem of Perspective").

9. Bender provides a systematic and thorough review of sociological and historical theories of community, which I do not do here. As I do, Bender offers a critique of the Romantic narrative that locates "community" as a premodern social formation preceding "society." He brings various historical evidence to bear to argue that community, as a quality of experience, persists alongside society. I argue that community, as a discourse and practice, not only persists but is actually produced within and necessary to modern society.

10. The term *Romantic,* while a technical term for the artistic and philosophical reaction, emblematized by Burke and Wordsworth, that occurred at the turn of the nineteenth century, has come to stand for the nostalgic retrospective yearning for lost idealized community, no matter where in history such yearning may appear, and I will use it in this latter way throughout the book.

11. Bell is particularly clear on this point. He elaborates the autonomy of values from value as a division of society into discrete domains, the economic, the political and the cultural, which act upon each other in different ways, and with regard to which one might take up different political orientations: he himself claims to be a socialist with regard to the economy, a political liberal, and a conservative with regard to culture *(Cultural Contradictions).*

12. Skocpol offers a dissenting opinion, arguing that in fact government is an important partner to nongovernmental efforts. Beginning, inevitably, with an invocation of Tocqueville, she actually uses Tocqueville to argue not for the independence of community from both the state and economy, but rather to argue for the interdependence of democratic civic associations with a strong national state. She also argues, against the trend, that nongovernmental efforts are not best when smallest and most local, pointing out that many of the most important organizations operating at local levels are actually chapters of national federations ("Don't Blame Big Government").

13. Putnam's statistical arguments for the decline of associational life in the United States ("Bowling Alone") have been persuasively refuted by Ladd *(The Ladd Report).*

14. Putnam may overly constrain his own claims: in an article critical of Putnam's focus on face-to-face organizations, Debra Minkoff argues that national social movement organizations do in fact also generate social capital. If Minkoff is correct, then the hegemonizing effects of the organizations Putnam celebrates would also be found in a much wider range of types of organizations—national organizations and political organizations as well as bowling leagues ("Producing Social Capital").

15. Spivak's argument draws on Diane Elson's reading of Marx's theory of value as a "value theory of labor," rather than a labor theory of value. Elson argues that the significance of Marx's theory of value is that it points out that, under the capitalist mode of production, labor is determined by value (rather than value by labor) ("Value Theory"). This reading is important in that it suggests that labor is not the material ground or origin of value or capital. I explore the implications of this alternative reading further in chapter 2.

16. Harry Braverman's *Labor and Monopoly Capital: The Degradation of Labor in the Twentieth Century* is a compelling update of the story.

17. I provide such a critique in chapters 2 and 5.

18. This mobility of labor is described by Sassen *(Mobility of Labor and Capital).*

19. "Particular Voices" is the title of an exhibit of photographs of gay and lesbian writers presented by the New York Public Library in 1998 (Giard, *Particular Voices).* I found the poem *Keeping Things Whole* by Mark Strand on the subway. Barnes and Noble sponsors "Poetry in Motion," a program that puts poems where ads would normally be on New York subways and buses. This poem seemed to me to capture both the concept of supplementarity—simultaneous completion and displacement—and to personalize it, to name particularity as the supplement to abstraction in much the way I mean to suggest. While Strand's celebration of wholeness is certainly against the Derridean grain, the ephemerality of wholeness indicated here

does also seem to capture the very temporary temporality of the efficacy of the supplement (Strand, *Poems*).

20. In California this threat was wielded to pass Proposition 187 in 1994, which restricted health, education, and welfare benefits for "illegal aliens." (Court battles have thus far prevented its implementation.) Protesters against the legislation, many of whom carried Mexican flags, were widely perceived as harming their own cause by flaunting an antiassimilationist stance.

21. See especially Harvey's "Class Structure and Residential Differentiation," in *The Urban Experience.*

22. By *individual* I mean a particular kind of subject, variously termed bourgeois, liberal, or abstract, who understands himself or herself as a rational, self-interested, and property owning individual (even when that property is limited to that individual's body) with some sort of internal and motivating selfhood, desire, etc. See MacPherson, *Political Theory.*

23. See Gordon, "Work of Corporate Culture."

24. LEAGUE is one of many "employee resource groups" enabled by AT&T.

25. Lubiano refutes this argument by pointing out that the divisions in society being taken up in a positive way now by various minority groups have their origin in the history of racism in this country ("Multiculturalism").

26. Omi and Winant call this discursive move the "immigrant analogy" (*Racial Formation,* 17).

27. See Epstein ("Gay Politics") for a discussion of the implications of treating gays and lesbians as an ethnic group.

28. During the NEA controversy, one of Sen. Jesse Helms's principal legislative and rhetorical strategies for limiting the art that could be funded by the NEA was to equate discrimination against "the religious community" with discrimination against African Americans and other historically oppressed groups.

29. Bellah's ethnographic descriptions *(Habits)* of the ways that people typically "get involved" in protecting their residential enclaves confirms Harvey's point.

2. The Performance of Production and Consumption

1. The critique of orthodox Marxism is reiterated so frequently that I cannot name all the locations here. Raymond Williams makes this point in *Marxism and Literature,* citing Lukács's earlier critique, and in fact, Williams offers a reading of Marx against orthodox Marxism that at a number of points closely resembles the argument I make here. Two particularly influential recent iterations are Laclau and Mouffe's *Hegemony and Socialist Strategy* and Lowe and Lloyd's introduction to *The Politics of Culture in the Shadow of Capitalism.*

2. I apply the notion of performativity very differently than Butler does. She uses it in a psychoanalytically grounded discussion of identity. To the extent that she is concerned with politics, she seems to focus on generating an improved identity politics: the existence of subjects with the appropriate identity is still cast as the automatic basis for community or collective action, but she would like to acknowledge disidentification in addition to identification as modes of community membership, thus opening a space for difference (see especially "Critically Queer" in *Bodies*).

3. In *Bodies That Matter* Butler distances herself from the term *theatrical,* which she used in "Performative Acts" and in *Gender Trouble,* apparently as part of her effort to shed the connotation of preexisting subjecthood.

4. She frequently substitutes the word "production" for "construction" in *Bodies That Matter,* again as a way of emphasizing constraint against connotations of voluntarism. The term *production* appears many, many times throughout the text, generally in lists of phrases attempting to generate the particular version of social construction she has in mind; *materialization* is another important term for her.

5. Cindy Patton also recognizes that the performative nature of identity means not that one is free to be any identity but rather that to achieve identity one is constrained to follow its rules: "Identities suture those who take them up to specific moral duties. Identities carry with them a requirement to act, which is felt as 'what a person like me does'" ("Tremble, Hetero Swine," 147).

6. In this chapter, I use the Tucker anthology as the source for all Marx quotations, including these from *The German Ideology,* except those taken from the *Grundrisse.* Tucker was used most often in the classes and reading groups in which I first read Marx, so these are the translations that determined my interpretations of Marx. In comparing Tucker's translation of *Capital* with the Ben Fowkes translation of volume 1, I have found Fowkes's language simply less lively, so have stuck with Tucker. In this chapter, all references to *Capital* are from Tucker, unless Fowkes's name is given.

7. Williams quotes the first thesis on Feuerbach in support of this reading (*Marxism and Literature,* 30).

8. Thanks to Russell Berman for this insight.

9. See Diane Elson, "The Value Theory of Labour," on the relation between various "aspects" and "forms of appearance" of labor, value, and the commodity.

10. Ernesto Laclau and Chantal Mouffe make this point: "Since the worker is capable of social practices, he could resist the imposed control mechanisms and force the capitalist to use different techniques. Thus, it is not a pure logic of capital which determines the evolution of the labour process; the latter is not merely the place where capital exerts its domination, but the ground of struggle" (*Hegemony and Socialist Strategy,* 79).

11. Waring's arguments are primarily a case against the discipline of economics and generally do not elaborate a new theory of value. In fact, she offers little self-conscious discussion of how she knows these things really are valuable, resorting to commonsense appeals to the value, for example, of time spent physically laboring or the beauty of untarnished nature, each of which—physical work, beauty—is, like money, a system of value that hierarchizes not only things but people (Waring, *If Women Counted*).

12. The lack of freedom involved in their choices has been analyzed by many theorists, including Baudrillard *(Mirror of Production),* Adorno and Horkheimer *(Dialectic of Enlightenment),* Marcuse *(One Dimensional Man)* and, more recently, Stuart Ewen *(Captains of Consciousness).* All are concerned with the construction of the consumer by the capitalist producer. To the extent that cultural studies scholars suggest that it is through discretionary spending that subcultures or individuals express themselves, they make the mistake of assuming that there is some preexisting, choosing subject. Kim Gillespie argues that in any case most people have very little discretionary income; thus, their ability to express themselves through their

consumptive practices is quite limited (personal communication). I am arguing that it is precisely these differential constraints that make consumption a subject-constructing behavior and that expressive possibilities are derived precisely from a system of constraints.

13. See, for instance, Stuart Hall, "Encoding/Decoding"; Dick Hebdige, *Subculture;* and John Fiske, "Jeaning of America," in his *Understanding Popular Culture.*

14. As Lauren Berlant and Elizabeth Freeman point out, the Gap has, for many years, done a prominent advertising campaign using gay celebrities and gay styles to sell its clothing to straight people ("Queer Nationality").

15. See, for example, John D'Emilio, "Capitalism and Gay Identity," and Louise Tilly and Joan Wallach Scott, *Women, Work, and the Family.*

16. *Culminated* is probably the wrong word here as the evolution from post–Civil War robber baron capitalism to post–World War II Fordism was not a continuous or necessary process and was shaped by intense and violent labor struggles and by the Great Depression, which instigated a dramatic restructuring of labor-capital relations. Martyn J. Lee accounts for the shift from pre-Fordism to Fordism as a shift from an extensive to an intensive mode of accumulation (*Consumer Culture Reborn,* see especially 73–74).

17. The characterizations of post-Fordism and flexible accumulation offered in this chapter are gleaned primarily from Harvey's *Condition of Postmodernity.* His characterization of changes in the location and composition of commodity production is reiterated by Lee in *Consumer Culture Reborn,* which is not surprising since both rely on "regulation school" theorists, principally: Michel Aglietta *(Capitalist Regulation);* Scott Lash and John Urry *(End of Organized Capital);* and Michael J. Piore and Charles F. Sabel *(Second Industrial Divide).* As I will discuss in detail in chapter 5, there are many problems with Harvey's and Lee's narratives, most especially their claims for a decisive epochal shift in the structure of capitalism. And as I note there, the empirical claims for a shift are much disputed. Lee acknowledges that "the argument that the sort of mass-production/mass-consumption economy which dominated the post-war years is now in rapid decline simply does not stand up to empirical scrutiny" (*Consumer Culture,* 111). And in more recent work Harvey also acknowledges that the shift may be more of an adjustment to financial systems than a dramatic transformation. Harvey and Lee both dismiss the concerns of the doubters by noting that while these changes may not be statistically dominant, they are an increasing trend and have already come to dominate the ideology, the discursive construction, of capitalism; certainly this info-service-niche-marketed capitalism is the image of capitalism being promoted throughout the popular media. What this ideological, if not statistical, dominance means is that the social relations implied by these new forms of production probably exceed and motivate the implementation of these forms.

18. An article in the *New York Times* about a strike, over outsourcing, at one General Motors parts plant in Anderson, Indiana, reported, "Local [union] officials are heavily influenced by the national leadership, but their re-election depends on how well they serve their small constituencies. That some of the outsourcing GM wanted to do at Anderson involved sending work to other GM plants did not lessen the local union leaders' anxiety about the declining number of jobs in their community" (Bennett, "Job Cuts and Grassroots"). Harvey points to the fact that towns and cities act in an entrepreneurial mode, competing with each other for tax base

by going to great lengths to get businesses to settle within their borders (*Postmodernity*, 171).

19. My sources for this characterization of labor-capital relations are (1) the debate over the North American Free Trade Agreement (NAFTA), which I absorbed through media representations (primarily the *New York Times* and National Public Radio), and, more important, (2) informal interviews with my father, who, as a labor lawyer for AT&T, participated in AT&T's triannual national collective bargaining. During the 1992 bargaining process, he gave me a patient and thoughtful lesson in how AT&T, which sees itself as a progressive leader and innovator in business practices, viewed the claims of labor unions (as regressive, not in the modern world) and in the various rhetorical and financial techniques AT&T brought to bear to get the unions to get with the program (downsizing, outsourcing, etc.). Prominent among these were (1) discussions of competition facing the company; (2) stock as part of wages; (3) less hierarchical shop floor management; and (4) outplacement, education, and retraining programs.

20. It is not clear to me that people are as unknowing as Marx suggests. However, as Slavoj Zizek argues, we all act as if we did not know, which is effectively as good as a lack of awareness (*Sublime Object*, 31).

21. On this point, Parker cites Hannah Arendt *(The Human Condition)* who makes a rather different antiproductivist argument based on the notion that production is the realm of necessity and that what is truly human is the political realm purged of all necessity. She makes a further distinction between the repetitive labor of reproduction and the production of works of art, which is neither truly unproductive nor mere animalistic existence.

As noted earlier, Marx does not count heterosexual reproduction as production per se. In fact, he seems to feel, not unlike Marilyn Waring (*If Women Counted*, 286), that the inscription of sexual relations in market terms is a corruption of what should be valued on its own distinct terms (*1844 Manuscripts*, 105). But I am not here particularly interested in Marx's views of heterosexuality or homosexuality except to the extent that, as Parker argues, they form a metaphoric basis for his analysis of production and unproductivity, respectively.

22. Parker relies heavily on Eve Kosofsky Sedgwick in his argument here, citing her assertion of the tie between self-display and sexuality in the nineteenth century (straight men do not engage in self-display). Separately, in explicitly antihomophobic projects, she does engage in celebrations of heterogeneity: for instance, *Epistemology of the Closet* begins with an elaboration of the sheer variety of possible sexual preferences (and possible definitions of sexual preference), all of which have been condensed into the binary homo vs. hetero; and *Tendencies* begins with an attempt to separate out the diverse pieces of identity that have all been condensed into gender. However, I am not sure that Sedgwick ties heterogeneity, theatricality, and homosexuality to an antiproductivist stance as Parker does, since she also claims to be fascinated with the productivity of performativity—the ability of the speech act to produce the reality it describes.

23. While Stallybrass uses the *Eighteenth Brumaire* to locate in Marx a recognition of the importance of the political (a representational or discursive realm with some independence from economic determinism), Parker focuses on Marx's condemnation of this independence and thus finds Marx in a self-contradiction, rejecting performative, discursive, and rhetorical strategies even while he uses them.

I'm not sure what the point is of catching Marx in a self-contradiction; it seems to me more politically useful to see Marx recognizing and offering a useful strategy than to posit Marx as the enemy and to throw out, along with Marx's clear and repugnant homophobia—which Parker has very valuably uncovered—his very potent analysis of social production and change.

24. Because Phelan's mode of articulation is primarily Lacanian she is interested in reproduction, both in the sense of culture, the Symbolic, and in the sense of procreation and women's roles therein (explicitly giving homosex an especially un[re]-productive role).

25. Phelan and Baudrillard might argue that in looking to representational excess for liberation they are precisely not looking to exteriority, but I find the term *excess* rather mystical and mystifying, yet another invocation of the emergence of something out of nothing.

26. The role that Phelan gives to performance is not far from the role Theodor Adorno sets out for lyric poetry in "Lyric Poetry and Society": both are expressions of that unformed human spirit I referred to earlier. However, in both cases this role is so clearly demarcated by the realm of the produced, the formed, that one can read the quality of the formed world by the nature of the protests of this unformed subjectivity.

27. Phelan does recognize that the notion that performance does not produce is something of a fantasy. She is aware that her own work, for instance, turns performance into production: "Writing about it necessarily cancels the 'tracelessness' inaugurated within this performative process" (*Unmarked*, 149).

28. Phelan cites in this context J. L. Austin's discussion of performative utterances and specifically focuses on the promise (*Unmarked*, 149). Pratt specifically cites the focus on the promise as a tip-off to the assumption of the intentional a priori subject underlying the theory ("Ideology and Speech Act Theory," 62).

29. In "Praxis and Performativity," Andrew Parker offers a critique of Marxian appeals to a Real that is prior to a mediated secondary superstructure of consciousness and representation. He suggests that a theory of performativity makes a radical break with this theory of praxis because it does not distinguish between these two levels. He proposes that the two might be brought together by reading performativity as constitutive of praxis, especially of the dialectical efficacy of praxis that produces "representations presumably alien to its own essential structure" (271). While I would have to argue with the presumption of alienness, insofar as that presumption is attributed to Marx, I find Parker's argument for locating performativity as constitutive of whatever is presented as the Real—be it praxis, use value, performance, or homosex—insightful and useful.

3. Not for Profit?

1. The essays in Odendahl and O'Neill's collection, *Women and Power in the Non-Profit Sector,* argue that nonprofit production is to a significant extent gendered female—in the United States the majority of volunteers, paid staff, and clients of nonprofits are women, though the larger the organization the less likely this is to be true, and the higher up one goes in the decision-making hierarchy of any particular organization, the more likely one is to find a man in the job.

2. The story I was told by Ann and others while I was in Tupelo is reiterated in an article in the *Northeast Mississippi Daily Journal.* The Web site of the newspaper

shows that the paper is owned by a nonprofit organization called Create: "Create was started in 1972 by the late George A. McLean. Create's purpose is to stimulate private giving by individuals and businesses in order to enhance the quality of life in Northeast Mississippi." The Web site gives the newspaper, rather than McLean personally, responsibility for the establishment of the Rural Community Development Council program in the 1930s, for working with other business leaders to establish the Community Development Foundation in 1948, and for the building of warehouses in the 1950s and 1960s "to support local industrial development." http://www.djournal.com/djournal/site/pages/specialsections/125/125th.htm.

3. The paper was actually founded in 1872 and became a daily in 1936, which appears to be the approximate time McLean became active.

4. What I mean here by dominant discourse is quite literally the discourse of the dominant, the capitalists and government policymakers who have been instrumental in the development of what they call the "nonprofit sector."

5. In U.S. academic literature, nonprofits are generally defined against business and government as a "third sector." The third sector analysis is based on a rational-choice economic model that assumes that consumer desire drives the creation of organizations that produce a variety of goods. According to this model, while for-profit firms and governments are the most efficient producers of some goods, nonprofits are the most efficient producers of those goods about which consumers cannot gain adequate information to make a rational choice and that therefore require the consumer to trust the producer. In this model, philanthropists are cast as consumers who purchase social rather than individual goods through their contributions to nonprofits. Grønbjerg contests this economic analysis in its own terms, arguing that "Nonprofits have both strategic and dynamic relations to the public and for-profit sectors and do not play a passive role in compensating for the general shortcomings in the political or market systems, as most observers implicitly assume. Nonprofit, public, and market actors can and do advance their own interests, creating an iterative process of strategic action and response. As a result, relations among the three sectors are constantly developing" ("Markets, Politics, and Charity," 137).

6. The interviews represented in this section were all conducted in July 1991. My representations of the interviews here are, of course, quite drastically edited; I spent anywhere from one to three hours with each of the people I interviewed, which yielded on average about fifty transcribed pages per interview.

7. Ken Dixon, a local African American gay theater actor and director, was the artistic director at Theater Rhinoceros from 1988 to 1991.

8. Bruce Sievers (political scientist and executive director of the Walter and Elise Haas Fund) is typical: "Growing out of traditions dating from classical and medieval times, the American philanthropic impulse was incorporated into the fabric of emergent Colonial culture. . . . historic traditions of religious charity and patronage blended in pre-Revolutionary America into a new phenomenon—voluntary giving for positive social purposes as a shared community value. By the time Alexis de Tocqueville visited the newly formed United States, the traditions of charitable giving and informal self-help associations had developed into what he described as a uniquely American blend of organizational life" ("Philanthropy," 2). A long quote from Tocqueville immediately follows that passage.

9. His reference to Israel here is mystifying and is not explained further in the text.

10. In *The Rise of Professionalism*, Magali Safatti Larson argues that a significant part of the ethos of professionalism is precisely "community."

11. The panel was chaired by William Julius Wilson. The presenters were Ronald B. Mincy, a program officer from the Ford Foundation; Jeffery M. Johnson, the president and chief executive officer of the National Center for Strategic Nonprofit Planning and Leadership, which runs the Partners project; Marilyn Ray Smith of the Child Support Enforcement Division of the Massachusetts Department of Revenue; and Stan MacLaren, a Boston-area activist working in the context of "community-based organizations."

12. Gellner defines civil society as "a cluster of institutions and associations strong enough to prevent tyranny, but which are, nevertheless, entered freely rather than imposed either by birth or by awesome ritual" ("Importance," 42). Oxhorn says: "Civil society is a rich social fabric formed by a multiplicity of territorially and functionally based units . . . and by their collective capacity simultaneously to resist subordination to the state and to demand inclusion into national political structures. . . . Strong civil societies are thus synonymous with a high level of 'institutionalized social pluralism'" ("Controlled Inclusion," 251–2). He goes on to exemplify his idea with reference to "organizations ranging from handicraft workshops and soup kitchens, to cultural, youth and women's groups, to organizations which are dedicated to the defence of human rights and the struggle for transitions from authoritarian to democratic regimes," in other words, a highly typical array of NGOs (260). And Giner defines civil society as "a historically evolved sphere of individual rights, freedoms and voluntary associations whose politically undisturbed competition with each other in the pursuit of their respective private concerns, interests, preferences and intentions is guaranteed by a public institution called the state" ("Civil Society," 304). He, like Oxhorn, imagines these associations to be "non-profit organizations and all sorts of philanthropic projects" (316).

13. Where Keane's arguments against post-Marxism suggest that all forms of Marxism tend toward central planning and thus totalitarianism, Meadwell makes what appears to me a more sophisticated argument against Habermasian theories, such as that offered by Arato and Cohen, suggesting that they tend not toward Soviet-style totalitarianism but rather toward "republicanism," which he argues is an antimodern and "illiberal" communalism requiring social conformity (Keane, *Civil Society;* Meadwell, "Post-Marxism"; Arato and Cohen, *Civil Society and Political Theory*).

14. Gellner's choice of metaphor is quite telling since, of course, furniture does not arrange itself according to its own volition but is rather arranged by some person according to that person's needs or desires. Keane, who opposes his position to Gellner's by claiming that he is offering a nonfoundationalist version of civil society, that is, a version that does not depend on a substantive notion of the good, nonetheless also proposes national identity as this normative supplement. Keane echoes Gellner's distinction between premodern communalism and national cultural homogeneity by carefully differentiating nationalism (bad) from national identity (good).

15. See, for instance, Ritchey-Vance's *The Art of Association: NGOs and Civil Society in Colombia* (published by the Inter-America Foundation); Hellinger, Hellinger, and O'Regan's *Aid for Just Development;* Carroll's *Intermediary NGOs: The Supporting Link in Grassroots Development;* Reilly's *New Paths to Democratic Development in*

Latin America: the Rise of NGO-Municipal Collaboration; or Clark's *Democratizing Development: The Role of Voluntary Associations.*

16. "While NGOs had been active in smaller numbers in the preceding decades, they expanded in the 1980s as individuals and international agencies sought to build a democratic counterweight to the military regimes that were dominating [Latin America]. The economic crisis of the 1980s also encouraged the growth of NGOs that sought solutions to worsening poverty" (Ewig, "Strengths and Limits," 75).

17. Carroll dates the mainstream "discovery" of NGOs to approximately 1985, when a World Bank staff working paper was produced that concluded that NGOs were superior to other types of aid agencies (*Intermediary NGOs,* 1).

18. In June 1982, at the onset of the crisis, the top nine U.S. banks' exposure to Mexico was more than 50 percent of their primary capital, and their exposure to Latin America as a whole was 179 percent (King, "Confrontation and Accommodation").

19. Phillips names this focus on microadjustment a "third wave" of development and notes that the emphasis on poverty alleviation and democratization is just one component of a larger shift to neoliberalism, that is, a strong emphasis on free markets in which people are enabled (or forced) to help themselves in the absence of government involvement *(Third Wave of Modernization).*

20. It is crucial to recognize that tiny loans to poor individuals have by no means replaced huge loans to nations; these loans are inevitably tied to structural adjustment policies that persist in creating the poverty and displacement NGOS and microcredit seek to address.

21. A number of audience members at Vinelli's Hauser Center presentation (7 December 1999) vociferously affirmed, citing their field experience, the claim that women are more responsible and more likely to use the loans in ways that have "social" or at least household-wide benefit.

22. The more appropriate conclusion of his argument would in some sense be Simmel's *Philosophy of Money,* a celebration of the social productivity of commodity exchange. On one hand, Simmel argues, against the utilitarians, that exchanges are based in assessments of the usefulness not of the objective value of the objects but rather of the subjective (and thus social) value of the personal sacrifice entailed in obtaining the object (82). He claims that exchange produces value (such as personal satisfaction) in excess of the value of the goods exchanged (84). And further, he points to the social goods, such as personal freedom or social superiority, that accrue to the possessors of money (215).

23. Badgett and Cunningham's study, which surveyed people who were on the mailing lists of gay organizations (those respondents who did not self-identify as gay or lesbian were eliminated from the analysis), was intended to determine "motivations and barriers" for giving and volunteering. Asked about their motivations, those surveyed responded as intentional individuals, overwhelmingly identifying "altruism" (the desire to help other gay people, 85 percent) and "social and political change" (also 85 percent) as primary motivations. Framed in this way, the study excluded the possibility that participation might actually constitute rather than result from gay identity. Despite the fact that the study itself overdetermined the subjectivity of those surveyed, the survey actually indicates that participation involves a process of subject formation. Forty-seven percent indicated that a desire to meet other gay people was a primary motivation. First-time involvement, while also

substantially motivated by altruism (83 percent) was also frequently motivated by the desire to be "more out about one's sexual orientation" (42 percent) and often occurred in response to a perceived threat (an antigay political candidate or referendum, 45 percent; an experience of discrimination, 29 percent; or simply an antigay comment, 45 percent).

24. Unlike the literature on nonprofits in the United States, which is almost exclusively celebratory, the literature on NGOs in developing countries is rich with critiques. Interestingly, one of the most trenchant critiques (Hudock, *NGOs*) is actually based on a sociological theory—resource dependence—that is quite standard fare in U.S. sociology. Despite the availability of this theory, it has rarely been mobilized, in the U.S. context, to propose, as Hudock does, that nonprofits are instruments of hegemony building. While discussions of elite philanthropy often suggest that such philanthropy is the tool by which the wealthy preserve their wealth and consolidate their power (see, for instance, Hall, *Inventing;* McCarthy, *Noblesse Oblige;* Grønbjerg, "Markets"; and Jenkins, "Channeling"), these discussions do not generally pose the question of hegemony as a question of subject construction. Joshua Gamson's article on the New York gay film festival is quite unique in asking, "How do resource dependencies and the characteristics of the *institutional environment* shape collective identity articulations?" ("Organization and Shaping," 527). Without making recourse to sociological theory, Alexandra Chasin *(Selling Out)* offers an analysis very much in line with the critiques of development NGOs, describing the impact of various kinds of fund-raising on the programs, culture, and inclusiveness of gay nonprofits.

25. The NGO system is regularly described as composed of layers of organizations ranging from well-endowed Northern international organizations, to intermediary organizations (the direct recipients of international funds that operate on a national level in Southern countries), to local membership organizations, which receive some or no support from intermediary organizations.

26. Carroll points out that even the most apparently grassroots organizations operating in "indigenous traditional communities" are subject to the "internal stratification" found in those communities (*Intermediary NGOs,* 157). Nancy Marie Robertson makes this point in a completely different context in her discussion of the power dynamics between black and white women in the formation of the YMCA in the early twentieth century in the United States ("Kindness or Justice?"). And Inderpal Grewal describes the construction of imperialist masculinity in the human rights efforts undertaken by Sikh men in the United States on behalf of Sikh women in India ("On the New Global Feminism"). While feminists such as Robertson and Grewal are concerned to analyze and intervene in the production of inequities at local as well as global levels, Carroll more or less dismisses the problem, saying, "a measure of inequality both in participation and in benefit distribution is a fact of life, as is factionalism, clientelism, and vulnerability to external manipulation" (*Intermediary NGOs,* 157).

27. Edwards and Hulme's paper was originally written for a workshop sponsored by Save the Children Fund–U.K., for which Edwards worked. Financial support for the workshop was provided by the Swedish International Development Authority and the U.K. Overseas Development Administration.

28. Likewise, Fernando and Heston write: "The majority of large NGOs did not evolve from the communities in which they work but were started by charismatic

leaders, and their organizations are hierarchically structured and bureaucratic, especially when they expand the scale of their activities" ("NGOs between States," 11).

29. See Bebbington, "New States, New NGOs?" and Edwards and Hulme, "Too Close for Comfort." Bebbington worked for the U.K. Overseas Development Administration and has served as a consultant to the World Bank.

30. On philanthropy as reciprocity, see Michael P. Moody's "Pass It On."

4. The Perfect Moment

1. A lengthy front page article, titled "Activists Protest Fundies' Easter," appeared the week after Easter 1992 in the San Francisco gay weekly, the *Bay Area Reporter*, replete with photographs. It read in part: "About 250 gays and lesbians led by the Bible Thumpers, a Queer Nation action group, marched from 8 A.M. to 2 P.M. on the side walk in front of Sacramento's Capital Christian Center on Easter Sunday to protest the homophobic teachings and political agenda of the Rev. Glen Cole.... Michael Cooney and Pamm Schrade who head the 'Set Free' ministry to reform gays looked sadly upon the demonstrators. 'I wish they knew we don't hate them. I want them to know they don't have to be gay,' Cooney said. 'Homosexuality is a sin and a damnation and has brought destruction to every civilization that has allowed it to flourish,' Cole said."

2. The public controversy began when Donald Wildmon's American Family Association brought to the attention of Congress and the public the exhibition of Andre Serrano's "Piss Christ." Both the exhibiting gallery and Serrano had received funding from the NEA. The public debate accelerated with the cancellation of an exhibition of Robert Mapplethorpe's photographs, "The Perfect Moment," by the Corcoran Gallery (Washington, D.C.), which was attempting to prevent a congressional backlash against the NEA. It continued with the NEA's defunding and refunding of an exhibition at the Artists' Space Gallery (New York) of works dealing with AIDS and with the defunding of four performance artists—Tim Miller, Holly Hughes, John Fleck, and Karen Finley (the "NEA Four")—three of whom are gay or lesbian, the fourth a feminist. There were several congressional battles over, and at various points the imposition of, content restrictions on all grants. These restrictions then resulted in court battles.

Marking the "Piss Christ" controversy as the initiating event for the larger battle over the arts erases some important congressional attacks on the NEA and the arts that occurred during the Reagan years, both with regard to the budget of the agency and the content of works funded. I choose to start here because it was with this event that the popular news media began its extensive coverage and at approximately this time that I became aware of the issue. For a full chronology, see Richard Bolton's *Culture Wars* (331ff).

3. There were different strategies in place for regulating content at different points in the controversy. Jesse Helms regularly proposed amendments to NEA legislation that listed specific content that could not be funded. These amendments never became law. What did become law were requirements, in 1989, that grants not be given for work that the courts would find "obscene" as defined by the 1973 *Michael Anthony Miller v. California Supreme Court* decision (113 Sup. Ct. 2360) and, in 1990, that grants be given in accord with "general standards of decency." In addition, the

NEA itself included an oath in its grant contracts for 1990 that required recipients to pledge not to produce "obscene" work. Both the obscenity oath and the decency clause were ultimately struck down in court, in *Bella Lewitzky Dance Foundation v. National Endowment for the Arts* (754 F. Supp. 744 [U.S. Dis. 1991]) and *Karen Finley, John Fleck, Holly Hughes, Tim Miller, and the National Association of Artists' Organizations v. National Endowment for the Arts* (795 F. Supp 1457 [U.S. Dis. 1992]), respectively.

4. The bulk of my research was conducted from 1991 to 1993. I started following the controversy in a casual way, reading newspapers and listening to National Public Radio. I interviewed approximately forty people: arts advocates and administrators, conservative Christian organization members and staff, employees of the NEA, and congressional staff. I attended arts activist planning meetings, public forums held by arts organizations meant to provoke "grassroots" activism, and I attended services at a variety of churches.

5. A People for the American Way pamphlet similarly has it both ways: "we" are, on one hand, "a passionate band of advocates"—sounds like David against Goliath—and on the other, "we" are "the rest of us" threatened by "a small, but highly organized, minority determined to impose their religious beliefs and narrow-minded values . . . the Helmses, Falwells, and Borks of this world."

6. GLAAD/SFBA video *The Fundamentalist Obsession;* Donna Minkowitz, "Undercover with the Religious Right" in *Out* and "Dancing on Your Grave" in *POZ;* L. A. Kauffman "Spy in the House of God" in *SF Weekly.*

7. One of the most famous instances of this genre is the video *The Gay Agenda.* The *American Family Association Journal* includes a twenty-four page insert, "Homosexuality in America: Exposing the Myths"; the journal of Concerned Women for America, *Family Voice,* did a special issue, "Militants Penetrate the Mainstream"; and *Focus on the Family* featured a cover story, "New Life, New Lifestyles" consisting of three first-person narratives by ex-gays Jami Breedlove, Vera Plechash, and David Davis. There are organizations and journals devoted to tracking both gays and Christians, though these generally operate under conservative and liberal political labels rather than being explicitly Christian or gay. *The Lambda Report* is a conservative journal tracking gays. Among the many organizations tracking the Christian right and publishing newsletters are Political Research Associates (Cambridge, Mass.), which publishes *The Public Eye,* and the Institute for First Amendment Studies (Great Barrington, Mass.), run by Skipp Porteous, which publishes *Freedom Writer; Culturewatch* is published using the resources of the Data Center (Oakland, Calif.).

8. The primary concern of AFA is television: they monitor television shows for sex, violence, and "anti-Christian bigotry" and mount boycott campaigns against the advertisers sponsoring programs they deem unacceptable. The NEA was for them a sidelight, though they made quite a stir with it.

9. David Wojnarowicz's work portraying Christ with a hypodermic needle in his arm was specifically featured in AFA mailings. Wojnarowicz wrote an essay for the catalogue of the Artists' Space show, "Witnesses: Against Our Vanishing" (16 November 1989 to 6 January 1990) that responds to Christian (Roman Catholic) legitimation of the government's inaction on AIDS as well as the attacks on the arts by Helms. This was the show that was funded by the NEA and then defunded and refunded (with the specific constraint that the funds not be used for the catalog) by the newly appointed and shell-shocked chairman of the NEA, John Frohnmayer.

10. Statewide battles have been fought in Colorado, Oregon, Maine, and Iowa. Colorado's initiative passed and was overturned by the Supreme Court. While the statewide initiative in Oregon lost, many local antigay rights initiatives in that state have been passed.

11. The National Association of State Arts Agencies supported this proposal and thus created one of many significant rifts within the arts lobby.

12. Janet R. Jakobsen, "Can Homosexuals End Western Civilization as We Know It?"

13. See Oswald Spengler's "Decline of the West" as discussed in Carlston (*Thinking Fascism*). While the Jew, another central character in the story of decline, was not a central figure in the NEA controversy as far as I know, it does appear in the critique offered by Wildmon of film and television. In *Home Invaders,* as evidence of the anti-Christian bias of Hollywood, Wildmon offers statistics on the domination of the television industry by Jews (21). This legacy is often recalled in the hyperbolic characterizations of the religious right as fascist or Nazi offered by gay people from time to time, and in the license that the Christian right seems to give to neo-Nazi groups such as the Christian Identity movement. During a conversation about the NEA controversy, a friend of mine, who is a gay man and performer, claimed that "they" were "scapegoating" gay artists as the Nazis had scapegoated Jews. While it is certainly debatable whether one can hold the Donald Wildmons of the world responsible for the activities and beliefs of other groups, it seems clear that the prominence of their racist, homophobic, sexist, exclusionary discourse provides an umbrella of legitimacy and acceptability for more extreme and violent articulations of Christianity and nationalism. Conservative Christian organizations celebrated a recent Supreme Court decision allowing the Ku Klux Klan to post a cross in a public park. In an interesting reversal, conservative Christian leaders frequently speak of liberals as "Nazis."

14. Schechner deploys this cliché in "Political Realities" (8).

15. Pastor Phil Pringle of the Christian City Church, Sydney, Australia, speaker at the Spiritual Warfare Conference, Jubilee Christian Center, San Jose, California, April 25, 1992.

16. Witness, for instance, the campaign for and passage of ballot measure 187 in California, denying a variety of social welfare benefits, including health care and education, to "illegal" immigrants.

17. Holly correctly characterizes the logic of the Christian right. The catch-22 in which expression is taken as evidence of worthiness for rights but all expression by gay people is by definition unworthy, because by definition obscene, was regularly reiterated. Christians frequently sought to prove that the NEA was funding obscenity by simply listing organizations and exhibitions by and for gay people that had been funded without any discussion of the content of the artwork. For instance, a letter to members of the House of Representatives dated 23 October 1991 and signed by Phyllis Schlafly, Eagle Forum; Beverly LaHaye, Concerned Women for America; Louis P. Sheldon, Tradition Values Coalition; Gary Bauer, Family Research Council; Robert P. Dugan, National Association of Evangelicals; Paul Weyrich, Coalition for America; Richard Land, Christian Life Commission of the Southern Baptist Convention; Donald Wildmon, American Family Association; and Ralph Reed, Christian Coalition, offers as "a few examples of the indecency that has been funded": "The 1991 San Francisco International Film Festival, a lesbian stage performance entitled *No Trace of the Blond,* which will use two teen-aged girls as the main per-

formers, and *Tongues Untied* about black homosexual life which was funded under an NEA grant to Public Television's *Point of View* series."

18. Conservative Christians have a history of factionalism and what they call separation, which is the unwillingness to deal with those who have theological differences. However, their desire to participate in national affairs, both in 1942 with the founding of the National Association of Evangelicals (Wells and Woodbridge, "Introduction," 13) and more recently, in the creation of organizations such as the Moral Majority and the Christian Coalition, has required them to tolerate such differences, to articulate a kind of Christian pluralism. As the general counsel of the NAE explained to me, "To join the National Association of Evangelicals...you have to subscribe to a seven statement tenet of faith, which is our fundamental Christian belief...And our group, we try to stress what unites us rather than what divides us...We have profound theological disagreements within our own constituency, you know, between Calvinism and Arminianism...there are those differences."

Christina used the notion of Christian pluralism to include Christians in the pluralism of the nation, to make an analogy between Christians and ethnic groups, an analogy that has been applied to gays as well. "I mean, you know, I'm an Anglo American, a WASP and I have tended to lump Latinos all into one big lump, you know, they speak Spanish, they come from South America, they're them out there....what I've discovered is that when we talk about Asians and when we talk about Latinos, we're actually talking about an enormous spectrum of different cultures...I would posit that the Christian church is no different. The same kind of diversity exists, even though there are certain things in common, that are important things."

5. Kinship and the Culturalization of Capitalization

1. *Flexibility* is generally characterized as involving just-in-time supplying of both human and material means of production, outsourcing, horizontal management, and diversity management. See Emily Martin's *Flexible Bodies* for a fuller account of the discourse of flexibility.

2. *Post-Fordism* was coined by regulation school theorists, but now is used quite widely and loosely. *Flexible specialization* is Piore and Sabel's term *(Second Industrial Divide)*. *Flexible accumulation* is David Harvey's coinage *(Condition of Postmodernity)*. *Disorganized capital* is Claus Offe's term *(Disorganized Capitalism)*, but Lash and Urry also describe "the end of organized capitalism" *(End of Organized Capital)*.

3. In *Modernity at Large*, Arjun Appadurai offers a particularly celebratory account of the flows of people and information (he has not much at all to say about capital), arguing that such flows are the basis for new practices of imagination. His emphasis on flows has been criticized by numerous scholars who point to the blockages and constraints that both impel and prevent the movements of people and information.

4. Paul Krugman's critique of the economic discourse of national "competitiveness" in *Pop Internationalism* is another version of this view, as is Reich's critique of "economic nationalism" in *The Work of Nations*.

5. They put *indigenous* in scare quotes.

6. Appadurai, similarly, offers a dialectical model, arguing for the emancipatory potential of local, cultural appropriations: "The megarhetoric of developmental modernization . . . is often punctuated, interrogated, and domesticated by the micronarratives of film, television, music and other expressive forms, which allow modernity to be rewritten more as vernacular globalization and less as a concession to large-scale national and international policies. . . . These subversive micronarratives also fuel opposition movements" (*Modernity*, 11). Stuart Hall's two essays in *Culture, Globalization, and the World System* are additional examples of this kind of argument, as is Lisa Lowe's *Immigrant Acts*.

7. Lowe and Lloyd's work is also an effort to disrupt such narratives, to contest "understandings of transnationalism [that] assume a homogenization of global culture that radically reduces possibilities for the creation of alternatives" (*Politics of Culture*, 1).

8. While Harvey seems to be criticizing the popular version of the globalization narrative here, a similar critique has been offered with regard to the academic regulation school version. Hirst and Zeitlin point out that the regulation school account can be criticized both as too Marxist and by Marxists for envisioning the establishment of a functionally determined structure instead of describing contestations over an open process ("Flexible Specialization").

9. Paul Krugman, for instance, argues against the claims that developed countries have deindustrialized in "Fantasy Economics" and *Peddling Prosperity*.

10. Dirlik does suggest that some (modern, constructed) version of the local might be a site of resistance, but differentiates his notion of the local from the celebrations of diversity found in much cultural studies scholarship ("The Local in the Global"). I'm not sure that his argument is really so different from that found in Hall or Lowe and Lloyd, though his sober emphasis on the role of the local as a supplement to the global is quite useful.

11. Jakobsen's essay ("Queer Is? Queer Does?") addresses the analogy between Jews and Queers. She argues that we need to move beyond an analogic understanding to a recognition of a complicity in the construction of the categories. She points out that the coarticulation of Jews and Queers in Cold War rhetoric posited them not as merely analogous but as acting together to subvert America. This Cold War antisemitic and antihomosexual discourse, she argues, played a crucial part in postwar racist resurgence, consolidating white supremacy, rendering blacks the visible enemy in contrast to the invisible, Jewish-Queer enemies. She hopes that we can appropriate this complicity, this negative articulation of cooperation between Jews and Queers, as a potential positive space of alliance.

12. Adam Smith and David Ricardo articulate a notion of nations in competition with each other that has persisted up to the present, a notion that sets up a binary division between "us" and "other" nations. But they also initiate a comparative discourse: both describe a world of national economies that are comparable to each other on the basis of their wealth, productive abilities in various industries, and soil quality. Brought together, the comparative (analogic) and competitive (binary) frameworks suggest that nations can be ranked in relation to each other and that some division of productive tasks will be to the advantage of all.

Bibliography

Abelove, Henry, Michèle Aina Barale, and David M. Halperin. "Introduction." In *The Lesbian and Gay Studies Reader,* edited by Henry Abelove, Michèle Aina Barale, and David M. Halperin. New York: Routledge, 1993.

Adorno, Theodor. *The Jargon of Authenticity.* Translated by Knut Tarnowski and Frederic Will. London: Routledge and Kegan Paul, 1973.

———. "Lyric Poetry and Society." *Telos* 20 (summer 1974): 56–71.

Adorno, Theodor, and Max Horkheimer. *The Dialectic of Enlightenment.* Translated by John Cumming. New York: Herder and Herder, 1972.

Agamben, Giorgio. *The Coming Community.* Translated by Michael Hardt. Minneapolis: University of Minnesota Press, 1993.

Aglietta, Michel. *A Theory of Capitalist Regulation: The U.S. Experience.* London: Verso, 1987.

Althusser, Louis. "Ideology and Ideological State Apparatuses." In *Lenin and Philosophy and Other Essays,* translated by Ben Brewster. New York: Monthly Review Press, 1971.

American Family Association. *American Family Association Journal.* Tupelo, Miss. Published monthly.

———. "Homosexuality in America: Exposing the Myths." *American Family Association Journal* 18, no. 10 (October 1994): 1–24. Special supplement.

Amin, Ash, ed. *Post-Fordism: A Reader.* Cambridge, Mass.: Blackwell, 1994.

Amin, Ash, and K. Robins. "The Re-emergence of Regional Economies? The Mythical Geography of Flexible Accumulation," *Environment and Planning D: Society and Space* 8, no. 1 (1990): 7–34.

Anderson, Benedict. *Imagined Communities.* London: Verso, 1983.

———. "Introduction." In *Mapping the Nation,* edited by Gopal Balakrishnan. London: Verso, 1996.

Anzaldúa, Gloria. *Borderlands/La Frontera: The New Mestiza.* San Francisco: Spinsters/Aunt Lute, 1987.

Appadurai, Arjun. "Disjuncture and Difference in the Global Cultural Economy." *Public Culture* 2, no. 2 (spring 1990): 1–24.

————. *Modernity at Large: Cultural Dimensions of Globalization.* Minneapolis: University of Minnesota Press, 1996.

Arato, Andrew, and Jean Cohen. *Civil Society and Political Theory.* Cambridge: MIT Press, 1992.

Arendt, Hannah. *The Human Condition.* Garden City, N.Y.: Doubleday, 1959.

Arian, Edward. *The Unfulfilled Promise: Public Subsidy of the Arts in America.* Philadelphia: Temple University Press, 1989.

"Asian Values Revisited." *The Economist,* 25 July 1998, 23–28.

Austin, J. L. *How to Do Things with Words.* 2nd ed. Cambridge: Harvard University Press, 1975.

Badgett, M. V. Lee, and Nancy Cunningham. "Creating Communities: Giving and Volunteering by Gay, Lesbian, Bisexual and Transgender People." Published by the Institute for Gay and Lesbian Strategic Studies (Amherst, Mass.) and the Working Group on Funding Lesbian and Gay Issues (New York), 1998.

Balakrishnan, Gopal, ed. *Mapping the Nation.* London: Verso, 1996.

Balibar, Etienne. "Racism as Universalism." In *Masses, Classes, Ideas,* translated by James Swenson. New York: Routledge, 1994.

Balmer, Randall. *Mine Eyes Have Seen the Glory: A Journey into the Evangelical Subculture in America.* New York: Oxford University Press, 1989.

Barber, Benjamin R. *A Place for Us: How to Make Society Civil and Democracy Strong.* New York: Hill and Wang, 1998.

Barnet, Richard J., and John Cavanagh. *Global Dreams.* New York: Simon and Schuster, 1994.

Bataille, Georges. "The Psychological Structure of Fascism." In *Visions of Excess: Selected Writings, 1927–1939,* edited by Allan Stoekl, translated by Allan Stoekl, Carl Lovitt, and Donald Leslie. Minneapolis: University of Minnesota Press, 1985.

Baudrillard, Jean. *The Mirror of Production.* Translated by Mark Poster. St. Louis: Telos, 1975.

Bebbington, Anthony. "New States, New NGOs? Crisis and Transition among Rural Development NGOs in the Andean Region." *World Development* 25, no. 11 (1997): 1755–65.

Bell, Daniel. *The Cultural Contradictions of Capitalism.* New York: Basic Books, 1976.

Bellah, Robert N. "Civil Religion in America." *Daedalus* 96 (winter 1967): 1–21.

Bellah, Robert N., Richard Madsen, William M. Sullivan, Ann Swidler, and Steven M. Tipton. *Habits of the Heart: Individualism and Commitment in American Life.* New York: Harper and Row, 1985.

————. *The Good Society.* New York: Vintage, 1991.

Bender, Thomas. *Community and Social Change in America.* Baltimore: The Johns Hopkins University Press, 1978.

Benhabib, Seyla. "Feminism and Postmodernism: An Uneasy Alliance." *Praxis International* 11, no. 2 (July 1991): 137–49.

————. *Situating the Self: Gender, Community and Postmodernism in Contemporary Ethics.* Cambridge, England: Polity Press, 1992.

Bennett, James. "Job Cuts and Grassroots." *New York Times,* 17 August 1994, National edition, A17, 19.

Berlant, Lauren, and Elizabeth Freeman. "Queer Nationality." *Boundary* 2 no. 19 (1992): 149–80.

Berman, Russell A. "Beyond Localism and Universalism: Nationhood and Solidarity." *Telos* 105 (fall 1995): 43–56.

Bhabha, Homi K. "A Good Judge of Character: Men, Metaphors, and the Common Culture." In *Race-ing Justice, En-gendering Power: Essays on Anita Hill, Clarence Thomas, and the Construction of Social Reality,* edited by Toni Morrison. New York: Pantheon, 1992.

———. *The Location of Culture.* London: Routledge, 1994.

———, ed. *Nation and Narration.* London: Routledge, 1990.

Bloom, Allan. *The Closing of the American Mind.* New York: Simon and Schuster, 1987.

Bolton, Richard, ed. *Culture Wars.* New York: New Press, 1992.

Bourdieu, Pierre. *Outline of a Theory of Practice.* Cambridge: Cambridge University Press, 1977.

———. *Distinction: A Social Critique of the Judgement of Taste.* Cambridge: Harvard University Press, 1984.

Bowles, Samuel, and Herbert Gintis. *Democracy and Capitalism: Property, Community and the Contradictions of Modern Social Thought.* New York: Basic Books, 1987.

Bowles, Samuel, David M. Gordon, and Thomas E. Weisskopf. *After the Waste Land: A Democratic Economics for the Year 2000.* Armonk, N.Y.: M. E. Sharpe, 1990.

Boyer, Robert. *The Regulation School: A Critical Introduction.* Translated by Craig Charney. New York: Columbia University Press, 1990.

Bramen, Carrie Tirado. *Finding "An Innocent Way Out": The Literature and Politics of Cultural Pluralism, 1880–1925.* Ph.D. diss., Stanford University, 1994.

Braverman, Harry. *Labor and Monopoly Capitalism: The Degradation of Work in the Twentieth Century.* New York: Monthly Review Press, 1974.

Breines, Wini. *Community and Organization in the New Left: 1962–1968.* New York: Praeger, 1982.

Brenner, Neil. "Global, Fragmented, Hierarchical: Henri Lefebvre's Geographies of Globalization." *Public Culture* 10, no. 1 (1997): 135–67.

Brown, Wendy. *States of Injury: Power and Freedom in Late Modernity.* Princeton, N.J.: Princeton University Press, 1995.

Burlingame, Hal. "LEAGUE Conference Keynote Address." San Francisco, California, 6 April 1995.

Butler, Judith. "Performative Acts and Gender Constitution: An Essay in Phenomenology and Feminist Theory." *Theater Journal* 40, no. 4 (December 1988): 519–31.

———. "The Force of Fantasy: Feminism, Mapplethorpe, and Discursive Excess." *Differences* 2, no. 2 (1990): 105–25.

———. *Gender Trouble.* New York: Routledge, 1990.

———. "Contingent Foundations: Feminism and the Question of 'Postmodernism,'" *Praxis International* 11, no. 2 (July 1991): 150–65.

———. *Bodies That Matter: On the Discursive Limits of Sex.* New York: Routledge, 1993.

———. "Against Proper Objects." *Differences* 6, no. 2/3 (1994): 1–26.

———. "Merely Cultural." *Social Text* 52/53 (fall/winter 1997): 265–78.

———. *The Psychic Life of Power.* Stanford: Stanford University Press, 1997.

Butler, Judith, and Joan W. Scott, eds. *Feminists Theorize the Political.* New York: Routledge, 1992.

Calhoun, Craig. "The Public Good as a Social and Cultural Project." In *Private Action and the Public Good,* edited by Walter W. Powell and Elisabeth S. Clemens. New Haven: Yale University Press, 1998.

Carlston, Erin. *Thinking Fascism: Sapphic Modernism and Fascist Modernity.* Ph.D. diss., Stanford University, 1995.

Carnegie, Andrew. "The Gospel of Wealth," Essays on Philanthropy, no. 1. Bloomington: Indiana University Center on Philanthropy, 1993.

Carroll, Thomas F. *Intermediary NGOs: The Supporting Link in Grassroots Development.* West Hartford, Conn.: Kumarian Press, 1992.

Chase-Dunn, Christopher. *Global Formation: Structures of the World-Economy.* Cambridge, Mass.: B. Blackwell, 1989.

Chasin, Alexandra. *Selling Out: The Gay and Lesbian Movement Goes to Market.* New York: St. Martin's Press, 2000.

Chatterjee, Partha. *Nationalist Thought and the Colonial World: A Derivative Discourse.* Minneapolis: Zed Books, 1993.

Chaves, Mark. "The Religious Ethic and the Spirit of Nonprofit Entrepreneurship." In *Private Action and the Public Good,* edited by Walter W. Powell and Elisabeth S. Clemens. New Haven: Yale University Press, 1998.

Chinni, Dante, et al. "Everyday Heros: A Tribute to Americans Who Care." *Newsweek,* 29 May 1995, 26.

Clark, John. *Democratizing Development: The Role of Voluntary Associations.* West Hartford, Conn.: Kumarian Press, 1991.

Coats, Dan, and Rick Santorum. "Civil Society and the Humble Role of Government." In *Community Works,* edited by E. J. Dionne Jr. Washington, D.C.: Brookings Institution Press, 1998.

Cohen, Ed. "Who Are 'We'? Gay 'Identity' as Political (E)motion (A Theoretical Rumination)." In *Inside/Out: Lesbian Theories, Gay Theories,* edited by Diana Fuss. New York: Routledge, 1991.

Concerned Women for America, "Militants Penetrate the Mainstream." *Family Voice* 16, no. 5 (May 1994). Special issue.

Cox, Kevin, ed. *Spaces of Globalization: Reasserting the Power of the Local.* London: Guilford Press, 1997.

Crosby, Christina. "Dealing with Differences." In *Feminists Theorize the Political,* edited by Judith Butler and Joan W. Scott. New York: Routledge, 1992.

Curry, Richard O., ed. *Freedom at Risk: Secrecy, Censorship, and Repression in the 1980s.* Philadelphia, Temple University Press, 1988.

Dayton, Donald W., and Robert K. Johnston, eds. *The Variety of American Evangelism.* Knoxville: University of Tennessee Press, 1991.

De Genova, Nicholas. "Gangster Rap and Nihilism in Black America: Some Questions of Life and Death." *Social Text* 43 (fall 1995): 89–132.

Delphy, Christine. *Close to Home: A Materialist Analysis of Women's Oppression.* Edited and translated by Diana Leonard. Amherst: University of Massachusetts Press, 1984.

D'Emilio, John. "Capitalism and Gay Identity." In *Lesbian and Gay Studies Reader,* edited by Henry Abelove, Michèle Aina Barale, and David M. Halperin. New York: Routledge, 1993.

Derrida, Jacques. *Of Grammatology.* Translated by Gayatri Chakravorty Spivak. Baltimore: The Johns Hopkins University Press, 1974.

————. *Given Time: 1. Counterfeit Money.* Translated by Peggy Kamuf. Chicago: University of Chicago Press, 1992.

————. *Specters of Marx.* Translated by Peggy Kamuf. New York: Routledge, 1994.

Diamond, Sara. *Spiritual Warfare: The Politics of the Christian Right.* Boston: South End Press, 1989.

DiIulio, John J., Jr. "The Lord's Work: The Church and Civil Society." In *Community Works*, edited by E. J. Dionne Jr. Washington, D.C.: Brookings Institution Press, 1998.

Dionne, E. J., Jr., ed. "Introduction: Why Civil Society? Why Now?" In *Community Works*. Washington, D.C.: Brookings Institution Press, 1998.

Dirlik, Arif. "The Postcolonial Aura: Third World Criticism in the Age of Global Capitalism." *Critical Inquiry* 20 (winter 1994): 328–56.

————. "The Global in the Local." In *Global/Local*, edited by Rob Wilson and Wimal Dissanayake. Durham: Duke University Press, 1996.

Dorado, Sylvia. "Microfinance Organizations: Collaborating to Bring Innovative Solutions to Ingrained Problems." Lecture presented at the Radcliffe Public Policy Center, 2 February 2000.

Douglas, Mary. Foreword to *The Gift: The Form and Reason for Exchange in Archaic Societies,* by Marcel Mauss, translated by W. D. Halls. New York: W. W. Norton, 1990.

Duggan, Lisa. "Making It Perfectly Queer." *Socialist Review* 22, no. 1 (January–March 1992): 11–32.

Edwards, Michael, and David Hulme. "Too Close for Comfort? The Impact of Official Aid on Nongovernmental Organizations." *World Development* 24, no. 6 (1996): 961–73.

Ehrenhalt, Alan. "Where Have All the Followers Gone?" In *Community Works,* edited by E. J. Dionne Jr. Washington, D.C.: Brookings Institution Press, 1998.

"El Plan de Santa Barbara." In *Youth, Identity, Power: The Chicano Movement,* by Carlos Muñoz Jr. London: Verso Press, 1989.

Elshtain, Jean Bethke. "Not a Cure All: Civil Society Creates Citizens, It Does Not Solve Problems." In *Community Works,* edited by E. J. Dionne Jr. Washington, D.C.: Brookings Institution Press, 1998.

Elson, Diane. "The Value Theory of Labour." In *Value: The Representation of Labour in Capitalism.* London: CSE, 1979.

Engels, Freidrich. *The Origin of the Family, Private Property, and the State.* 1884. New York: Penguin, 1972.

Epstein, Stephen. "Gay Politics, Ethnic Identity: The Limits of Social Constructionism." *Socialist Review* 17, no. 3–4 (May–August 1987): 9–54.

Escobar, Arturo. "Imagining a Post-Development Era? Critical Thought, Development and Social Movements." *Social Text* 31/32 (1992): 20–56.

————. *Encountering Development.* Princeton: Princeton University Press, 1995.

Etzioni, Amitai. *The Spirit of Community: Rights, Responsibilities, and The Communitarian Agenda.* New York: Crown Publishers, 1993.

Ewen, Stuart. *Captains of Consciousness.* New York: McGraw-Hill, 1976.

Ewig, Christina. "The Strengths and Limits of the NGO Women's Movement Model: Shaping Nicaragua's Democratic Institutions." *Latin American Research Review* 34, no. 3 (1999): 75–102.

Fabian, Johannes. *Time and the Other: How Anthropology Makes Its Object.* New York: Columbia University Press, 1983.

Fanon, Frantz. *The Wretched of the Earth.* New York: Grove Press, 1963.

Feldman, Shelley. "NGOs and Civil Society: (Un)stated Contradictions." *Annals of the American Academy of Political and Social Science* 554 (November 1997): 46–65.

Ferber, Marianne A., and Julie A. Nelson, eds. *Beyond Economic Man: Feminist Theory and Economics.* Chicago: University of Chicago Press, 1993.

Ferguson, Sarah. "The Communitarian Manifesto." *Village Voice,* 18 August 1992, 17.

Fernando, Jude L., and Alan W. Heston. "NGOs between States, Markets, and Civil Society." *Annals of the American Academy of Political and Social Science* 554 (November 1997): 8–21.

Feuerbach, Ludwig. *The Essence of Christianity.* New York: Harper, 1957.

Fiske, John. *Understanding Popular Culture.* New York: Routledge, 1989.

Focus on the Family. "New Life, New Lifestyles." *Focus on the Family Magazine* 18, no. 3 (March 1994): 2–5.

Foley, Michael W., and Bob Edwards. "Escape from Politics? Social Theory and the Social Capital Debate." *American Behavioral Scientist* 40, no. 5 (March–April 1997): 550–61.

Foucault, Michel. *The Order of Things: An Archaeology of the Human Sciences.* New York: Random House, 1970.

———. *Discipline and Punish: The Birth of the Prison.* Translated by Alan Sheridan. Pantheon Books, 1977.

———. *The History of Sexuality, Volume I: An Introduction.* Translated by Robert Hurley. New York: Random House, 1978.

———. "What Is an Author?" Translated by Josué V. Harari. In *The Foucault Reader,* edited by Paul Rabinow. New York: Pantheon Books, 1984.

———. "Rethinking the Public Sphere: A Contribution to the Critique of Actually Existing Democracy." In *Habermas and the Public Sphere,* edited by Craig Calhoun. Cambridge: MIT Press, 1992.

Fraser, Nancy. "What's Critical About Critical Theory? The Case of Habermas and Gender." In *Unruly Practices,* edited by Nancy Fraser. Minneapolis: University of Minnesota Press, 1989.

———. "False Antithesis: A Response to Seyla Benhabib and Judith Butler," *Praxis International* 11 no. 2 (July 1991): 166–77.

———. "Heterosexism, Misrecognition, and Capitalism: A Response to Judith Butler." *Social Text* 52/53 (fall/winter 1997): 279–89.

Frazer, Elizabeth, and Nicola Lacey. *The Politics of Community: A Feminist Critique of the Liberal-Communitarian Debate.* Toronto: University of Toronto Press, 1993.

Fukuyama, Francis. *Trust: The Social Virtues and the Creation of Prosperity.* New York: Free Press, 1995.

Fundamentalist Obsession, The. Gay and Lesbian Alliance Against Defamation/San Francisco Bay Area Chapter, 1993. Videocassette.

Gagnier, Regenia. "On the Insatiability of Human Wants: Economic and Aesthetic Man." *Victorian Studies,* winter 1993, 125–53.

———. "Is Market Society the *Fin* of History?" In *Cultural Politics at the Fin de Siècle,* edited by Sally Ledger and Scott McCracken. Cambridge: Cambridge University Press, 1994.

Gamson, Joshua. "The Organization and Shaping of Collective Identity: The Case of Lesbian and Gay Film Festivals in New York." In *A Queer World,* edited by Martin Duberman. New York: New York University Press, 1997.

Gay Agenda, The. The Report. Los Angeles: Antelope Valley Springs of Life Ministries, 1992.

Gellner, Ernest. "The Importance of Being Modular." In *Civil Society: Theory, History, Comparison,* edited by John A. Hall. Cambridge, Mass.: Blackwell, 1995.

Giard, Robert. *Particular Voices: Portraits of Gay and Lesbian Writers.* Cambridge: MIT Press, 1997.

Gibson-Graham, J. K. *The End of Capitalism (As We Knew It).* Cambridge, Mass.: Blackwell, 1996.

Giner, Salvador. "Civil Society and Its Future." In *Civil Society: Theory, History, Comparison,* edited by John A. Hall. Cambridge, Mass.: Blackwell, 1995.

Ginsburg, Faye. "The Word-Made Flesh: The Disembodiment of Gender in the Abortion Debate." In *Uncertain Terms: Negotiating Gender in America,* edited by Faye Ginsburg and Anna Tsing. Boston: Beacon Press, 1990.

Goldberger, Paul. "To Gain Subsidies, Must Art Be Useful? Must It Be Sweet?" *New York Times,* 11 January 1995, National edition.

Gordon, Avery. "The Work of Corporate Culture: Diversity Management." *Social Text* 13, no. 3 (fall/winter 1995): 3–30.

Gramsci, Antonio. *Selections from the Prison Notebooks.* Edited and translated by Quintin Hoare and Geoffrey Nowell Smith. New York: International Publishers, 1971.

Grewal, Inderpal. "On the New Global Feminism and the Family of Nations: Dilemmas of Transnational Feminist Practice." In *Talking Visions,* edited by Ella Shohat. Cambridge: MIT Press, 1998.

Grønbjerg, Kirsten A. "Markets, Politics, and Charity: Nonprofits in the Political Economy." In *Private Action and the Public Good,* edited by Walter W. Powell and Elisabeth S. Clemens. New Haven: Yale University Press, 1998.

Guha, Ranajit. *Dominance Without Hegemony: History and Power in Colonial India* Cambridge: Harvard University Press, 1997.

Guha, Ranajit, and Gayatri Spivak. *Selected Subaltern Studies.* New York: Oxford University Press, 1988.

Habermas, Jürgen. *The Theory of Communicative Action, Vol. I. Reason and the Rationalization of Society.* Translated by Thomas McCarthy. Boston: Beacon Press, 1984.

———. *The Structural Transformation of the Public Sphere.* Cambridge: MIT Press, 1991.

———. "Struggles for Recognition in the Democratic Constitutional State." Translated by Shierry Weber Nicholsen. In *Multiculturalism and "the Politics of Recognition": An Essay* by Charles Taylor, with commentary by Amy Gutmann et al. Princeton: Princeton University Press, 1992.

———. "The European Nation-State: On the Past and Future of Sovereignty and Citizenship." *Public Culture* 10, no. 2 (winter 1998): 397–417.

Hall, Peter Dobkin. *"Inventing the Nonprofit Sector" and Other Essays on Philanthropy, Voluntarism, and Nonprofit Organizations.* Baltimore: The Johns Hopkins University Press, 1992.

Hall, Stuart. "Encoding/Decoding." In *Culture, Media, Language: Working Papers in Cultural Studies, 1972–79,* edited by S. Hall, D. Hobson, A. Lowe, and P. Willis. London: Hutchinson, 1980.

———. "The Local and the Global: Globalization and Ethnicity." In *Culture, Globalization, and the World System: Contemporary Conditions for the Representation of Identity,* edited by Anthony D. King. London: Macmillan, 1991.

———. "Old and New Identities, Old and New Ethnicities." In *Culture, Globalization, and the World System: Contemporary Conditions for the Representation of Identity,* edited by Anthony D. King. London: Macmillan, 1991.

Halley, Janet. "Sexual Orientation and the Politics of Biology: A Critique of the Argument from Immutability." *Stanford Law Review* 46 (1994): 503.

Hansmann, Henry. "Economic Theories of Nonprofit Organization." In *The Nonprofit Sector: A Research Handbook,* edited by Walter W. Powell. New Haven: Yale University Press, 1987.

Haraway, Donna. "A Manifesto for Cyborgs: Science, Technology, and Socialist Feminism in the 1980s." *Socialist Review* 15, no. 80 (March–April 1985): 65–107.

———. "Situated Knowledges: The Science Question in Feminism and the Privilege of Partial Perspective." *Feminist Studies* 14, no. 3 (fall 1988): 575–99.

Haraway, Donna, and David Harvey. "Nature, Politics, and Possibilities: A Debate and Discussion." *Environment and Planning D: Society and Space* 13 (1995): 507–27.

Harding, Susan. "Convicted by The Holy Spirit: The Rhetoric of Fundamental Baptist Conversion." *American Ethnologist* 14 (1987): 167–81.

———. "If I Should Die Before I Wake: Jerry Falwell's Pro Life Gospel." In *Uncertain Terms: Negotiating Gender in America,* edited by Faye Ginsburg and Anna Tsing. Boston: Beacon Press, 1990.

———. "Representing Fundamentalism: The Problem of the Repugnant Cultural Other." *Social Research* 58, no. 2 (summer 1991): 373–93.

Hart, Lynda. "Karen Finley's Dirty Work: Censorship, Homophobia, and the NEA." *Genders* 14 (fall 1992): 1–15.

Harvey, David. *The Urban Experience.* Baltimore: The Johns Hopkins University Press, 1989.

———. *The Condition of Postmodernity.* Cambridge, Mass.: Blackwell, 1990.

———. "Globalization in Question." *Rethinking Marxism* 8, no. 4 (1995): 1–17.

———. "The Body as an Accumulation Strategy." *Environment and Planning D: Society and Space.* 16, no. 4 (August 1998): 401–22.

Hauser Center for Nonprofit Organizations. *The Opening of the Hauser Center for Nonprofit Organizations: Edited Proceedings of the April 1997 Inaugural Conference.* Harvard University, 1997.

Hebdige, Dick. *Subculture: The Meaning of Style.* London: Methuen, 1979.

Hellinger, Stephen, Douglas Hellinger, and Fred M. O'Regan. *Aid for Just Development.* Boulder: Lynne Rienner Publishers, 1988.

Herrnstein Smith, Barbara. *Contingencies of Value.* Cambridge: Harvard University Press, 1988.

Himmelfarb, Gertrude. "Second Thoughts on Civil Society." In *Community Works,* edited by E. J. Dionne Jr. Washington, D.C.: Brookings Institution Press, 1998.

Hirst, Paul, and Jonathan Zeitlin. "Flexible Specialization versus Post-Fordism: Theory, Evidence, and Policy Implications." *Economy and Society* 20, no. 1 (February 1991): 1–56.

Honig, Bonnie. *Political Theory and the Displacement of Politics.* Ithaca: Cornell University Press, 1993.

hooks, bell. *Ain't I a Woman: Black Women and Feminism.* Boston: South End Press, 1981.

Howe, Richard G. "Homosexuality in America: Exposing the Myths." *American Family Association Journal* 18, no. 10 (October 1994): 2–15.

Hudock, Ann C. *NGOs and Civil Society: Democracy by Proxy?* Cambridge, England: Polity Press, 1999.

Hummon, David. *Commonplaces: Community Ideology and Identity in American Culture.* Albany: State University of New York Press, 1990.

Hunter, James Davison. *American Evangelicalism: Conservative Religion and the Quandary of Modernity.* New Brunswick, N.J.: Rutgers University Press, 1983.

———. *Culture Wars.* New York: Basic Books, 1991.

Independent Sector. www.independentsector.org.

Jakobsen, Janet R. "Agency and Alliance in Public Discourses about Sexualities." *Hypatia* 10, no. 1 (winter 1995): 133–54.

———. "Deconstructing the Paradox of Modernity: Feminism, Enlightenment, and Cross-Cultural Moral Interactions." *Journal of Religious Ethics* 23, no. 2 (fall 1995): 333–66.

———. "Queer Is? Queer Does? Normativity and Resistance." *GLQ: A Journal of Lesbian and Gay Studies* 4, no. 4 (1998): 511–36.

———. *Working Alliances and the Politics of Difference: Diversity and Feminist Ethics.* Bloomington: Indiana University Press, 1998.

———. "Can Homosexuals End Western Civilization as We Know It? Family Values in a Global Economy." In *Queer Globalizations: Citizenship and the Afterlife of Colonialism,* edited by Arnaldo Cruz-Malavé and Martin Manalansan. New York: New York University Press, 2002.

James, Estelle. "The Nonprofit Sector in Comparative Perspective." In *The Nonprofit Sector: A Research Handbook,* edited by Walter W. Powell. New Haven: Yale University Press, 1987.

Jenkins, J. Craig. "Channelling Social Protest: Foundation Patronage of Contemporary Social Movements." In *Private Action and the Public Good,* edited by Walter W. Powell and Elisabeth S. Clemens. New Haven: Yale University Press, 1998.

Johnson, Jeffery M. *Strengthening Fragile Families Initiative: The Ford Foundation.* 2nd ed. Washington, D.C.: National Center for Strategic and Nonprofit Planning and Community Leadership, 1999.

Joseph, Miranda. "Constructing Gay Identity and Community: The AIDS Plays of Theatre Rhinoceros." *Theatre InSight* 3, no. 1 (spring 1991): 6–11.

Kandiyoti, Deniz. "Identity and Its Discontents: Women and the Nation." In *Colonial Discourse and Post-Colonial Theory: A Reader,* edited by Patrick Williams and Laura Chrisman. New York: Columbia University Press, 1994.

Kaplan, Caren, Norma Alarcón, and Minoo Moallem, eds. *Between Woman and Nation: Nationalisms, Transnational Feminisms, and the State.* Durham: Duke University Press, 1999.

Kauffman, L. A. "Spy in the House of God." *SF Weekly* 13, no. 30 (September 21, 1994): 12–14.

Kazanjian, David. "Racial Governmentality: Thomas Jefferson and the African Colonization Movement in the United States." *Alternation: Journal of the Centre for the Study of Southern African Literature and Languages* 5, no. 1 (1998): 39–84.

Keane, John. *Civil Society: Old Images, New Visions.* Stanford: Stanford University Press, 1998.

Kermode, Frank. "Whose History Is Bunk?" *New York Times Book Review,* 23 February 1992.

King, Robin. "Confrontation and Accommodation: A Multi-Actor Approach to Mexican External Debt Policy and Macroeconomic Management." Ph.D. diss., University of Texas at Austin, 1991.

Klein, Christina. *Cold War Orientalism.* Berkeley: University of California Press. Forthcoming.

Knight, Robert H. "The National Endowment for the Arts: Misusing Taxpayers' Money." *The Heritage Foundation Backgrounder* 803 (18 January 1991): 1–19.

Krieger, Susan. *The Mirror Dance: Identity in a Women's Community.* Philadelphia: Temple University Press, 1983.

Krugman, Paul. "Fantasy Economics." *New York Times,* 26 September 1994, National edition, A15.

———. *Peddling Prosperity.* New York: Norton, 1994.

———. *Pop Internationalism.* Cambridge: MIT Press, 1996.

Laclau, Ernesto. *New Reflections on the Revolution of Our Time.* London: Verso, 1990.

Laclau, Ernesto, and Chantal Mouffe. *Hegemony and Socialist Strategy: Towards a Radical Democratic Politics.* London: Verso, 1985.

Ladd, Everett Carll. *The Ladd Report on Civic America.* New York: Free Press, 1998.

Larson, Magali Safatti. *The Rise of Professionalism.* Berkeley: University of California Press, 1977.

Lasch, Christopher. *The Culture of Narcissism.* New York: Warner Books, 1979.

Lash, Scott, and J. Urry. *The End of Organized Capital.* Cambridge, England: Polity Press, 1987.

Lee, Martyn J. *Consumer Culture Reborn: The Cultural Politics of Consumption.* New York: Routledge 1993.

Lefebvre, Henri. *The Production of Space.* Translated by Donald Nicholson-Smith. Cambridge, Mass.: Blackwell, 1991.

Levine, Daniel. "Immigrant/Ethnic Mutual Aids Societies, c. 1880s–1920: A Proposal for a Typology." Essays on Philanthropy, no. 18. Bloomington: Indiana University Center on Philanthropy, 1995.

Levy, Dan. "Arrests at Unruly Board Meeting." *San Francisco Chronicle,* 9 November 1993, final edition, A15.

Lienesch, Michael. *Redeeming America: Piety and Politics in the New Christian Right.* Chapel Hill: University of North Carolina Press, 1993.

Lipietz, Alain. *Mirages and Miracles: The Global Crisis in Fordism.* London: Verso, 1987.

———. *Towards a New Economic Order: Postfordism, Ecology and Democracy.* Translated by Malcolm Slater. New York: Oxford University Press, 1992.

———. "Post-Fordism and Democracy." In *Post-Fordism: A Reader,* edited by Ash Amin. Oxford: Blackwell, 1994.

Lorde, Audre. *Sister Outsider.* Trumansburg, N.Y.: Crossing Press, 1984.

Lowe, Lisa. *Immigrant Acts: On Asian American Cultural Politics.* Durham: Duke University Press, 1996.

Lowe, Lisa, and David Lloyd, eds. *The Politics of Culture in the Shadow of Capital.* Durham: Duke University Press, 1997.

Lubiano, Wahneema. "Multiculturalism: Negotiating Politics and Knowledge." *Concerns* 22, no. 3 (fall 1992): 11–21.

Lukács, Georg. "Reification and the Consciousness of the Proletariat." In *History and Class Consciousness: Studies in Marxist Dialectics,* translated by Rodney Livingstone. Cambridge: MIT Press, 1971.

Lukenbill, Grant. *Untold Millions: Positioning Your Business for the Gay and Lesbian Consumer Revolution.* New York: HarperCollins, 1995.

Lyotard, Jean-François. *The Postmodern Condition: A Report on Knowledge.* Translated by Geoff Bennington and Brian Massumi. Minneapolis: University of Minnesota Press, 1984.

MacDonald, Laura. *Supporting Civil Society: The Political Role of Non-Governmental Organizations in Central America.* New York: St. Martin's Press, 1997.

Macpherson, C. B. *The Political Theory of Possessive Individualism: Hobbes to Locke.* Cambridge: Oxford University Press, 1962.

Mander, Jerry, and Edward Goldsmith, eds. *The Case Against the Global Economy and for a Turn Toward the Local.* San Francisco: Sierra Club Books, 1996.

Mansbridge, Jane. "Feminism and Democracy." *The American Prospect* 1 (spring 1990).

Marcuse, Herbert. *Eros and Civilization: A Philosophical Inquiry into Freud.* New York: Vintage, 1955.

———. *One-Dimensional Man.* Boston: Beacon, 1964.

Marston, Sallie A. "Citizen Action Programs and Participatory Politics in Tucson." In *Public Policy for Democracy,* edited by Helen Ingram and Steven Rathgeb Smith. Washington, D.C.: Brookings Institution, 1993.

Martin, Biddy, and Chandra Mohanty. "Feminist Politics: What's Home Got to Do with It?" In *Feminist Studies, Critical Studies,* edited by Teresa de Lauretis. Bloomington: Indiana University Press, 1986.

Martin, Emily. *Flexible Bodies.* Boston: Beacon, 1994.

Marx, Karl. *The Eighteenth Brumaire of Louis Bonaparte.* New York: International Publishers, 1963.

———. *Grundrisse.* Translated by Martin Nicolaus. New York: Vintage, 1973.

———. *Political Writings.* Edited by David Fernbach. New York: Vintage Books, 1974.

———. *Capital.* Volume 1. Translated by Ben Fowkes. New York: Random House, 1977.

———. *Capital.* Volume 1. In *The Marx-Engels Reader.* 2nd ed. Edited by Robert C. Tucker. New York: Norton, 1978.

———. *Capital.* Volume 2. Translated by David Fernbach. London: Penguin Books in association with New Left Review, 1978.

———. "Critique of the Gotha Program." In *The Marx-Engels Reader.* 2nd ed. Edited by Robert C. Tucker. New York: Norton, 1978.

———. *The German Ideology: Part I.* In *The Marx-Engels Reader.* 2nd ed. Edited by Robert C. Tucker. New York: Norton, 1978.

———. *Manifesto of the Communist Party.* In *The Marx-Engels Reader.* 2nd ed. Edited by Robert C. Tucker. New York: Norton, 1978.

———. "On Imperialism in India." In *The Marx-Engels Reader.* 2nd ed. Edited by Robert C. Tucker. New York: Norton, 1978.

————. "On the Jewish Question." In *The Marx-Engels Reader*. 2nd ed. Edited by Robert C. Tucker. New York: Norton, 1978.

————. "Theses on Feuerbach." In *The Marx-Engels Reader*. 2nd ed. Edited by Robert C. Tucker. New York: Norton, 1978.

Marx, Karl. *Economic and Philosophic Manuscripts of 1844*. Translated by Martin Milligan. Amherst, N.Y.: Prometheus Books, 1988.

Marx, Karl, and Frederick Engels. *Ireland and the Irish Question*. Moscow: Progress Publishers, 1971.

Matsuda, Mari J., et al. *Words That Wound: Critical Race Theory, Assaultive Speech, and the First Amendment*. Boulder: Westview Press, 1993.

Mauss, Marcel. *The Gift: The Form and Reason for Exchange in Archaic Societies*. Translated by W. D. Halls. New York: W. W. Norton, 1990.

Mayer, Margit. "Post Fordist City Politics." In *Post-Fordism: A Reader*, edited by Ash Amin. Oxford: Blackwell, 1994.

McCarthy, Kathleen D. *Noblesse Oblige: Charity and Cultural Philanthropy in Chicago, 1849–1929*. Chicago: University of Chicago Press, 1982.

McClure, Kirstie. "On the Subject of Rights: Pluralism, Plurality and Political Identity." In *Dimensions of Radical Democracy: Pluralism, Citizenship, Community*, edited by Chantal Mouffe. London: Verso, 1992.

Mead, Walter Russell. "Asia Devalued." *The New York Times Magazine*, 31 May 1998, 38–39.

Meadwell, Hudson. "Post-Marxism, No Friend of Civil Society." In *Civil Society: Theory, History, Comparison*, edited by John A. Hall. Cambridge, Mass.: Blackwell, 1995.

Memmi, Albert. *The Colonizer and the Colonized*. Boston: Beacon, 1965.

Meyer, Sarah Elizabeth. *From the Ground Up: Coalition Building in the Arts*. Master's thesis. New York: Columbia University, 1990.

Miami Theory Collective, ed. *Community at Loose Ends*. Minneapolis: University of Minnesota Press, 1991.

Miller, Neil. *In Search of Gay America*. New York: Harper and Row, 1989.

Minkoff, Debra C. "Producing Social Capital: National Social Movements and Civil Society." *American Behavioral Scientist* 40, no. 5 (March–April 1997): 606–19.

Minkowitz, Donna. "Undercover with the Religious Right." *Out* (February–March 1994): 56–61.

————. "Dancing on Your Grave." *POZ* 5 (December 1994–January 1995): 44–47, 71.

Moody, Michael P. "Pass It On: Serial Reciprocity as a Principle of Philanthropy." *Essays on Philanthropy*, no. 13. Bloomington: Indiana University Center on Philanthropy, 1994.

Moore, Michael, dir. *Roger and Me*. Burbank, Calif.: Warner Home Video, 1990.

Moores, Lew. "CAC Jury a Collage of Interests." *Cincinnati Enquirer* 28 September 1990, 1.

Moraga, Cherríe, and Gloria Anzaldúa, eds. *This Bridge Called My Back*. New York: Kitchen Table Woman of Color Press, 1983.

Mouffe, Chantal. "Democratic Citizenship and the Political Community." In *Dimensions of Radical Democracy: Pluralism, Citizenship, and Community*, edited by Chantal Mouffe. London: Verso, 1992.

————. Preface to *Dimensions of Radical Democracy: Pluralism, Citizenship, and Community*, edited by Chantal Mouffe. London: Verso, 1992.

Moynihan, Daniel P. *The Negro Family: The Case for National Action.* Washington, D.C.: Office of Policy Planning and Research. U.S. Department of Labor, March 1965.

Moynihan, Daniel P., with Nathan Glazer. *Beyond the Melting Pot.* 2nd ed., Cambridge: MIT Press, 1970.

Mozzochi, Jonathan, Gillian Leichtling, and Steve Gardiner. "The New Right and the Christian Right." *NGLTF Action Kit: Fight The Right (March on Washington Edition).* Washington, D.C.: NGLTF Policy Institute, 1993.

Mydans, Seth. "Crisis Aside, What Pains Indonesia Is the Humiliation." *New York Times,* 10 March 1998, A9.

Nancy, Jean-Luc. *The Inoperative Community.* Edited by Peter Connor, translated by Peter Connor et al. Minneapolis: University of Minnesota Press, 1991.

National Association of Artists' Organizations. *Bulletin.* Washington, D.C.: National Association of Artists' Organizations. Published bimonthly.

National Center for Strategic Nonprofit Planning and Community Leadership. *Annual Report: 1998.* Washington, D.C.: National Center for Strategic Nonprofit Planning and Community Leadership, 1998.

———. *Strengthening Fragile Families Initiative.* 2nd ed. Washington, D.C.: National Center for Strategic Nonprofit Planning and Community Leadership, 1999.

National Gay and Lesbian Task Force Policy Institute. *Anti-Gay/Lesbian Violence, Victimization, and Defamation in 1991.* Washington, D.C.: NGLTF Policy Institute, 1992.

———. *NGLTF Action Kit: Fight the Right (March on Washington Edition).* Washington, D.C.: NGLTF Policy Institute, 1993.

Negri, Antonio. *Marx Beyond Marx: Lessons on the Grundrisse.* Translated by Harry Cleaver, Michael Ryan, and Maurizio Viano. Brooklyn: Autonomedia, 1991.

Nelson, Julie A. "The Study of Choice or the Study of Provisioning? Gender and the Definition of Economics." In *Beyond Economic Man: Feminist Theory and Economics,* edited by Marianne A. Ferber and Julie A. Nelson. Chicago: University of Chicago Press, 1993.

Neuhaus, Richard John, and Micheal Cromartie, eds. *Piety and Politics: Evangelicals and Fundamentalists Confront the World.* Washington, D.C.: Ethics and Public Policy Center, 1987.

Newton, Kenneth. "Social Capital and Democracy." *American Behavioral Scientist* 40, no. 5 (March–April 1997): 562–74.

Nicholson, Linda J., ed. *Feminism/Postmodernism.* New York: Routledge, 1990.

Nietzsche, Friedrich. *On the Genealogy of Morals.* Translated by Walter Kaufman and R. J. Hollingdale. New York: Vintage Books, 1989.

Northeast Mississippi Daily Journal. www.djournal.com.

Odendahl, Teresa, and Michael O'Neill, eds. *Women and Power in the Non-Profit Sector.* San Francisco: Jossey-Bass, 1994.

Offe, Claus. *Disorganized Capitalism: Contemporary Transformations of Work and Politics.* Cambridge: MIT Press, 1985.

Ohmae, Kenichi. *The End of the Nation State: The Rise of Regional Economies.* New York: Free Press, 1995.

Omi, Michael, and Howard Winant. *Racial Formation in the United States: From the 1960s to the 1980s.* New York: Routledge and Kegan Paul, 1986.

O'Neill, Michael. *America's Third Sector.* San Francisco: Jossey-Bass, 1989.

Oxhorn, Philip. "From Controlled Inclusion to Coerced Marginalization: The Struggle for Civil Society in Latin America." In *Civil Society: Theory, History, Comparison,* edited by John A. Hall. Cambridge, Mass.: Blackwell, 1995.

Packard, William. *Evangelism in America: From Tents to TV.* New York: Paragon House, 1988.

Padmore, George. *Pan-Africanism or Communism? The Coming Struggle for Africa.* New York: Roy Publishers, 1956.

Parker, Andrew. "Unthinking Sex: Marx, Engels, and the Scene of Writing." In *Fear of a Queer Planet,* edited by Michael Warner. Minneapolis: University of Minnesota Press, 1993.

———. "Praxis and Performativity." *Women and Performance* 8 (1996): 265–73.

Pateman, Carole. *The Sexual Contract.* Cambridge, England: Polity Press, 1988.

Patner, Andrew, ed. *Alternative Futures: Challenging Designs for Arts Philanthropy.* Washington, D.C.: Grantmakers in the Arts, 1994.

Patton, Cindy. "Tremble, Hetero Swine." In *Fear of a Queer Planet,* edited by Michael Warner. Minneapolis: University of Minnesota Press, 1993.

Peck, Jamie, and Adam Tickell. "Searching for a New Industrial Fix: The After-Fordist Crisis and the Global-Local Disorder." In *Post-Fordism: A Reader,* edited by Ash Amin. Oxford: Blackwell, 1994.

Phelan, Peggy. *Unmarked: The Politics of Performance.* New York: Routledge, 1993.

Phillips, Derek L. *Looking Backwards: A Critical Appraisal of Communitarian Thought.* Princeton, N.J.: Princeton University Press, 1993.

Phillips, Lynne, ed. *The Third Wave of Modernization in Latin America: Cultural Perspectives on Neoliberalism.* Wilmington, Del.: Scholarly Resources, 1998.

Piore, Michael. "Economic Identity/Sexual Identity." In *A Queer World,* edited by Martin Duberman. New York: New York University Press, 1997.

Piore, Michael, and Charles F. Sabel. *The Second Industrial Divide: Possibilities for Prosperity.* New York: Basic Books, 1984.

Poovey, Mary. "The Production of Abstract Space." In *Making a Social Body.* Chicago: University of Chicago Press, 1995.

Postone, Moishe. "Anti-Semitism and National Socialism." In *Germans and Jews since the Holocaust,* edited by Anson Robinach and Jack David Zipes. New York: Holmes and Meier, 1986.

Powell, Walter W. Preface to *The Nonprofit Sector: A Research Handbook,* edited by Walter W. Powell. New Haven: Yale University Press, 1987.

Powell, Walter W., and Elisabeth S. Clemens. Introduction to *Private Action and the Public Good,* edited by Walter W. Powell and Elisabeth S. Clemens. New Haven: Yale University Press, 1998.

Pratt, Mary Louise. "Ideology and Speech Act Theory." *Poetics Today* 7, no. 1 (1986): 59–72.

Pratt, Minnie Bruce. "Identity: Skin, Blood, Heart." In *Yours in Struggle: Three Feminist Perspectives on Anti-Semitism and Racism,* by Elly Bulkin, Minnie Bruce Pratt, and Barbara Smith. New York: Long Haul Press, 1984.

———. "Poetry in Time of War." In *Rebellion: Essays 1980–1991.* Ithaca, N.Y.: Firebrand Books, 1991.

Putnam, Robert D. "The Prosperous Community." *American Prospect* 13 (spring 1993): 35–42.

———. "Bowling Alone: America's Declining Social Capital." *Journal of Democracy* 6, no. 1 (January 1995): 65–78.

Reagon, Bernice Johnson. "Coalition Politics: Turning the Century." In *Home Girls: A Black Feminist Anthology,* edited by Barbara Smith. New York: Kitchen Table Women of Color Press, 1987.

Reich, Robert B. *The Work of Nations.* New York: Random House, 1991.

Reilly, Charles A. "Public Policy and Citizenship." In *New Paths to Democratic Development in Latin America: The Rise of NGO-Municipal Collaboration,* edited by Charles A. Reilly. Boulder: Lynne Rienner Publishers, 1995.

Reisman, David, with Nathan Glazer and Reuel Denney. *The Lonely Crowd.* 1961. Abr. ed. with 1969 preface. New Haven: Yale University Press, 1989.

Reynolds, Charles H., and Ralph V. Norman, eds. *Community in America: The Challenge of Habits of the Heart.* Berkeley: University of California Press, 1988.

Ribuffo, Leo P. *The Old Christian Right: The Protestant Far Right from the Great Depression to the Cold War.* Philadelphia: Temple University Press, 1983.

Ricardo, David. *On the Principles of Political Economy and Taxation.* Edited by Pierro Sraffa. Cambridge: Cambridge University Press, 1951.

Ritchey-Vance, Marion. *The Art of Association: NGOs and Civil Society in Colombia.* Rosslyn, Va.: Inter-America Foundation, 1991.

Rivers, Eugene F. III. "High Octane Faith and Civil Society." In *Community Works,* edited by E. J. Dionne Jr. Washington, D.C.: Brookings Institution Press, 1998.

Robertson, Nancy Marie. "Kindness or Justice? Women's Associations and the Politics of Race and History." In *Private Action and the Public Good,* edited by Walter W. Powell and Elisabeth S. Clemens. New Haven: Yale University Press, 1998.

Robinson, Amy. "Forms of Appearance of Value: Homer Plessy and the Politics of Privacy." In *Performance and Cultural Politics,* edited by Elin Diamond. New York: Routledge, 1996.

———. "The Ethics of Analogy." Lecture presented at the Stanford Humanities Center, 20 March 1997.

Rooney, Ellen. "Who's Left Out? A Rose by Any Other Name Is Still Red; Or, the Politics of Pluralism." *Critical Inquiry* 12 (spring 1985): 550–63.

Roxas, Sixto K. "Principles for Institutional Reform." In *Development: New Paradigms and Principles for the Twenty-First Century.* Rethinking Bretton Woods, vol. 2, edited by Jo Marie Greisgraber and Bernhard G. Gunter. London: Pluto Press, 1996.

Rubin, Gayle. "The Traffic in Women: Notes on the 'Political Economy' of Sex." In *Toward an Anthropology of Women,* edited by Rayna R. Reiter. New York: Monthly Review Press, 1975.

Said, Edward W. *Culture and Imperialism.* New York: Alfred Knopf, 1993.

Salamon, Lester. "The Rise of the Nonprofit Sector." *Foreign Affairs* 73, no. 4 (July–August 1994): 109–22.

Samantrai, Ranu. *AlterNatives: Black Feminism in the Postimperial Nation.* Stanford: Stanford University Press, 2002.

Sandel, Michael J. *Liberalism and the Limits of Justice.* New York: Cambridge University Press, 1982.

Sandoval, Chela. *Methodology of the Oppressed.* Minneapolis: University of Minnesota Press, 2000.

Sassen, Saskia. *The Mobility of Labor and Capital.* Cambridge: Cambridge University Press, 1988.

Sayre, Robert, and Michael Lowy. "Figures of Romantic Anti-Capitalism." In *Spirits of Fire,* edited by G. A. Rosso and Daniel P. Watkins. Rutherford: Fairleigh Dickinson University Press, 1990.

Schambra, William A. "All Community Is Local: The Key to America's Civic Renewal." In *Community Works,* edited by E. J. Dionne Jr. Washington, D.C.: Brookings Institution Press, 1998.

Schechner, Richard. "Enough Already: Political Realities, the NEA, and You," *Village Voice* 24 July 1990.

Schlesinger, Arthur M., Jr. *The Disuniting of America: Reflections on a Multicultural Society.* Knoxville, Tenn.: Whittle Direct Books, 1991.

Scott, Allen J., and Michael Storper. "High Technology Industry and Regional Development." *Regional Science* 112 (1987): 215–32.

———, eds. *Production, Work, Territory: The Geographical Anatomy of Industrial Capitalism.* Boston: Allen and Unwin, 1986.

Sedgwick, Eve Kosofsky. *Epistemology of the Closet.* Berkeley: University of California Press, 1990.

———. *Tendencies.* Durham: Duke University Press, 1993.

Sennett, Richard. *The Fall of Public Man.* London: Faber and Faber, 1977.

Shah, Nayan. *Contagious Divides: Epidemics and Race in San Francisco's Chinatown.* Berkeley: University of California Press, 2001.

Sievers, Bruce. "Can Philanthropy Solve the Problems of Civil Society?" Essays on Philanthropy, no. 16. Bloomington: Indiana University Center on Philanthropy, 1995.

Simmel, Georg. "The Stranger." In *Conflict: The Web of Group Affiliations.* Translated by Kurt H. Wolff and Rienhard Bendix. New York: Free Press, 1964.

———. *The Philosophy of Money.* 2nd ed. Translated by Tom Bottomore and David Frisby. London: Routledge, 1990.

Skocpol, Theda. "Don't Blame Big Government: America's Nonprofits Thrive in a National Network." In *Community Works,* edited by E. J. Dionne Jr. Washington, D.C.: Brookings Institution Press, 1998.

Smith, Adam. *The Theory of Moral Sentiments.* Edited by D. D. Raphael and A. L. Macfie. Indianapolis: Liberty Press, 1976.

———. *Wealth of Nations.* 1776. Amherst: Prometheus Books, 1991.

Smith, Anthony. *The Ethnic Origins of Nations.* Oxford: Blackwell, 1986.

Smith, Brian H. *More Than Altruism: The Politics of Private Foreign Aid.* Princeton: Princeton University Press, 1990.

Smith, Neil. "The Satanic Geographies of Globalization: Uneven Development in the 1990s." *Public Culture* 10, no. 1 (1997): 169–89.

Solomon, Lawrence. "Micro-Credit's Dark Underside." *World Press Review,* August 1998, p. 3. Reprinted from *Next City,* winter 1997–1998.

Soros Foundation. www.soros.org.

Spengler, Oswald. *The Decline of the West.* New York: Alfred A. Knopf, 1926.

Spivak, Gayatri. "Scattered Speculations on the Question of Value." In *In Other Worlds: Essays in Cultural Politics.* New York: Methuen, 1987.

———. "Can the Subaltern Speak?" In *Marxism and the Interpretation of Culture.* Urbana: University of Illinois Press, 1988.

Stacey, Judith, and Susan Elizabeth Gerard. "'We Are Not Doormats': The Influence of Feminism on Contemporary Evangelicals in the United States." In *Uncertain Terms: Negotiating Gender in America,* edited by Faye Ginsburg and Anna Tsing. Boston: Beacon Press, 1990.

Stallybrass, Peter. "Marx and Heterogeneity: Thinking the Lumpenproletariat." *Representations* 31 (summer 1990): 69–95.

Stanley, Alessandra. "For Ambitious Entrepreneurs, All Europe Is Just One Nation." *New York Times,* 24 December 1998, A1, 10.

Steinfels, Peter. "Ideas and Trends." *New York Times,* 24 May 1992, E6.

Stoler, Ann Laura. *Race and the Education of Desire.* Durham: Duke University Press, 1995.

Storper, Michael. "Territories, Flows, and Hierarchies in the Global Economy." In *Spaces of Globalization: Reasserting the Power of the Local,* edited by Kevin Cox. New York: Guilford Press, 1997.

Strand, Mark. *Poems: Reasons for Moving, Darker and the Sargentville Notebook.* New York: Alfred A. Knopf, 1997.

Tendler, Judith. "Turning Private Voluntary Organizations into Development Organizations: Questions for Evaluation." Discussion paper no. 12, A.I.D., Washington, D.C., 1982.

Thomas, Anthony. "Thy Kingdom Come . . . Thy Will Be Done." Corporation for Public Broadcasting, 1986.

Thrift, Nigel. "A Phantom State? International Money, Electronic Networks, and Global Cities." In *Spatial Formations.* London: Sage Publications, 1996.

Tilly, Louise, and Joan Wallach Scott. *Women, Work, and the Family.* New York: Routledge, 1989.

Tocqueville, Alexis de. *Democracy in America.* New York: Vintage, 1945.

Tonnies, Ferdinand. *Community and Society.* 1887. Edited and translated by Charles P. Loomis. New York: Harper, 1957.

Trachtenberg, Alan. *The Incorporation of America: Culture and Society in the Gilded Age.* New York: Hill and Wang, 1982.

Vance, Carol. "The War on Culture." *Art in America,* September 1989, pp. 39–64.

———. "Misunderstanding Obscenity." *Art in America* (May 1990): 49–61.

———. "Negotiating Sex and Gender in the Attorney General's Commission on Pornography." In *Uncertain Terms: Negotiating Gender in America,* edited by Faye Ginsburg and Anna Tsing. Boston: Beacon Press, 1990.

———. "Reagan's Revenge: Restructuring the NEA." *Art in America,* November 1990, pp. 49–55.

Vinelli, Andrés. "Managing Microfinance Organizations: The Perils of Financial Sustainability." Unpublished manuscript. Presented at Hauser Center for Nonprofit Organizations, Harvard University, 7 December 1999.

Walby, Sylvia. *Theorizing Patriarchy.* Oxford: Oxford University Press, 1990.

Waring, Marilyn. *If Women Counted: A New Feminist Economics.* San Francisco: Harper and Row, 1988.

Warner, Michael, ed. *Fear of a Queer Planet: Queer Politics and Social Theory.* Minneapolis: University of Minnesota Press, 1993.

Watt, David Harrington. *A Transforming Faith: Explorations of Twentieth-Century American Evangelicalism.* New Brunswick, N.J.: Rutgers University Press, 1991.

Weber, Max. *The Protestant Ethic and the Spirit of Capitalism.* Translated by Talcott Parsons. London: Harper Collins Academic, 1930.

Weinbaum, Alys. "Engels' Originary Ruse: Race, Reproduction, and Nation in the Story of Capital." Paper presented at the Pembroke Center, Brown University, Providence, R.I., April 1998.

Weisbrod, Burton A. *The Nonprofit Economy.* Cambridge: Harvard University Press, 1988.

Wells, David B., and John D. Woodbridge. Introduction to *The Evangelicals: What They Believe, Who They Are, Where They Are Changing,* 9–19. Nashville: Abingdon Press, 1975.

————, eds. *The Evangelicals: What They Believe, Who They Are, Where They Are Changing.* Nashville: Abingdon Press, 1975.

Weston, Kathleen M. "Production as Means, Production as Metaphor: Women's Struggle to Enter the Trades." In *Uncertain Terms: Negotiating Gender in America,* edited by Faye Ginsburg and Anna Tsing. Boston: Beacon Press, 1990.

————. *Families We Choose: Lesbian and Gay Kinship.* New York: Columbia University Press, 1991.

————. "Do Clothes Make the Woman? Gender, Performance Theory, and Lesbian Eroticism." *Genders* 16 (1993): 1–21.

Weston, Kathleen M., and Lisa B. Rofel. "Sexuality, Class, and Conflict in a Lesbian Workplace." In *The Lesbian Issue: Essays From Signs,* edited by Estelle B. Freedman et al. Chicago: University of Chicago Press, 1985.

White, Mel. *Stranger at the Gate: To Be Gay and Christian in America.* New York: Simon and Schuster, 1994.

Wildmon, Donald. *The Home Invaders.* Wheaton, Ill.: Victor Books, 1986.

Wilkerson, Isabel. "Obscenity Jurors Were Pulled Two Ways But Deferred to Art." *New York Times,* 10 October 1991, B1.

Williams, Raymond. *The Country and the City.* New York: Oxford University Press, 1973.

————. *Marxism and Literature.* Oxford: Oxford University Press, 1977.

Wolfe, Alan. "Is Civil Society Obsolete? Revisiting Predictions of the Decline of Civil Society in *Whose Keeper.*" In *Community Works,* edited by E. J. Dionne Jr. Washington, D.C.: Brookings Institution Press, 1998.

Wright, Melissa. "Mexican Women, American Business and the Materials of Values." Paper presented at American Anthropological Association, Washington, D.C., November 1997.

————. "The Dialectics of Still Life: Murder, Women, and Maquiladoras." *Public Culture* 11, no. 3 (1999): 453–74.

Wuthnow, Robert. "Rediscovering Community: The Cultural Potential of Caring Behavior and Voluntary Service." In Essays on Philanthropy, no. 7. Bloomington: Indiana University Center on Philanthropy, 1992.

Yanagisako, Sylvia. *Culture and Capital: The Cultural Production of Italian Family.* Princeton: Princeton University Press, 2002.

Young, Iris Marion. "The Ideal of Community and the Politics of Difference." *Social Theory and Practice* 12, no. 1 (spring 1986): 1–26.

————. *Justice and the Politics of Difference.* Princeton: Princeton University Press, 1990.

Yunis, Muhammad. "The Grameen Bank." *Scientific American,* November 1999, pp. 114–19.

Yuval-Davis, Nira, and Floya Anthias, eds. *Woman-Nation-State.* MacMillan: London, 1989.

Zaretsky, Eli. *Capitalism, the Family, and Personal Life.* New York: Harper and Row, 1986.

Žižek, Slavoj. *The Sublime Object of Ideology.* London: Verso, 1989.

Index

NEA controversy voices: Ann, 71, 136; Christina, 125–28, 130, 133, 196n18; Holly, 131–32; Jane, 141; Mrs. Allen, 134, 142, 143; Pastor Allen, 128, 133–34, 136; Rebecca, 140; Wayne, 136–37; Allen Wildmon, 70, 137; Donald Wildmon, 7, 9, 70–71, 136, 137, 195n13
Negri, Antonio, 16
new social movements, xvii, xxviii, 32–33, 60. *See also* social movements
NGLTF (National Gay and Lesbian Task Force), 121
niche markets: gays and lesbians, 22–23, 43, 44–45, 49, 51, 139–40, 186n14; racial, 49, 53–54; religious, 139–40, 143, 144, 149
Nietzsche, Friedrich, 100–101
nongovernmental organizations: capitalism, 95–100, 153–55; civil society, 95–96, 190n12; communal relationships, 98–100, 113–16, 192n26, n28; Communism and, 89–91, 93–95; critiques of, 113–17, 192n24; debt crisis, 96–97, 98–100, 191n20, n22; definitions, 87, 192n25; development, 95–100, 154–55, 191n16, n17, n19, n20, 192n24; funding of, 114; history of, 86–92; as voluntary associations, 113–16. *See also* development
nonprofit organizations: capitalism, 70, 71–75, 87–93; Communism and, 83–86, 87, 89–93, 117; community and, 69–70, 111, 121; definitions, 70, 87, 189n5; Fordism and, 92; Hauser Center for, 92, 112–14, 191n21; hegemony and, 73–74, 109–11, 192n24; history of, 86–88, 91–92, 111; nation-state, 28, 72, 87–93; performativity of, 75; race/ethnicity in, xxii–xxiv; Romantic narratives of 70, 72, 73; in Tupelo, Mississippi, 70–71, 133, 136–38; as voluntary association, 86; women and, 188n1, 191n22. *See also* faith-based organizations; voluntarism

Odendahl, Teresa: and Michael O'Neill, 188n1
Ohmae, Kenichi, 147–48, 155, 162, 166

O'Neill, Michael, 86: and Teresa Odendahl, 188n1
Oxhorn, Phillip, 190n12

Parker, Andrew, 61–65, 67, 187n21, n22, 188n29
particularity/abstraction: definitions, xxxii; globalization, 147–48, 174; liberalism and, xxi–xxii, 26–28; Marx on, 13–17, 20; in NEA controversy, 139–40, 143–45; rights discourse, 144; social hierarchies, 3, 17; subject formation, 94–95, 109; temporality and, 17, 183n19; Theatre Rhinoceros and, xxxvi; value and, 13–17, 20–21, 139–40. *See also* analogies; binary oppositions
particularity/universality, xviii–xix, xxi–xxii, xxxii, 6, 18–19. *See also* particularity/abstraction
Partners for Fragile Families, 92–93, 117
Patton, Cindy, 185n5
Peck, Jamie: and Adam Tickell, 151
Penniston, Pam, 80–86, 100
People for the American Way, 120, 124, 140–41, 194n5
performance, xxxii, 60–67, 186n26, n27, n30
performativity: for capitalism, xxxi–xxxvi, 63; of capitalism, xxxi–xxxvi; of consumption, 33–34; definitions, 33–34, 63, 184n2; of gender, 33–34; of identity, xxv–xxvi, 33–36, 184n2, 185n3, n5; praxis and, 188n29; of production, xxxii–xxxiii, 30–36, 117, 185n4; speech act theory and, 33, 66–67, 187n22
Phelan, Peggy, 64, 65–67, 188n24, n25, n26, n27
philanthropy, 89–90, 108–9, 112–13, 189n5, 189n8, 191n23
Phillips, Lynne, 95, 191n19
Piore, Michael, 146, 148, 152–53; and Charles F. Sabel, 46, 48, 152–53, 156, 158–59, 166, 196n2
pluralism, xxi, 21–25, 25–28, 139–41, 157, 196n18. *See also* diversity; multiculturalism

Miranda Joseph is associate professor of women's studies at the University of Arizona.